Connecting Generations

Connecting Generations

Integrating Aging Education and Intergenerational Programs with Elementary and Middle Grades Curricula

Barbara M. Friedman
Intergenerational Educator and Consultant

Foreword by
Robert N. Butler, M.D.

Allyn and Bacon
Boston   London   Toronto   Sydney   Tokyo   Singapore

Series Editor: Virginia Lanigan
Series Editorial Assistant: Bridget Keane
Manufacturing Buyer: Suzanne Lareau

Copyright © 1999 by Allyn & Bacon
A Viacom Company
Needham Heights, MA 02494

Internet: www.abacon.com

Library of Congress Cataloging-in-Publication Data

Friedman, Barbara (date)
    Connecting generations : integrating aging education and intergenerational
programs with elementary and middle grades curricula / Barbara M. Friedman :
foreword by Robert N. Butler
        p.   cm.
    Includes bibliographical references and index.
    ISBN 0-205-27513-3
    1. Aging—Study and teaching (Elementary)—United States. 2. Intergenerational
relations—Study and teaching (Elementary)—United States. 3. Children and adults—
Study and teaching (Elementary)—United States. I. Title.
HQ1064.U5F755   1999
305.26'071—DC21   98-30551
                                                                                                    CIP

Printed in the United States of America
10 9 8 7 6 5 4 3 2 1   02 01 00 99 98

To
Mark
for love that empowers me

To
Amy and David
for constantly encouraging me

To
Gaga
who taught me how to live and, in the end,
taught me how to die

Contents

Chapter 4   **Psychological Aspects of Aging**   **88**

Chapter Overview   88

Intergenerational Program Suggestions   88

Chapter 5   **Historical Perspectives of Aging**   **108**

Chapter Overview   108

Intergenerational Program Suggestions   108

Chapter 6   **The Biology of Aging**   **151**

Chapter Overview   151

Intergenerational Program Suggestions   151

Chapter 7   **Evaluation of Intergenerational Programs**   **187**

Foreword

Fifty years ago, this book would not have been needed, because in 1940 only 7 percent of Americans lived to be 90. Old age was the domain of the lucky few. It is difficult for us to comprehend that in less than 100 years humanity has made greater gains in life expectancy from birth than in the preceding 50 centuries of human history. For example, at the start of the American Revolution, the average life expectancy for both sexes was 35 years and only 2 percent lived to be 65. Even at the turn of the century, one could reasonably expect to live only to the age of 50. Today, we are likely to live longer than our parents and to see our children mature and grow older.

Why are we seeing this extraordinary shift in the demographic landscape? We can point with pride to improved public health, nutrition, education, and medical advances, which have all played a critical role. Diseases once believed to be natural and inevitable are now preventable and, as in the case of smallpox, obsolete. Moreover, medical interventions can now retard age-related diseases and processes of aging.

Today, one has only to open the daily newspaper to realize that science is on the brink of extraordinary breakthroughs that have the potential to expand life expectancy even further. We can reasonably look forward to a time when living to age 100—and beyond—will be a cause for celebration, but not amazement.

Every generation has produced its share of individuals who lived to great old age and who continued to be productive virtually to the end of their lives. We know of extraordinary people whose creativity and brilliance ripened with age, beginning with Sophocles (89) and extending to Benjamin Franklin (84), Johann Wolfgang von Goethe (83), Florence Nightingale (90), and Georgia O'Keeffe (99). We know that Edgar Degas (83) achieved greatness as a painter after 50, and that he continued to grow more creative in his old age. However, notwithstanding individual cases of longevity in the past, our contemporary experience is very different, because of the sheer numbers of healthy older adults in the population. Within the next decade, baby boomers, who now comprise one-third of the nation's population, will reach their 60s. Between 2020 and 2030, one of five Americans will be over 65, making them the largest generation of older persons in U.S. history. The odds are in favor of a vital, active, experienced, engaged, and useful older population.

We are privileged to witness the evolution of a new stage of life. No longer biological, fixed, and immutable, old age identity has become a social and cultural construct that will undergo further transformation as the twenty-first century unfolds. Our stereotypes of older persons no longer apply. At the same time, the growing numbers of fruitfully occupied older people is incompletely understood, because it is so new, and because we have had so little experience dealing with this phenomenon.

Humanity is exploring a new frontier, and society at all levels is being challenged to develop new institutions and social arrangements to accommodate the longer life expectancy.

Teachers are at the forefront of this demographic revolution. Nowhere can we find a better opportunity to change mind sets than by educating young persons in the first third of life to develop an understanding and appreciation of the richness of life in the final third. By integrating aspects of aging into every subject—from life sciences to civics and mathematics—students will learn to accept the later years of life as a natural part of living and aging. I envision a time when the art and science of growing old are an integral part of every child's learning experience. When students study biological sciences, they will learn about the physiology of aging. When they are taught economics, youngsters will be introduced to the concept of productive aging and the continuing contributions to society of older persons. Students can develop an understanding of Social Security and pension funds, their importance to the growth of the economy, and the maintenance of financial security in old age.

The twenty-first century could be the century when we actually celebrate in thought and deed the 25 more years of life expectancy that we have at the end of the century than we had at the beginning. The historian, Philippe Aries, wrote that the seventeenth century marks the discovery of childhood. Perhaps future generations will look back on the twentieth and twenty-first centuries and observe that it was the era when a serious analysis of the milestones of the life course and of old age began.

ROBERT N. BUTLER, M. D.

Preface

One beautiful spring day, as I was rushing from one meeting to another, I noticed an older woman with a child about three years old standing near a small pond. The sun danced on the ripples of the water and it reflected onto them so that they too seemed all aglitter. And they were giggling. Hard. The scene was so enticing that I pulled over to the side of the road just to watch. I expected to see something strange or surprising that would account for their laughter. Instead, I saw them methodically pick up pebbles and sometimes alternately, sometimes simultaneously, toss them into the water. That was all. A simple, playful game. Why, I thought, could that be giving them so much pleasure?

Suddenly the answer appeared simple. It was not the game that made them laugh, nor was it the effects of the game, but rather that they were happy just being together. And the sheer beauty of their connection was joyous. They also both had that one luxury that I did not have—time to spare and time to share. I drove to my meeting realizing that most of us in the middle years of life don't have the time we desire to share simple pleasures. I was grateful that older adults do, yet I was sobered by the knowledge that all too often the young and the old, who can share so much, do not connect as often as they should.

The moment at the pond happened many years ago. That, and the death soon after of my beloved grandmother, "Gaga," inspired me to pursue a career in intergenerational education. It seemed to be a reasonable extension of my years as a high school biology teacher, because biology textbooks never seemed to delve into aging as part of a normal life cycle; somehow the adult years appeared as the endpoint of one's biological development. Since I began in the field, I have worked on intergenerational program development with many educators and taught aging education curricula to hundreds of schoolchildren. And in those years, my involvement, and the field, has changed dramatically.

In my early years as a consulting/visiting teacher, I was often responding to issues that focused specifically on the two generations involved in the program who too often had little interaction with each other. I was delighted to see changes in stereotypic ageist attitudes and behaviors as a result of my programs, and I appreciated the ability to develop curricula that taught students that the process of aging is a normal part of our life cycle. That too was the goal of the intergenerational movement in the early 1980s. An added benefit for me was that I always learned more than I taught. A certain "magic" happens when these generations interact that always makes me both humble and grateful.

As an example, I remember so clearly the nine-year-old immigrant Jewish girl whom I randomly paired in a pen-pal program with an older woman who had no family (and who, I might add, had to be coerced into joining the program). After the 20-week program, pen pals finally met. I knew something important had happened in their relationship, because they greeted each other with a hug that was more than perfunctory. I didn't know how important it was until six months later when I received a phone call from the woman. She exclaimed, "I just had to tell you how wonderful my grandchild is." I replied, "Rita, I thought you had no family?" "Oh, not biologically," she said, "but you gave me a family when you gave me a pen pal." "You see," she continued, "I helped that little girl adjust to America and we really formed quite an emotional attachment. We decided to stay in touch. This summer when I needed cataract surgery and had no family to help me, she and her dad and mom were wonderfully supportive. Then, just yesterday they came to my house and asked me if it was okay if they bought a home near me so they could take care of me for the rest of my life!"

Magic!

And as if that wasn't enough, she continued, "You know I am an Arab." (I did not know. Actually I had guessed she was Jewish and the pairing would result in commonality!) "My new family and I have talked a lot about the Israeli–Arab problems. I've been so angry for so long, but not anymore. If we can love each other so much, why can't they?"

Magic!

Intergenerational interactions such as this one are simply win-win, mutually beneficial situations. They recognize a human need and create a support system for people that empowers them to function individually as well as contribute to their community. As a result of my understanding the importance of this type of intergenerational interaction, my prototype for programming had developed into a mutual-needs-oriented goal. Through interaction with colleagues, I knew that this was the direction in which all of us were moving in the late 1980s.

Now, something especially important has evolved in the intergenerational field and in my own personal involvement in it. As intergenerational programs are becoming more frequent in our communities (for reasons that will be discussed later), they are systematically beginning to address the important needs of those communities. Often, the programs have become crucial to the community's health, well-being, and development. We need these kind of programs: they respond to pressing social situations that threaten to break down, rather than build, community; they allow all generations to come together in mutual respect and acknowledged need, not be pulled apart by those who would say one needs to step aside to allow the other to blossom; they encourage the best in each of us to flourish through community service; and they prepare our youngsters for their own aging, and for empathizing with the generation for whom they will be caregivers. In 1993 I began working with high school students and older adults in Hingham, Massachusetts, to develop programs in which these two generations, working together, identify community needs and then build their intergenerational program around those needs. They work side by side and, therefore, view each other as equally important and equally productive participants in the projects.

This point needs to be stressed: Intergenerational programs must be part of a larger context in order to achieve their greatest potential. They should be a means to a greater end: building communities that nurture and provide service to their own. This was brought to everyone's attention by the Presidents' Summit in Philadelphia in April 1997, which advocated greater service by everyone in a *combined* effort to help our children read. In October 1996, a Wingspread Conference, "2000 and Beyond: Building an Action Plan for the Intergenerational Movement" convened. The conference provided information for a monograph outlining an intergenerational strategy to build caring communities. Titled "Strengthening the Social Compact: An Intergenerational Strategy," the monograph focuses on strategies and a vision for the future. In addition, it identifies the changes that have occurred in the intergenerational field. Comparing this conference with a similar one held in 1980, Carol Tice, President of Lifespan Resources and a participant of both conferences, says in the monograph:

> In 1980, the emphasis was on setting an agenda that would foster and sustain intergenerational programs. In 1996, our discussions were not about intergenerational programs per se, but about how intergenerational programs and policy perspectives were integral parts of a strategy to build a caring society in which all generations are served and contribute to community. As such, intergenerational approaches have become vehicles for achieving a good society, not ends in themselves—part of a broader concern about maintaining and enhancing an engaged and caring community.

The philosophy of the field has moved in a more universal, needs-based direction, as have my efforts as a consultant to guide practitioners. I find that practitioners generally believe in that philosophy. Yet those who wish to engage in programming often have difficulty actually developing programs to fit that strategy. And educators have even more difficulty finding the time to integrate programming into a school day, or to incorporate aging education into a school curricula. Educators are quick to agree with educational research that advocates the importance of aging education to accompany intergenerational programs (Glass & Trent, 1980; Newman, 1985; McGuire, 1987; Pratt, 1992; Aday, Sims, McDuffy, & Evans, 1996), but they are often overwhelmed with special curricula that intrude into basic skills education. Teachers are indeed overburdened by days in which they need to accomplish more than the hours will allow.

The question that we might need to ask, therefore, is whether the philosophy inherent in the intergenerational strategies is moving faster than the practice of programming and curriculum in our communities. If so, how can educators from schools and from various agencies that develop intergenerational programs move in that direction? This book is intended to be one resource to assist in that process.

I hope that this book will aid in the understanding of program development that will contribute to building communities; and that it will help in the understanding of proactive aging education curricula as a way to allow students to make universal and personal connections and to understand and sustain relationships with the people with whom they are interacting. Specifically, the lessons in the curriculum will assist educators in integrating aging information into preexisting curricula so that it becomes part of the curriculum web already in place, not an addition to it. It *can* be user friendly. It *can* be incorporated into everyday lessons.

But even those who are eager to begin, and eager to be converted to the merits of this programming, sometimes have difficulty believing that students in grades 2 through 8 can really conceptualize information about aging and an aging society. My answer, quite simply, after years of actually doing it, is I know they can. Teachers, senior center directors, parents, and I are continually amazed at the insight and empathy students exhibit. I certainly agree that older children may understand more, or on a deeper level, than younger students, but young children *do* think about the subject. We need to remember that and never minimize our expectations of children. Even if they do not understand at the same level, the exposure to this type of thinking is crucial if we are to develop awareness and more global, critical thinking about aging issues.

STRUCTURE OF THIS BOOK

Chapters 1 and 2 focus on the development of good intergenerational programming. In the terminology I will be using, programs are the service, or project, aspect of the intergenerational work being done. Program suggestions are made in Chapter 3 and in succeeding chapters. The lessons are parts of the aging education curriculum that will help students understand the older people in the program.

For each lesson, learner outcomes are listed for aging issues and also for probable, preexisting academic curricula. There is also a section on what specific academic disciplines, and what specific areas of those disciplines, can integrate with the lesson. These two sections should facilitate integration. Aging education can be incorporated into math, English language arts, fine arts, science, physical education, health, and social studies curricula. These are guidelines for using your same lesson plans, but incorporating aging issues into them. These lessons will stimulate you to begin the process, and then provide motivation to use your own creativity to expand the curriculum to meet your classroom needs.

The lessons are designed for the middle elementary grades (4, 5). Each chapter also has suggestions on how to adapt the lesson for lower grades (2, 3) or for middle school grades (6, 7, 8).

Appropriate age-level trade books, with a brief annotation, are listed for each chapter. In many cases, one book is appropriate reading for different lessons; if a book has an obvious possible double use, I have listed that book in the bibliography for each chapter. Other times, I have chosen the lesson for which I feel it is most appropriate. Trade books that are wonderful intergenerational reading in general, but do not directly fit into a particular lesson, have been listed in the Annotated Book List at the end of this text. These books should be used frequently to enrich the entire intergenerational experience. I have attempted to locate and list as many of these books as possible, but I am pleased to say that it has been an impossible task. The great volume of books with intergenerational themes being published is staggering.

Some lessons require, or suggest activities that require, magazines, newspapers, and even birthday cards that illustrate issues of aging and older adults. It would be a good idea to continually be aware of that need and begin collecting this media at the beginning of your exploration into aging education. Other lessons require students to interview older adults. It might also be advisable at the beginning of your exploration into aging education to discuss interviewing skills and strategies, perhaps through role playing with students. This can be done as part of an English lesson or separately. In the chapter on historical perspectives interviewing is especially important and I have provided some basic guidelines.

Suggestions, written as *"Note,"* are included about what might be generated in class either through the students' comments or through the teacher's lead. These are, of course, only suggestions, but they come from many years of teaching and refining this curriculum and, therefore, represent viable scenarios.

Finally, for each lesson, the "Terms Used" definitions are from the *Webster's New World Dictionary of the American Language, College Edition,* in an attempt to make them accessible to all grade levels.

I believe that teachers are the lifeblood of our society. If a healthy society depends on the interdependence of our generations, which it does, it surely depends on teachers to prepare students for that society. And in the process of doing that, be sure to enjoy watching the MAGIC! I welcome any comments and ideas. My e-mail address is mrfriedman@pol.net.

References

Aday, R. H., Sims, C. R., McDuffie, W., & Evans, E. (1996). Changing Children's Attitudes Toward the Elderly: The Longitudinal Effects of an Intergenerational Partners Program. *Journal of Research in Childhood Education, 10* (2), 143–151.

Glass, J. C., & Trent, C. (1980). Changing Ninth-Graders' Attitudes Toward Older Persons. *Research on Aging, 2* (4), 499–512.

Kingson, E., Corman, J., & Leavitt, J. K. (1997). *Strengthening the Social Compact: An Intergenerational Strategy.* Wingspread Conference Monograph, Generations United, Washington, DC.

McGuire, S. L. (1987). Aging Education in Schools. *Journal of School Health, 57* (5), 174–176.

Newman, S. (1985, November). *A Curriculum on Aging in Our Schools: Its Time Has Come.* Paper presented at Bridging the Gap Conference, Brookdale Institute and New York City Public Schools.

Pratt, F. (1992). *Why Teach About Aging?* Epilogue for Schools in an Aging Society, 6 volumes, State of Connecticut Department of Education and Department on Aging.

Acknowledgments

I wish to thank many people for helping this book become a reality.

For his constant support I thank my husband, Mark. From the first intergenerational program I orchestrated in 1984 to the final edit of this book, his insight helped refine my thinking and his encouragement inspired me.

To my first teacher, who continues to teach by example, I thank my mother Ruth Meshekow. As an older adult, she is simply beautiful.

My classroom teaching for thirteen years was invaluable in helping me develop curricula that would be responsive to the needs of elementary students. I had the privilege of working with many teachers, administrators, and Council on Aging directors, who are too numerous to list, but for whose support I am grateful. A few, however, do stand out. In their role as administrators, Robert Monson, Judith Daley, and Renee Rubin affirmed for me that the curriculum in intergenerational programming is crucial for the successful and sustainable outcomes of those programs. I thank them for their continual encouragement over many years of working together. As the first teachers to open to me their classrooms, and their hearts, I thank Evelyn Wonson, Bob McInnes, and Martha Gawthrop. Their emotions and responses in that first year of teaching made me know I was on the right track. I am grateful to Fran Pratt who, years ago, spent time and shared ideas with me about teaching aging. He provided, through his organization The Center for Understanding Aging, insights that led to the development of this aging curriculum.

In preparing this book I greatly appreciate the time spent by Rabbi Henry Zoob in reading the manuscript. His insight and suggestions were important. I thank Erik Hajer for his suggestions about exercise and older adults, Laura Pelger for her invaluable assistance with research, Erin Peterson for her artistic interpretation of older adults and youth—without the stereotypes.

I thank my editor, Virginia Lanigan, for taking a chance on me and providing guidance. To the editorial staff at Allyn and Bacon, Kris Lamarre and Bridget Keane, and to Janice K. Davis, Ladue School District and Dr. Jacqueline Collier, Centerville City Schools and Miami University, who reviewed the manuscript and made valuable suggestions, thank you for helping a new author get through the process and for making an imperfect manuscript better.

Finally, my deepest appreciation and gratitude must go to the wonderful students and older adults with whom I have had the privilege of working these many years. Their emotional attachment to each other has been inspiring and humbling. I shall always be grateful they chose to share themselves with me.

Somehow we have to get older people back close to growing children if we are to restore a sense of community, a knowledge of the past, and a sense of the future.

Margaret Mead

Erin Peterson © 1997

We reach backward to
our parents and forward
to our children to a future we
will never see, but about
which we need to care.

Carl Jung

Connecting Generations

Chapter **One**

Rationale for Intergenerational Programming and Curricula

he number of school-based, older adult agency-based, and community-based, intergenerational programs has increased dramatically in the last decade. There are many reasons for this.

CHANGING DEMOGRAPHICS

The growth of America's older population has dramatically changed in the twentieth century. From a moderate pace to a very rapid pace, the growth in the twentieth century of those over age 65 has far outpaced those under age 65. And the fastest growing segment of that over-age-65 group is the over-85-year-old category. The U.S. Census Bureau, "Sixty-Five Plus in the United States" (1995), states that

> During the 20th century the number of persons in the United States under age 65 has tripled. At the same time, the number aged 65 or over has jumped by a factor of 11! The elderly, who comprised only 1 in every 25 Americans (3.1 million) in 1900, made up 1 in 8 (33.2 million) in 1994. . . . According to the Census Bureau's "middle series" projections, the elderly population will more than double between now and the year 2050, to 80 million. By that year as many as 1 in 5 Americans could be elderly. Most of this growth should occur between 2010 and 2030 when the "baby boom" generation enters their elderly years. During that period, the number of elderly will grow by an average of 2.8 percent annually. By comparison, annual growth will average 1.3 percent during the preceding 20 years and 0.7 percent during the following 20 years. . . . The "oldest old"—those aged 85 and over—are the most rapidly growing elderly age group. Between 1960 and 1994, their numbers rose 274 percent. In contrast, the elderly population in general rose 100 percent and the entire U.S. population grew only 45 percent.

The decline in birth rates from many years ago when families were so large results in fewer children born and a smaller population of young people. Couple that with the increase in life span due to medical and engineering technology, and we begin to see one of the reasons for the demographic trends in America. In addition, the movement toward early retirement that is a phenomenon caused in part by corporate and business downsizing creates a situation in which many older adults find themselves with many productive years left after retirement. They need to find meaningful activities with which to occupy their time.

EDUCATION REFORM AND POLITICAL IMPERATIVES

Education reform in America in 1998 is advocating interdisciplinary, experiential education with outreach to the community. Academic outcomes emphasize what children can learn through their interactions with that community, by either doing something or seeing something modeled. Learning within the context of a community also provides the opportunity for students to see beyond and outside themselves and to make internal and attitudinal connections with that community.

This emphasis has come to be known as Community Service Learning (CSL) and advocates that students will learn substantially better, and classrooms will be substantially more exciting, when students are learning as they are doing. As stated by the Community Service Learning Center (1996), of Springfield, Massachusetts in their brochure:

> CSL is a strategy for school reform and community development—it revitalizes classrooms and renews communities. CSL places academic learning in a real-life context by having youth meet actual community needs while gaining mastery over important academic, employment, and social skills. Although CSL can be adapted to many situations—the classroom, the summer program, the community youth group—it requires a few simple steps that lead to impressive outcomes. It must
>
> > meet real community needs
> > allow students to direct their learning
> > incorporate time for reflection
> > and be linked with actual academic learning
>
> This teaching strategy can be best understood through examples such as:
>
> > a social studies class volunteers at a local soup kitchen while learning about issues of the homeless and hungry
> > a science class learns about pollutants while taking steps to eliminate all styrofoam products in their school

In addition, when financial resources are limited and school systems must be creative in securing financial stability to maintain their programs, the importance of recognizing community human resources is crucial. Due to their large numbers and availability in society, older adults are often asked to assist with school personnel needs and education reform imperatives.

But inadvertently, something unexpected also results. When older adults and students interact, a greater understanding by older adults for the needs of schools, students, and teachers occurs. This includes the recognition and acceptance of the need for increased funding. As a result, older adults often become advocates for schools and children. Conversely, those who normally work only with children begin to recognize that generational conflict does not have to be a certainty and that both generations have equally important needs. Sharing the financial resources and creating a society that is strong in its leadership and support for concerns that focus on every generation is a positive political outcome of intergenerational programming.

CHANGES IN MOBILITY, SOCIAL STRUCTURE, AND FAMILY STRUCTURE

Economic realities often dictate that families move frequently. High mobility means that children are no longer growing up with grandma and grandpa next door, and aunt and uncle around the corner, as was the case when today's older adults were growing up. This mobility reduces the possibility of nurturing and the passing on of historical perspectives that older generations ideally provide for youth. Many young people grow up with infrequent contact with their grandparents. From an older adult perspective, this mobility reduces the chance for them to be cared for by family members as they grow old. Whereas it was uncommon years ago for older adults to grow old outside the home of a family member (unless there was extreme need for constant medical care), today's plethora of nursing homes, assisted-living facilities, retirement complexes, and continuing-care facilities indicates that, for many and varied reasons, those days of family caretaking and constant family interactions are not as common.

Yet, even within this definitive change in society, there are still numbers of older adults living with their relatives. This may be due to a lack of the older adult having sufficient financial resources to live on his/her own or in a care facility. It may also be due to lack of sufficient financial resources of the family, resulting in two parents working and requiring the older adult to be available for child care. A third possibility might include cultural or ethical belief systems. In some cultures having an older relative in a care facility is unheard of, whereas in others it appears needed and humane.

Whatever the housing option, some of the outside care facilities are often located in serene settings that are, unfortunately, out of the mainstream of the community. Thus they tend to be isolated from the social structures that encourage generational interactions. Unless the generations come together in social clubs, religious institutions, or work-related situations, often little contact between them occurs. I am constantly surprised how many parents contact me and say, "My child cannot fulfill this request of yours because we do not know any older adults!" To fill that gap in their lives, people are embracing intergenerational programming for social and emotional reasons.

Finally, the stereotypic family of mother, father, two children and a dog no longer exists. The typical family of Norman Rockwell illustrations and the families on TV in the 1950s represented by *Father Knows Best* or *Ozzie and Harriett* are no longer the norm. Families come in as many varieties as people, and the multicultural, single-parent, or nontraditional family is too common to ignore. In addition, blood relations are no longer the only source of a family support system. Intergenerational programming provides its participants with the same nurturing and caring relationship and often provides greater support because of the voluntary nature of the interactions.

AGE-SEGREGATED SOCIETY RELATED TO HOUSING OPTIONS

As alluded to in the preceding section, alternative housing for older adults has increased dramatically, with both positive and negative impacts on the community and on society as a whole. While offering older adults a viable and protected environment for growing old, their frequent serene and idyllic location far from the mainstream of the community and their incredible in-house facilities contribute to a situation in which older adults never venture out into the community and, therefore, might never interact with other generations. Although older adults enjoy the company of those their own age, being constantly surrounded by one generation of people is unnatural. They begin to miss the vibrancy of youth. For this reason, many of these facilities are beginning to incorporate intergenerational activities into their daily planning, and many of the facilities are even being built with room to house child-care or preschool groups. This, of course, sets up ideal situations in which the two generations can interact on a regular basis.

YOUTH-CENTERED AND FITNESS-ORIENTED SOCIETY

Although slowly beginning to change, our society focus has been on the young as the productive members of society, whereas the old are viewed as passive consumers. This is reflected in both the print and electronic media, in the greeting card industry where age is a topic for negative humor, in the sports world, in fitness clubs, in advertisements, and in general attitudes.

We are bombarded with advertisements that suggest we be wary of the normal signs of aging, such as wrinkles, and that further suggest that we search for "effective" methods for remaining youthful looking. The implication that wrinkles are bad or undesirable is incorporated into our thinking and certainly into the psyche of impressionable children. Researchers believe that by the age of eight, children have incorporated these negative images of aging and it becomes their normative frame of reference (Rich, Myrick, & Campbell, 1983).

Companies that cater to fitness (such as sneaker manufacturers) have traditionally used young people in their ads. An active lifestyle has been the domain of the young, and slogans even used terminology associated with youth. Recently, as the baby boomers have begun to reach their fifties, sheer numbers alone have made corporations recognize that they need a marketing strategy that will cater to older people as well. These corporations are starting to shift to a philosophy that fitness is important for everyone, of every age.

TECHNOLOGY AND THE GENERATION GAP

As technology becomes increasingly sophisticated, it also becomes increasingly foreign to many older adults. Young children growing up with the use of computers, word processing, Internet access, the World Wide Web, and modem connections are comfortable and fluent with the terminology and concepts involved. They soon become aware that they know more than the older adults. This can create a wide generation gap, and even more important, a lack of respect for the wisdom and talents of older adults. To counter that, many successful intergenerational programs focus on the young teaching older adults how to access and use technology. Although this kind of program accentuates the fact that youth may know more than older people, it also provides a wonderful model for lifelong learning and for dispelling the myth that older adults can no longer learn.

Students learning about aging issues can use Internet access to learn more about governmental data on aging as well as information about aging agencies such as the American Association for Retired Persons (AARP) or the Retired Senior Volunteer Program (RSVP). Accessing this type of information will allow students to see the vast network of older adults who are active and vital to society and will minimize the effects of the generation gap.

GROWTH IN STATURE OF THE INTERGENERATIONAL FIELD

The increased stature of the intergenerational field is an important reason for advocating for intergenerational program development and should be used as part of the thinking when writing for grant money or defending thematic units in schools. For many years, intergenerational programming simply sought to create good feelings between generations as a way to change negative, stereotypic attitudes (Rich, Myrick, & Campbell, 1983; Cartensen, Mason, & Caldwell, 1982). Programming also attempted to provide the needed nurturing that older adults offer children; it was little more than putting the two generations together and watching the connections that are made in a loving, caring, and supportive environment.

Although these are still commendable goals, and the outcomes of any program should recognize that these emotional ties are substantive, today's intergenerational programming should attempt to address many of the most pressing social issues of the day. Needs-based program development creates highly sophisticated prototypes that are often initiated by older adults and elder agencies, by community- or city-based social service and public safety departments, and by the more typical outreach from schools and youth agencies. In addition, needs assessments are crucial to support the program development, and the process should include input from all facets of the community.

Some of these program prototypes include ones that outreach to the social isolation issues of elders in nursing homes, mentoring programs with teenage mothers and fathers, combined day-care facilities, friendly visiting to frail and homebound older adults, intergenerational community service corps, mentoring juvenile offenders, day-care centers partially staffed by older adults, telephone reassurance programs, violence prevention programs, social support for the disabled, and health-related programs.

This field no longer consists only of the "feel good" programs of the past; it is now viewed as a significant method of addressing important social problems and building community. Degree and certificate programs for intergenerational educators are being developed in institutions of higher education, and coursework for community leaders in this field is becoming available.

COMMUNITY DEVELOPMENT

Community development should reflect a community's best practices in an effort to achieve a more service-oriented, caring society. Community development can mean many different things. Business development, environmental concerns, or governmental issues are certainly part of the thinking. But community development must also include attention to the human needs and resources available. The nurturing of the community, by all its members and for all of its members, to achieve a more just and caring society must be part of the equation. Intergenerational programs can help in that effort.

WIN-WIN BENEFITS FOR ALL

Intergenerational programs have proved to be significantly beneficial for all participants. This would obviously include the youth and the older adults, but also includes the teachers, senior center directors, community organizers, and the actual community itself.

Students participating in intergenerational community service learning programs have been shown to increase their academic performance as well as their prosocial behavior. The Florida Learn and Serve K–12 (1994–1995) project has tracked outcome data for three parameters of student performance and has noted that students who were involved with community service learning programs showed an improvement in grade point average (GPA), an improvement in school attendance, and a decrease in discipline referrals. With students in these programs who are "at risk," the positive outcomes were even greater.

Older adults taking part in programs have received benefits that range from increased physical well-being (Fries, 1984; Leviton & Santa Maria, 1979) to higher levels of prosocial behavior and less solitary activity (Short-DeGraff & Diamond,

1996) to feelings of greater life satisfaction (Newman, 1982, 1988; Kocarnik & Ponzetti, 1991) and finally to increased memory function for those in school-based programs (Newman, Karip, & Faux, 1995).

Those who plan and administer the intergenerational programs have admitted to changes in their own attitudes about aging, in their relationships with the older adults in the program, and even in their attitude about their own aging.

Finally, if intergenerational programming has as one of its goals the building of a more caring society, then the community changes that occur as a result of that programming must certainly be viewed as a benefit for each individual in that community. Human needs that are often met include a greater sense of personal life satisfaction, greater well-being, enriched life activities, and higher self-esteem. In addition, intergenerational programming provides services to those parts of the population that are often most in need. The economic needs of the community are met through keeping older adults in their own homes with visiting and personal health programs, advocating for schools and voting for issues that provide schools with greater financial resources, and using all the resources of the community to meet the financial needs of that community. The political needs are met through a greater understanding of people for the needs of each other, thereby creating mutual advocacy and mutual support.

Intergenerational programming is truly a win-win situation.

References

Cartensen, L., Mason, S., & Caldwell, E. (1982). Children's Attitudes Toward the Elderly: An Intergenerational Technique for Change. *Educational Gerontology, 8,* 291–301.

Community Service Learning Center. (1996). Springfield, MA: Community Service Learning Center: Building Communities Together: Youth at the Center of Community Development and Learning. (Brochure).

Florida Learn & Serve K–12, 1994–1995. Florida State University Center for Civic Education and Service, and the Florida Department of Education.

Fries, J. (1984). The Compression of Morbidity: Miscellaneous Comments About a Theme. *Gerontologist, 24,* 354–359.

Kocarnik, R. A., & Ponzetti, J. J. (1991). The Advantages and Challenges of Intergenerational Programs in Long Term Care Facilities. *Journal of Gerontological Social Work, 16,* 97–107.

Leviton, D., & Santa Maria, L. (1979). The Adults Health & Development Program: Descriptive and Evaluative Data. *Gerontologist, 19,* 534–543.

Newman, S., (1982). *The Impact of Intergenerational Programs on Children's Growth and on Older Persons' Life Satisfaction.* Paper presented at a symposium, "Innovations Within Educational Gerontology." Available through Generations Together, Pittsburgh, PA, Order Number 02-82-230.

Newman, S., (1988). *The Impact of the School Volunteer Experience on the Well-Being of Older Persons.* Paper presented at the Gerontological Society of America. Available through Generations Together, Pittsburgh, PA, Order Number 02-88-285.

Newman, S., Karip, E., & Faux, R. B. (1995). Everyday Memory Function of Older Adults: The Impact of Intergenerational School Volunteer Programs. *Educational Gerontology, 21,* 569–580.

Rich, P., Myrick, R., & Campbell, C. (1983). Changing Children's Perceptions of the Elderly. *Educational Gerontology, 9,* 483–491.

Short-DeGraff, M. A., & Diamond, K. (1996). Intergenerational Program Effects on Social Responses of Elderly Adult Day Care Members. *Educational Gerontology, 22,* 467–482.

U.S. Census Bureau. (1995). *Sixty-Five Plus in the United States.* [On-line]. Available: http://www.census.gov/socdemo/www/agebrief.html

Suggested Reading

Handel, R. D. (1996). *Teachers as Family Literacy Learners: Report from the Field.* Paper presented at the annual meeting of the American Educational Research Association, New York, Available through ERIC, ED398176.

Malekoff, A. (1994). Action Research: An Approach to Preventing Substance Abuse and Promoting Social Competency. *Health & Social Work, 19* (1), 46–53.

Newman, S., & Brummel, S. (Eds.). (1989). *Intergenerational Programs, Imperatives, Strategies, Impacts, Trends.* New York: Haworth Press.

Rosenbaum, W. A., & Button, J. W. (1993). The Unquiet Future of Intergenerational Politics. *Gerontologist, 33* (4), 481–490.

Chapter **Two**

Program Development

WHAT MAKES A GOOD INTERGENERATIONAL PROGRAM

Among many issues and concerns in developing intergenerational programs, four main components should be carefully considered. Although each is not absolutely required for the program to be successful, most are, and each should be considered a goal to work toward achieving. The integration of these four ideas into program development will allow the program to be more meaningful and will create a program that can be sustained year after year.

1. **The Program Must Be Mutually Beneficial**

   Most intergenerational programs provide intrinsic, emotional benefits for everyone involved, and these are certainly valid indicators of the program's success. However, children and older adults who may have no prior involvement with community service, or are not convinced that intrinsic feelings will emerge, often need to see initial, extrinsic benefits that are readily identified. Once the programming has begun and the value, good feelings, and emotional rewards become obvious, the provision for extrinsic benefits is not as necessary; the call to service is often enough.

   For example, an elementary school class in a small northern town observes that many of its neighbors are older adults who have trouble shoveling snow from their front walks. As a community service project, students decide to shovel the snow for those neighbors.

   Scenario One: The teacher organized the program and Johnny, a student from the class, is assigned to shovel Mrs. Smith's driveway. After he shovels her front walk, she comes to the doorway and yells, "Thank you, Johnny"; he waves goodbye and goes back to school feeling good that he did a nice thing to help Mrs. Smith; and his effort contributes to the community service project the class planned. But, both Johnny and Mrs. Smith still have the following problematic feelings: Johnny still thinks of Mrs. Smith as "poor Mrs. Smith, she is too old and cannot shovel her walk," and although Mrs. Smith is glad that her walk is shoveled, it simply reinforces her feelings that she is getting old and useless. The psychological translation for both is that Mrs. Smith is a consumer in society, she is not a productive member.

Scenario Two: Johnny shovels Mrs. Smith's driveway; Mrs. Smith invites him in for cookies and milk to say thank you, and in conversation says, "You know I am a retired math teacher. If you have trouble with your math homework, I will be glad to help you. In fact, you can tell your teacher that I would love to come into your class and help all the students." Johnny still feels good that he did a nice thing to help Mrs. Smith and he contributed to his class service project, but now, although he knows she *cannot* shovel her walk, he knows what she *can* do—help him in math. Mrs. Smith is still glad that her walk is shoveled, but now, she feels good that she will give something back to the school and that she is still a valuable person. The psychological translation is that Mrs. Smith may be in need of some services from society, but she has much to offer and is a productive member of the community.

(Note: This scenario is, of course, an ideal situation. Often safety and liability concerns today preclude children from simply going in to a home for cookies and milk. But the program has many options for the same outcome: as an alternative, all the older adults whose walks have been shoveled are invited to the school at one time, or at lunchtime each day, where they can bring cookies, and they can interact and share their skills with the new friend who shoveled their walk.)

This scenario provides an opportunity for both members of the interaction to receive a service from the other, allowing each of them to feel good about him/herself *and* about the other person.

Once students have worked with intergenerational programs and aging curricula long enough to understand the value and worth of every human being regardless of age or circumstance of health, the extrinsic mutuality of a relationship is not as crucial. At that time, service projects can be mutual in the intrinsic feelings of worth and/or life satisfaction they offer each individual.

2. **The Program Must Be Ongoing**

Programs that are ongoing offer a greater chance for relationships to form, for empathy to develop, and for sustainability of interest. For example, a school is located near a nursing home, and the class has correctly assessed that the residents may be lonely and would want visitors.

Scenario One: The class develops a skit and song for each season and four times a year goes to the nursing home to present this show for the residents. The students are prepared for what they will experience in a nursing home setting, because the teacher and nursing home director have spoken to them at length in their classroom. During the first presentation, the skit is received with a modicum of interest by some, and some are so thrilled with the young children that they show that excitement by grabbing at them in an effort to hug or kiss them. Although the students were told to be prepared for this type of behavior, they are scared. The only actual interaction between student and nursing home resident is in the forced hello and goodbye activity that occurs for five minutes at the beginning and the end of the visit. The next season, when they visit the home, there may be different adults viewing the skit; some may have died; some do not choose to attend again.

Scenario Two: Students are paired individually, or in groups of two students for each older adult, with the residents of a nursing home. The nursing home activities director has worked with the teacher prior to this meeting to match older adults who have chosen to participate in the program with students of like interests, talents, temperament, and so on. At the first meeting, older adults and students spend time getting to know each other better; the activities or exercises designed for the entire visit are solely for this purpose. The activities are fun, nonthreatening, and such that everyone can easily do them. Biweekly meetings take place. Activities for each meeting are planned by the senior residents once a month and by the students once a month. Some of the activities may be physical, some may be academic, but all are social and interactive. Any show or presentation is inclusive of both generations and is presented to a third party—visiting guests of the older adults and students, for example. The program continues twice a month for the length of the school year. Substantive relationships form as the pairs get to relate regularly. If death occurs, which is always a possibility, the student should be given time to mourn before being asked to accept a new friend, and the class as a whole needs to deal with the death (see Chapter 6, Lesson 5 on death).

In the second scenario, students have access to the residents on a one-to-one basis and have the needed time to develop a relationship. The relationship, as well as the service, is real and meaningful.

3. **The Program Must Include Both a Service and an Educational Component**

A service learning curricula involves students' reflection on the service provided and its link to the academic subject at hand. But the service component of the curriculum must be supported by a learning component that provides contextual understanding to the experience of aging.

For example, while studying about "Neighborhoods," a third-grade class decides to interview older adults to find out what their neighborhood was like in the early 1920s. Students write a book about the neighborhood with the information obtained from the older adults; they include maps of their neighborhood and information about the demographics of the community then and now. They then present copies of the finished book to the library, to the local senior center, and to the town governmental offices. This is a good, reflective, intergenerational service learning project that uses the knowledge of the older adult population.

What this project example doesn't do is help the students better understand the people with whom they are interacting. So the type of learning curriculum that should be implied in the program development of any intergenerational project is an aging education curriculum—the content and reason for this book.

In this example of oral histories about a neighborhood, understanding the aging process from a sociological and psychological perspective would allow students to empathize with an older adult population that has experienced significant changes in its lifetime and has had to adapt to these changes. It would help them understand why there are nursing homes in the neighborhood, why there are senior centers, and what is happening within those doors. It would allow the students to view the world more globally and recognize the value of historical perspectives superimposed on present-day life.

In the example of students shoveling older adults' sidewalks, an aging education curriculum would allow the students to understand what happens to our bodies as we age and why shoveling snow may be difficult. It also would speak to the issue of housing options for older adults who may not be able to run a large home on their own and the economics of living on a limited income with no money to hire someone to shovel the snow. The students would better understand the need for their service. In conjunction with making the experience beneficial for all, that program is now truly meaningful.

In the example of nursing home visits, students need to not just be verbally prepared for what they may see, smell, or hear. They need to understand about the biology of aging and why the residents are in the home. They need to learn about the psychological needs of most residents and the human need for continued social interactions. This will create a greater empathy and again make the program more meaningful.

Intergenerational programming should also involve a curricular component for the older adults in the program. Although a course on child development is not what is being suggested, I am advocating that older adults do need to understand the particular stresses and needs of students today and the new developments in understanding the way students learn. Many older adults will say that they raised their own children and are certainly aware of what child development entails. That statement could be countered by suggesting that when they raised their children, the world, theories on education, and technology were certainly different. Today's children and today's schools need to be understood in order for the older adults to truly gain from the experience and offer the best they can to students who need to learn from them. Students need to know that the older adults working with them are "in touch" with their world. As the program evolves, regularly scheduled times should be included for the older adults to meet and learn from a structured, even if short, curriculum that has been developed with these needs in mind.

4. **The Program Should Strive for Young and Old Working Together**

Although there are many successful programs in which one group primarily "serves" another, as in the examples of one shoveling snow for another, or one providing information through interviews to another, a distinctive model of programming allows the young and old to work *together* to address a community need. In this model the impact of the service to the community and the mutuality of benefits is greater than the sum of its parts. Students and older adults see each other as equals in their efforts to reach a goal.

For example, a middle school class is studying pollution and local government in its science and social studies curricula, respectively. The teachers of the classes realize the opportunity for integration of their two curricula and encourage their classes to develop a goal of speaking to the local government about the need for recycling. Through their initial investigations, the students realize that recycling is not a new phenomenon; it used to be the norm. Consequently, they decide to invite older adults to be part of their study and their presentation to the legislators. They interview older adults and realize, for example, that years ago milk could only be obtained in bottles from the milkman who then collected the empty bottles and used them again. Teams of young and old work together in class and in the school library to research pollution issues together; they study how recycling would help their own local environment; and finally, they research and go through the proper procedures that allows them access to the local government for their presentation.

The local legislators listen to the presentation. They know the local newspapers are covering their meeting (a usual occurrence in many towns, although, as politically astute citizens, the students and older adults previously notified the reporters that the presentation would be happening!). The local officials certainly see the benefits of what the students and older adults are presenting. Normally, they wouldn't hesitate to institute townwide recycling, but the economic status of the town might make them hesitate about the expenditure of that kind of money. Yet, these elected officials are also focusing on the fact that both proud parents (middle-age voters) and older adults (known to be the most faithful voters) are either in the audience or actually standing before them with a proposal. It passes. They decide to commit to the proposal but enlist the services of town residents to find creative ways to fund the effort—a committee is set up to do this.

Aside from the obvious environmental benefit, the students and older adults have now viewed each other as equally important contributors to society. Age was irrelevant in the attainment of the goal; but the combination of generations made for a more powerful presentation. The feelings of accomplishment and of providing an important service to the community are unparalleled.

GETTING STARTED

In addition to these four components of good intergenerational programming, other important issues should be addressed. A brief presentation of each is described here for consideration when developing a plan.

Leadership

An intergenerational program should not be developed alone! A successful program needs the sense of ownership of many people—the students, the older adults, the administration of both the school and older adult network, the parents, members of the business and social community. Planning should involve everyone so that everyone has an investment.

However, one or two committed individuals must be selected for the overall leadership. It is these two individuals who will need to recruit the others for the program development. The leaders can be the teachers and older adult community leaders, but they can also be parents or other outside volunteers. So if you are reading this chapter and are feeling motivated to begin, speak to people involved with the older adult or youth population in your community and work together to decide who to involve and how to do it. The leaders must know this is hard work. It does not happen without planning and organization. But once it happens, the rewards are great and the return rate of involvement by others is high.

Coalition and Partnership Building

Once the primary leadership is in place, a coalition of partnerships should be developed to extend the planning process throughout the community. The following exercise is helpful in forming those partnerships.

List all the possible community connections to the older adult network and to the youth network. These can be in schools or after-school centers; in senior centers or housing for seniors; through religious organizations, clubs, service or volunteer organizations; or with local businesses or political groups. Also list all the connections in the community that may have an interest in being involved in an intergenerational program or those people who you think might be important in the execution of a program.

From this comprehensive list, decide what groups need to be involved for the project to be successful. Is a bank needed? a nursing home? a printer? parents? college students? community leaders? Approach these people with a basic plan of why you want a program to develop and, if you have decided on one, what the basic outline of that program will be. The word *basic* was used intentionally here, because although partners will want to know what they will be committing time and energy to, they should also be encouraged to have input into the project. This will allow for a sense of ownership to the project. Invite these people to be part of the planning group.

Now decide who will be the participants in the program. It will probably be your classroom and the local senior center or facility with whom you originally connected. But don't overlook other sources of participants. Invite representatives of these groups to join the planning group.

Keep in mind that the planning group should be small enough to be a workable group, that it should not be intimidating to anyone within the group, and that it should reach out into the community and represent that community generationally and culturally. Now that a group has been assembled, the real work begins.

Needs Assessment

Once the planning group is together, divide into smaller groups of three to four people. Look at the resources and the attributes of the community and make lists for the following categories:

- What are the good things about the community? What are the bad things?
- What are the physical needs? Is a playground in need of repair? Is there a wonderful open space for a fitness trail? Is recycling an issue in town?

- What are the social needs? Do students have anyplace to "hang out"? Are there many latch-key children in the community? Are there many home-bound elders?
- What are the academic needs? Are too many children reading below grade level? Are too many parents working two jobs and not able to help with homework? Are there older adults who want to learn computer skills? Are the schools in need of aides for teachers?
- What are the community resources? Are there churches, housing facilities, businesses nearby? What are the special interests and talents of the student and older adult population? Are there artists? engineers? woodworkers? musicians?

Once these questions are answered, analyze the results and pair up the needs and talents with a possible program. Be sure to keep in mind the four components of meaningful programs.

The planning group then needs to develop the outcomes desired from the program. The list should include academic goals, social goals, goals for the students and the teachers, and goals for older adult issues.

Funding Sources

Most intergenerational programs cost very little. Oral histories, friendly visiting, mentoring, and tutoring programs incur little expense. Often the most expensive component of a program is the transportation. It takes a certain amount of creative funding to meet the needs. Some options include:

- **State and federal agency grants.** Call agencies that deal with what you need and then request guidelines and grant options. Look to agencies that are interested in funding intergenerational interactions such as AARP, Area Agencies on Aging, Department of Education Grants, and Law Enforcement Agencies.
- **Foundations and corporations.** Check the areas of giving for each and then find a match for what you want to do. Apply after first discussing the project with someone in the headquarters.
- **In-kind funding.** Sometimes corporations are unable to provide grants, but may be delighted to provide in-kind funding. Do you need to publish a newspaper? They may be happy to do it in their printing department. Do you need a mini-van for transportation that they may have? A local market may be delighted to give you ice cream and cookies for your final wrap-up party.
- **Local education foundations.** This is a fast-growing source of funding for schools. As education reform seeks to make education more experiential, the chances of intergenerational programs being funded are increased.
- **Cooperative funding.** Remember that intergenerational programs involve different groups and each should be able to contribute. The human services departments in a community and schools may find it easier to fund half a program than the whole program.

Recruitment of Volunteers

Assuming that the students for the intergenerational program may be in a contained and accessible area—a classroom, an after-school program, a YM/WCA—the issue of recruitment will probably focus on recruiting older adults for the program. In some cases, the older adult population will also be self-contained as in a nursing home, but in many programs that will not be the case and older adults will need to be recruited.

The bad news is that although this should be relatively easy, it is not. Demographics certainly favors easy recruitment, but the reality is that so many older adults are so busy these days that it is hard to find those able to make long-term commitments. The good news is that once recruited, and they go through the program, they are hooked! The return rate for involvement is extremely high because the rewards and benefits are so high.

There are three ways to recruit older adults for a program. The first is a direct recruitment. This includes word of mouth, volunteers calling and explaining the program one on one, friends calling friends and saying, "I'm doing this, how about joining me?," and going to different older adult activities and speaking about the program. The second method of recruitment is an indirect method. This includes articles in newspapers and in church and senior center newsletters, flyers around town, or notices on bulletin boards. The third method of recruitment is a delegated recruitment in which different organizations involved in the program do the recruiting. For example, each person in the planning group representing their own organization/group is required to recruit a certain number of older adults for the program.

The first method is often the most time consuming, but it is also the most successful. Don't neglect the value of youth doing the recruiting—they can call grandparents, recruit older adults from their paper routes or other jobs, and speak at their local church or club.

Depending on the group and the program, there may be a need or desire to screen and/or interview older adults. If the program requires specific qualifications, they need to be delineated and an interviewing process is advisable. This might be the case for programs in which older adults work in day-care facilities.

Friendly visiting programs may require students to be alone with older adults, and schools may feel the need to initiate a child abuse/criminal record check. This may be the law in some cases, and in others it may just be custom, but police departments should be consulted for guidelines. In other cases, there may be a desire not to do any checks like this, because the older adults are recruited locally where they are well known and it would place a distrustful tone on the program. This needs to be discussed and reviewed with the administration of the participating organizations.

Orientation and ongoing training for older adult volunteers are crucial. The program should have regular hours and a set curriculum for workshops that teach child development and education practices and for time for reflection on issues pertaining to the children and to the program itself. There should be written job descriptions, a statement of expectations, and an agreed-upon commitment of both time spent and duration of the program. Training should be ongoing throughout the program so that issues that arise can be addressed.

Thanking the volunteers is a crucial part of any program planning process. Plan to thank them in many different ways. Certificates, parties, children's cards, presentations, and local press coverage go a long way in insuring their return next year. The visibility in local media is essential for future recruiting.

Developing an Action Plan

This is the time for all the logistics to be finalized and for the job descriptions to be completed. Issues that need to be considered are:

- transportation
- safety and accessibility issues
- emergency and/or medical needs
- staffing issues and clearly defined roles and responsibilities of each partner
- duration of the program and frequency of interactions
- plans for each interaction of program participants
- availability of food
- planning for a culminating event
- publicity for the program

There are bound to be many unexpected occurrences. Developing an action plan will help you anticipate as many as possible. Regularly scheduled meetings with the planning committee or with the leaders of the program are important to address anything unexpected.

Successful publicity generates excitement and provides for community building and development. Some things to consider in developing the public relations strategy for your program include making presentations within schools and school committee meetings and to community organizations; contacting local media, including cable TV, radio, and newspapers; advertising in newsletters representing local business, community, and religious groups; posting flyers for easy community access; and opening the culminating event to the community and to media for coverage.

Evaluation

During the program you must continually assess its effectiveness. Change what is not working and reinforce what is working. Be flexible. The suggestion that meetings be held regularly will assist in that effort. Keep a journal and note the changes you have made and why. That will help in refining the program for next year.

At the conclusion of the program, an evaluation is important to determine whether the goals have been met and to provide substance for future grant requests. The evaluation tool you use should reflect the whole program, but be aware that evaluations should meet the needs of your funders as well as the needs of the program. If your funder is a business or corporation, it may want to know what community changes have been achieved; if your funder is the local education foundation, it may be interested in how academic needs have been met; if the funder is the Area Agency on Aging, it may be interested in the older adult outcomes more than those of the students. Assessment strategies will be discussed in more detail in Chapter 7.

PROGRAM MODELS AND PROTOTYPES

There are four basic models of intergenerational programming. Each is a valuable prototype and each can produce meaningful programs. Yet in some, the four components mentioned at the beginning of this chapter are not inherent in the model and may need to be built in.

Youths Provide Service to Older Adults
Examples include:
- chore programs (such as students shoveling snow for older adults)
- friendly visiting programs, whether they occur in the homes of homebound older adults or in facilities such as nursing homes
- students serving meals at senior centers or meals on wheels
- students teaching older adults computer skills
- adopt a grandparent

Older Adults Provide Service to Youth
Examples include:
- tutoring and mentoring
- reading and literacy programs
- foster grandparent programs
- latch-key students in partnership with older adults
- volunteering in child-care facilities and preschool centers

Older Adults and Youth Provide Service for Each Other
Examples include:
- pen-pal programs
- phone-pal programs
- dance, choral, and theater productions
- arts projects
- student/older adult companionship programs

Older Adults and Youth Together Provide Service to the Community
Examples include:
- oral histories for community publications
- restoration and urban renewal projects
- companionship and friendly visiting for frail or homebound elders
- community events and productions
- creating an activity in the community—fitness trails, recycling centers

Another type of intergenerational program that is becoming more readily available is the development of facilities that care for, and house, both young and old. An example of this is joint child-care and adult-care facilities housed in corporate buildings in which the employees are caregivers for both generations. Corporations that are initiating this type of intergenerational center are finding that the productivity of the adult employees is greater when their worries about caregiving are relieved. Although the need is there and the intergenerational nature of the facility is obvious, this is not a program that is typical in its development plan and, as a result, will not be discussed in great detail in this book. However, once the center is established, the plans and components for any good intergenerational program discussed in this book should be followed for the facility to be successful.

Suggested Reading

Aday, R. H., Sims, C. R., McDuffie, W., & Evans, E. (1996). Changing Children's Attitudes Toward the Elderly: The Longitudinal Effects of an Intergenerational Partners Program. *Journal of Research in Childhood Education, 10* (2), 143–151.

Ames, B. D., & Youatt, J. P. (1994). Intergenerational Education and Service Programming: A Model for Selection and Evaluation of Activities. *Educational Gerontology, 20,* 755–764.

Ausherman, J. A., White, D. M., & Chenier, T. C. (1991). Junior High Health Teachers' Knowledge and Attitudes About Aging and Implementation of Aging Education. *Educational Gerontology, 17,* 391–401.

Corbin, D. E., Metal-Corbin, J., & Barg, C. (1989). Teaching About Aging in the Elementary School: A One-Year Follow-Up. *Educational Gerontology, 15,* 103–110.

Duggar, M. L. (1993). *Intergenerational Programs: Weaving Hearts and Minds.* Intergenerational Programs in the State of Florida. Available from Florida Education Center, Tallahassee, FL 32399-0400.

Firman, J., Gelfand, D. E., & Ventura, C. (1983). Intergenerational Service-Learning: Contributions to Curricula. *Educational Gerontology, 9,* 405–415.

Glass Jr., J. C., & Trent, C. (1980). Changing Ninth-Graders' Attitudes Toward Older Persons. *Research on Aging, 2* (4), 449–512.

Hausmann, H. S. (1994). *Promoting Positive Socialization in Fourth Grade Students Through Intergenerational Mentoring.* Practicum Paper available through ERIC, ED389636.

Hoot, J. L. (1981). Teaching Aging in the Public Schools, Results of an Exploratory Study. *Educational Gerontology, 7,* 331–337.

Kuehne, V. S. (1992). Older Adults in Intergenerational Programs: What Are Their Experiences Really Like? *Activities, Adaptation & Aging, 16* (4), 49–64.

Lyons, M. (1992). *A Guide to Developing Intergenerational Programs.* Glenn Woods Corporation, c/o Margaret Maher, Danvers, MA.

McDuffie, W., & Whiteman, J. (1989). *Intergenerational Activities Program Handbook* (3rd ed.). Binghamton, NY: Broome County Child Development Council.

McGuire, S. L. (1987). Aging Education in Schools. *Journal of School Health, 57* (5), 174–176.

Powers, W. G., Bailey-Hughes, B., & Ranft, M. (1989). Senior Citizens as Educational Resources. *Educational Gerontology, 15,* 481–487.

Scannell, T., & Roberts, A. (1994). *Young and Old Serving Together*. Washington, DC: Generations United.

Schools in an Aging Society. (1992). State of Connecticut Department of Education and Department on Aging, five booklets exploring program and curriculum development for high school students.

Strom R. D., & Strom, S. K. (1995). Intergenerational Learning: Grandparents in the Schools. *Educational Gerontology, 21*, 321–335.

Struntz, K., & Reville, S. (1985). *Growing Together: An Intergenerational Sourcebook*. Washington, DC: AARP, and Palm Springs, CA: Elvirita Lewis Foundation.

Tiemann, K. A., & Stone, M. D. (1992). Projective Aging: An Engaging Technique for Teaching Issues in Growing Older. *Educational Gerontology, 18*, 645–649.

Woodward, K. A. (1993). *Elementary School-Based Adopted Grandparent Programs: Combining Intergenerational Programming with Aging Education*. Paper presented at the annual meeting of the Association for Gerontology in Higher Education. Available through ERIC, ED361113.

Chapter Three

Sociological Aspects of Aging

CHAPTER OVERVIEW

T he program suggestions and lessons in this chapter will enable educators to help students discuss the issues of aging and older adults in our society. They will provide students with a broad view of the value we do, or do not, place on older adults as well as the circumstances that contribute to their life. In addition, they will help students recognize that there is a commonality between them and older adults and that the so-called generation gap is a gap in chronological age only.

INTERGENERATIONAL PROGRAM SUGGESTIONS

Pen-Pal Programs

Program: In this program students are paired with an older adult in a writing program with each group writing alternately every week. Teachers can either direct the correspondence or leave it up to the students. In either case teachers should discuss the kinds of things that can be written. Students will quickly run out of facts to share, such as my favorite flavor of ice cream, book, movie, and TV show; I have brothers and sisters; we went on a vacation to the Grand Canyon; I play soccer and baseball; I collect Barbie dolls. Discuss with students the need to share feelings, thoughts, and opinions as well as facts, for example, I still like a night light even though I am probably too old for one; my best friend and I had a fight; my parents are getting a divorce; I wish I got better grades in school; when we talk about wars it scares me.

Ask the students to be sure every letter has three paragraphs: one to tell something factual, one to share a feeling, and one to ask questions. Hold regular meetings with the older adults also, telling them what is being discussed in class and requesting them to answer all the students questions and ask some of their own.

At the conclusion of the program, plan an event so that pen pals have the opportunity to meet. The event should be relaxed and informal and allow for time to share and to get to know each other. A good way for them to "find" each other is for the students to be seated with a place next to them for their pen pal; older adults are temporarily outside the room. Students should have large name cards with their pen pal's name on it. At a signal they should hold the cards high and the older adults are invited inside. The older adults look for their own name on the card, and when they find it, they know the person holding the card is their pen pal.

Mutuality and Ongoing: A pen-pal program is a mutually beneficial prototype. Each group receives equal enjoyment in receiving their letters. It obviously integrates well with writing lessons. Think twice about checking the letters for spelling and grammar. These letters should be private and confidential, which allows for greater chance at real sharing and relationship building. If you want to use it as a vehicle for teaching writing—which it certainly should be—have the students work on editing and checking spelling on their own. You will be surprised at how willing, and even eager, they are to do that.

The program should continue for at least five months. An exchange of at least ten letters is important for building relationships. During this time you can explore with students the concept of pen-pal relationships. (Read *Dear Annie* by Caseley or discuss the play *Cyrano de Bergerac* by Rostand.)

Phone-Pal Programs

Program: This is very similar to the pen-pal program, but it focuses on students who are latch-key children (returning after school to an empty home) and older adults who are homebound elders. The program pairs these two groups, and the student is required to call the older adult every day when he or she arrives home from school. They chat on the phone, perhaps the older adult helps with some homework, suggests a schedule the student should follow that afternoon, and discusses the day's events. The student knows that the elder is there if he or she should decide to call again. For both partners, emergency numbers are available.

Arrange for the parents to meet the older adult, so that they can share their wishes about the productiveness of the child's time after school. If the program has an end point, you could plan an event or culminating activity; without an end point, you should periodically hold some kind of party or event that allows thank-yous to be shared.

Mutuality and Ongoing: The program allows both student and older adult to feel that the phone calls are providing a service to the other—the child knows the older adult is looking forward to his/her phone call as he/she has been at home all day, often without companionship; the older adult knows he/she is serving "in loco parentis" and the ritual phone call allows the adult to know the child has arrived home safely. Actually each partner is providing a check on the other, and when either senses something wrong they are instructed to call the emergency number.

The duration of the program usually follows parents' work schedules.

Intergenerational Literacy Programs

Program: Literacy programs take many forms. In family literacy programs, students and parents are taught reading skills at the same time. Parents are encouraged to read to their children at home, thereby creating a reinforcement for their own skill development and emphasizing the importance of reading. Although the focus may be on children, the adult learners are an important part of family literacy efforts. Other literacy programs involve older adults reading to children either in public and school libraries or in classrooms, or older adults tutoring children in reading skills within a classroom setting and usually with the guidance of the teacher. Even Start is an example of an existing literacy program that is a federal initiative but is state or locally funded. Many local districts have Even Start programs that are totally devoted to family literacy efforts.

Mutuality and Ongoing: Most literacy programs occur for the length of the school year. Because family literacy programs involve both adult learners and their children, they are often called intergenerational literacy programs. The other literacy efforts being made usually involve older adults. Although the most benefit is obtained from the student who is being aided, the older adult receives intrinsic benefits that are equally valuable. In an effort for the student to give back to the adult, he or she should be paired with an older adult whose needs match the student's talents.

Intergenerational Theater and Arts Projects

Program: Theater and art programs are exceptional in their ability to bring generations together in a shared project that can be presented to the community. Both the project and the intergenerational interaction nurture the heart and nurture creativity. A wide range of projects can be accomplished on almost any grade level, including

- theater productions based on oral histories or shared experiences
- dance and movement productions
- puppet shows
- murals and dioramas of neighborhoods
- violence-prevention productions
- variety or talent shows
- musical/choral productions
- designing and making quilts
- storytelling
- creating books (including bookbinding and cover design) of poems, essays, oral histories, or stories
- crafts projects, representing both older and more modern techniques

Mutuality and Ongoing: All the options for creative activities are done with generations working side by side. Thus each is viewed as an equal in the success of the project and each has an equal sense of ownership for the project. The project by its nature is long term, but even those that can be accomplished in a short time should be extended and made as comprehensive as possible to allow for relationship building.

Mentoring and Tutoring

Program: Mentoring programs rely on the older adult providing stability and modeling for youth, and tutoring programs increase the academic achievements and self-esteem of youth. In each case, the student and older adult are in a relationship that fosters trust, companionship, and growth. The programs can be formal or informal, but must be well structured, including a schedule for the interaction and a scheduled time for reflection and evaluation by all participants. The youth served can be

- teenage mothers and fathers—in this case the older adults may be a child-care provider (which would allow the teenager to remain in school), as well as a mentor in parenting techniques
- juvenile offenders—mentors are trained by probation officers and are required to meet with the youth on a prearranged schedule
- at-risk schoolchildren—tutored in or out of school
- children with disabilities

Mutuality and Ongoing: Although these types of programs usually involve older adults serving youth, the need in society is so great, and the older adults are so valuable, that initially it is not crucial to focus on the mutuality. However, as the youth become more able to succeed, they must begin seeing themselves as producers in society and not always in need of some assistance. Therefore, the mutuality becomes greater and the young people should be encouraged to serve the older adults in some way. The relationship should be such that the youth will know how to best serve the older adult. This type of program is ongoing by nature and is dependent on those involved as to how it proceeds.

Mediation Programs

Program: In this program older adults are part of a school mediation process and are available for informal mentoring following the mediation. The school has a policy that if a student misbehaves in a way that warrants a visit to a school administrator, the student is asked whether he or she would prefer punishment or mediation. If the answer is mediation, the student appears before a small group of students and older adults (recruited for this purpose), which mediates solutions to the behavior. An older adult is scheduled to go to the school each day. He or she may not be needed, but the schedule must be followed. The student is offered the chance to meet with the older adult on an informal basis in a mentorship relationship.

Mutuality and Ongoing: The program continues for the school year, and the older adults must be prepared to be involved on a regular basis. The school can decide whether any kind of mediation experience is necessary, but training both students and older adults for this mediation board is needed. Although there is no initial extrinsic mutual benefit in this program, the benefit for the older adult is derived from the mentoring relationship that can ensue. For the student, there is the opportunity to develop a relationship with an older adult.

Older Adults in Child Care

Program: These programs can occur with older adults working in child day care, in preschool, or as a teacher's assistant in elementary and middle schools. In all cases, older adults could be interviewed, and should be carefully trained, for the position. The level of assistance is determined by the administrator but should be important and integral to the program. Asking volunteers to do menial labors within the school setting is a sure way to avoid sustainability of the program. Rather, volunteers should be in positions in which they can make a significant difference to the program and the youth.

Mutuality and Ongoing: Even very young students can be involved in making this relationship mutually beneficial. Although the older adult is performing most of the service, the youth should work on small ways to make it reciprocal. Except for day care, which is an ongoing program, most often the time period is a school year.

Friendly Visiting

Program: Students are paired with frail or homebound older adults or those in nursing facilities and visit them on a regular basis. This is usually planned for older students if the visiting is one-on-one and especially if it occurs in their own time or schedule. This program requires a substantial amount of planning and preparation and should not be viewed as an easy intergenerational program because both groups are in contained locations and easy to reach.

First, students should have interacted with well elderly in a program or through community contacts before they are given the opportunity to meet with frail elderly. The reason for this is that if the student's initial contact is with frail elderly, that will become their normative frame of reference and stereotypes will simply be reinforced rather than positively changed. The transition from their knowing well, active, and productive older adults to being with some who are in need of substantial services is easier than the reverse. In many cases the friendly visiting does occur with well older adults in their own homes.

Second, the students must be well trained and prepared for visits to a nursing facility, and an aging education curriculum is especially important as it allows them to understand why these older adults are in need of such services and why they may respond to them in unfamiliar ways. Reflection and time to discuss what they feel and witness is an important part of this program. Programs exist in middle schools in which students are paired with nursing home residents and visit once or twice a week for an entire school year. Very often the students are at-risk academically or behaviorally and the residents are often in need as well.

Students and the older adults may do anything during the time of visiting, and although light chores may be acceptable, the time together is for being together, not for the student to do chores for the older adult.

Mutuality and Ongoing: The program could continue for the length of the school year as a scheduled event, but could also continue throughout the year on the student and older adult's own schedule. The longer the duration, the greater the relationship. During the visits the student should be instructed to gain from the older adult information and/or assistance that will benefit him/her as well, such as help with homework, oral history information, or writing poems and stories together. This way they both will be "serving" each other in a program of mutual benefit and respect.

Chore Programs

Program: Students work either in groups or as individuals to do chores for older adults who cannot perform them. Although this is an honorable program, it must be carefully directed so as not to reinforce the stereotype of older adults being consumers, rather than productive members, of society. This program can also include retired older adults who are engineers, woodshop workers, and so on who can work with students to actually build ramps and make modifications in homes for those with disabilities. That would allow students to work with older adults in service to other older adults—a doubly beneficial program. In addition, the project would incorporate other academic disciplines, such as math measurements, technology workshops, and design.

Mutuality and Ongoing: This program can vary in duration, so efforts should be made to make it a program of substance by investigating long-term projects such as home modifications. If the program is for younger students and small chores are the level that can be accomplished, then it is important to continue those chores for a significant length of time. An effort should be made by the older adult to give back something to the student and/or the school through tutoring, oral histories, craft work, and so on.

(An example of a chore program can be found in Chapter 2, Program Development, in the section on why good programs must be mutually beneficial.)

Suggested Reading

Barrow, G. (1996). *Aging, the Individual, and Society* (3rd ed.). St. Paul, MN: West Publishing Company.

Beal, R., & Berryman-Miller, S. (Eds.). (1988). *Dance for the Older Adult.* Reston, VA: The American Alliance for Health, Physical Education, Recreation, and Dance.

Caseley, J. (1991). *Dear Annie.* New York: Greenwillow Books.

Davis, S., & Ferdman, B. (1993). *Nourishing the Heart, A Guide to Intergenerational Arts Projects in the Schools.* New York: City Lore.

Frego, R. J. D. (1995, May). Uniting the Generations with Music Programs. *Music Educators Journal.*

Handel, R. D. (1996). *Teachers as Family Literacy Learners: Report from the Field.* Paper presented at the annual meeting of the American Educational Research Association, New York. Available through ERIC, ED398176.

Kaplan, M. (1994). *Side by Side, Exploring Your Neighborhood Through Intergenerational Activities*. Berkeley, CA: MIG Communications.

National Council on the Aging. (1994). *Family Friends, A Program Guide*. Washington, DC: Author.

Newman, S., Vander Ven, K., & Ward, C. (1992). *The Productive Employment of Older Adults in Child Care*. Generations Together: An Intergenerational Studies Program, University of Pittsburgh, University Center for Social and Urban Research, Pittsburgh, PA.

Perlstein, S., & Bliss, J. (1994). *Generating Community, Intergenerational Partnerships Through the Expressive Arts*. Brooklyn, NY: Elders Share the Arts.

Rostand, E. *Cyrano de Bergerac, A Treasury of the Theater*. (1963). Edited by J. Gassner, New York: Simon and Schuster.

Seefeldt, C. (1987). The Effects of Preschoolers' Visits to a Nursing Home. *Gerontologist, 27* (2), 228–232.

Lesson 1

Ageism and Stereotypes in Society

I had little expectations that seniors could do such interesting things.
I also didn't know that much about seniors and how they were so cool.
And I thought seniors couldn't do anything but sit on a rocking chair.
Boy all that changed when I started to write to my awesome pen-pal.
I'm really lucky to be doing this program it was great! I learned so
much about seniors and had fun at the same time.

—Ali, 4th grade

LESSON OVERVIEW

Students hear and probably use ageist expressions everyday. These expressions unconsciously affect their attitudes about aging. Although they are generally aware of gender bias and racism, the issue of ageism and age-related stereotypes are new to them. The recognition that ageism is an equally insidious form of discrimination, and the ramifications of that for a healthy society, is the topic under consideration here.

Learner Outcomes—Aging Issues
- Students will understand the meaning of the term *ageism* and its relation to other forms of discrimination.
- Students will discover the prevalence of ageism in society.
- Students will recognize that ageism is directly applicable to them.

Learner Outcomes—Integration with Academic Curricula
- Students will learn interviewing skills through oral and written communication.
- Students will perform simple math addition through compilation of collected data.
- Students will form hypotheses.
- Students will transfer data into basic bar graphs.
- Students will make inferences from the interpretation of data.

This lesson integrates with
Math: the evaluation and development of graphs; math compilation
Language Skills: interviewing techniques—oral communication
Literature: reading books with critical evaluation of ageist issues

GRADE ADJUSTMENTS

For grades two and three, teachers may want to have students interview people in small groups. Rather than graphs, the results can be tabulated and blocks can be placed in towers to simulate the graph itself. But the words and the concept of discrimination are important to retain as part of the lesson.

For middle school students, this can be made more sophisticated by interviewing larger numbers, by increasing the number and complexity of questions asked, and by focusing on reasons for their hypotheses and hypothesizing a more global perspective than the small sample interviewed. Once discriminatory issues are identified, the discussion can lead into business "downsizing" by offering early retirement options to relatively young-older people. What does that mean for our society and for the retiree who now has many more years left of what should be a productive life?

TERMS USED

Ageism	discrimination against people on the basis of age
Stereotypes	an unvarying, fixed, or conventional expression, notion, character, or mental pattern, having no individuality
Hypothesis	a principle that is supposed or taken for granted in order to draw a conclusion to prove the point in question
Bar Graph	a method of measuring in which a bar is used to show the measurement
Population	a group of individuals

MATERIALS NEEDED

graphing chart paper

PROCEDURE

Day 1
1. Ask students to describe an older adult.
   This can either be done by drawing pictures or through words.
2. Write the words on the board or have the students draw on the board.
   Note: Do not discourage any words; negative words are important. Probable words might include sad, lonely, fat, mean, witch, grumpy, slow, sick, kind, generous, geezer, biddy, old maid, sweet.
   Probable pictures might include squiggly lines on faces, canes, short, stooped over, unkempt, in wheelchairs.
3. Ask students what these words or drawings are saying about being old—is being old portrayed as good or bad? What do they think other people think about being old? How do they know?
4. Identify and define the words *stereotype* and *ageism* with them.
5. Ask students how the words and drawings they just drew fit into the definitions.
6. Now elicit discussion about how the students feel they are discriminated against because of their age.

Note: Probable answers might include: older people cut in front of them in lines; salespeople do not help them as readily as they do adults; store personnel follow students around; adults do not let them help with certain jobs.

You will need to discuss the difference between discrimination and age-related safety issues because you might also get answers such as "I'm not allowed to drive, to go on all the amusement park rides alone, ride my bike into town alone."

7. Assign the accompanying assignment. There should be equal numbers of students in each of the four age-group categories: elementary students (ages 6–12), teenagers (ages 13–19), adults (ages 20–60), older adults (ages 61–   ).

8. Review or discuss good interviewing techniques.

Day 2

1. Prepare bar graphs that look like figures 3–1.1 and 3–1.2:

   Note: The bar graphs may be created using a computer or copied from the figure presented in this chapter. For younger students, you may choose to leave more space between the numbers on the graph allowing for greater accuracy.

2. Review with or present to the class information about a bar graph.

3. Ask students to hypothesize what the graph they are to do will look like. Which age group will have known the word *ageism* the most? least? Which age group will have experienced ageism the most? least?

4. Have students work in groups of age categories. Ask them to tally the results of their interviews for questions 1 and 2 and then enter the results on the class bar graph.

5. Discuss the results.

   Note: The bar graph may show varied results depending on the demographics of your community. As the population of older adults continues to increase, demographers are beginning to divide them into "young-old" and "old-old" categories. You may find that a high number in the "adult" category have experienced discrimination. You may, therefore, want to divide the adult category into two smaller age group categories. This is also a wonderful opportunity to discuss business downsizing and early retirement issues.

6. Suggestions for discussion about the graph can include

   Variations to the hypothesis and why

   Reasons for the results

   The kinds of ageism people faced (see number 3 of the homework assignment)

   The correlation between knowing the definition of ageism and experiencing it

SUGGESTIONS FOR FURTHER ACTIVITY

1. Have students write a paragraph about being old intentionally using ageist words and stereotypes. Then have them rewrite the paragraph using nonageist words.

2. Have students compose a class letter to the local newspaper outlining the results of their survey and urging the town to be nonageist.

Figure 3–1.1   Do You Know What Ageism Is?

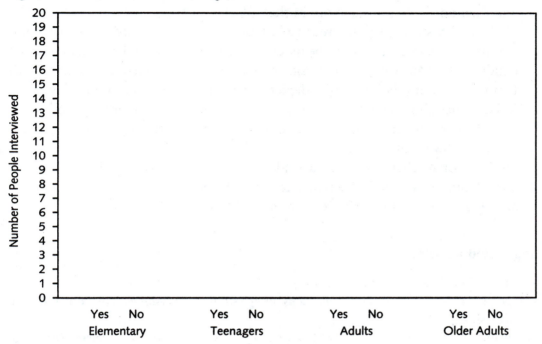

Students will fill in the graph based on the results of their interviews and answer tallies.

Figure 3–1.2   Have You Experienced Ageism?

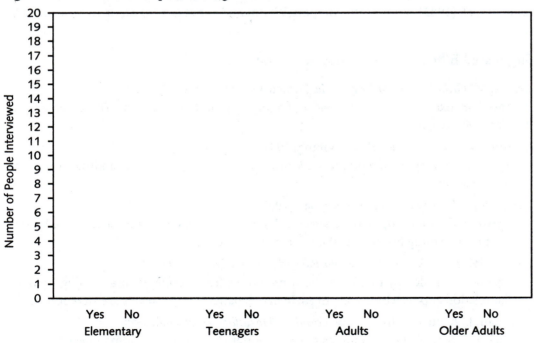

3. Have students prepare a bulletin board for the school identifying ageist words and then nonageist words to use in their place.

4. Have students role play different ages. Discuss stereotypes and ageist behavior, and then ask some students to be older adults, some to be adults, and some to be children. Students can design masks to help create their persona—decide with them if they want their masks to depict stereotypes or not. Try to role play a typical day, including activities such as going to the supermarket, driving, and shopping. Be sure students know it is acceptable to act out stereotypes. Discuss with students how it felt.

5. Students or teacher can select a trade book in which ageist attitudes are displayed. Students would role play and place the emphasis on the ageist activity, and then "rewrite" the script to eliminate the ageist activity.

Suggested Reading

Ageism. (1984, August–September). *Aging*.

Cooper, B. (1988). *Over the Hill: Reflections on Ageism Between Women*. Freedom, CA: The Crossing Press.

Coupland, N., & Coupland, J. (1993). Discourses of Ageism and Anti-Ageism. *Journal of Aging Studies, 7* (3), 279–301.

Goyer, A., Couper, D. P., & Donorfio, L. (1995). *Images of Aging in America, Children's Attitudes*. Washington, DC: AARP.

Mor-Barak, M. (1995). The Meaning of Work for Older Adults Seeking Employment: The Generativity Factor. *Aging and Human Development, 41* (4), 325–344.

Nussel, Jr., F. H. (1982). The Language of Ageism. *Gerontologist, 22* (3), 273–276.

Shonfeld, D. (1982). Who Is Stereotyping Whom and Why? *Gerontologist, 22* (3), 267–272.

Suggested Bibliography for Use with This Lesson

Beil, K. M. *Grandma According to Me*. Delacorte, 1992.

Ages 5–8. Example of negative view of aging by grandma but wonderful acceptance of it by granddaughter.

Carlson, N. *A Visit to Grandma's*. Viking, 1991.

Ages 5–8. A very unstereotypic view of a Thanksgiving visit to Grandma in her new condo in Florida.

Cosgrove, S. *Grampa-Lop*. Stern & Sloan, 1988.

Ages 1–5. Grampa-Lop may be a very old, gray bunny who is of no use to the older rabbits, but to the young bunnies of the thicket, he is magic.

Fox, M. *Winifred Gordon McDonald Partridge*. Kane, Miller, 1985.

Ages 5–8. A little boy discovers about memories from residents in a nursing home. A special relationship develops with an Alzheimer's patient. Illustrations are stereotypic.

Hoffman, J., & Burroughs, M. *My Grandma Has Black Hair*. Dial, 1988.

Ages 5–8. Stereotypes abound as granddaughter realizes her grandma doesn't fit those stereotypes.

Hurd, E. *I Dance in My Red Pajamas.* Harper & Row, 1982.

Ages 1–8. Mother and Father tell Jenny not to make noise when visiting her grandparents, but Jenny knows better—they aren't too old for noise and fun. Breaks stereotypes.

Khasa, D. K. *Tales of a Gambling Grandma.* Clarkson Potter, 1986.

Ages 8–11. Grandma tells stories of an active, adventurous life. Breaks stereotypes.

MacDonald, B. D. *Scarecrowell.* Lippincott, 1992.

Ages 5–8. Nathan is afraid of his neighbor, old Mrs. Crowell, until she befriends him and shares the beauty of her garden with him.

Mathis, S. B., *The Hundred Penny Box.* Viking, 1975.

Ages 8–11. Treatment of older adult by mother is sometimes stereotypic. Love of a boy for his great-great-aunt, their games, and his protectiveness of her.

McDonald, M. *The Potato Man.* Orchard Books, 1991.

Ages 5–11. Grandpa shares his story of how the potato man in his old neighborhood taught him an important lesson.

Rylant, C. *Miss Maggie.* Dutton, 1983.

Ages 8–11. Miss Maggie appears to be a witch to Nat and he is scared of her. When he realizes she has feelings, his stereotypic view disappears and they become friends.

Schwartz, D. *Supergrandpa.* Lothrop, 1991.

Ages 5–11. True story of an old man disregarding the blatant ageism that was thrust on him by judges in the Tour de Sweden.

Uchida, Y. *The Wise Old Woman.* McElderry, 1994.

Ages 5–11. A Japanese tale about a village that discriminates against old people. An old woman's wisdom saves the village from a marauding conqueror.

Wayland, A. H. *It's Not My Turn to Look for Grandma!* Knopf, 1995.

Ages 6–8. A "romp and stomp" picture book about an energetic grandma whose behavior sometimes makes her family very nervous.

Wilson, C. *A Treasure Hunt.* National Institutes of Health, 1980.

Ages 8+. *A Treasure Hunt* was written in the hopes that it will encourage children to be active in the lives of the elderly and make them aware of the special ways in which some older people try to deal with the prejudice that surrounds the world in which they live.

Ageism in Society

Name _____

My assigned age category is _____

Choose any three people in your assigned age category. Ask each of them the following three questions. Record their answers. *Note:* If the answer to question 1 is no, then you must tell them what ageism is in order for them to answer questions 2 and 3.

1. Do you know what ageism is?

   Person 1   yes _____   no _____

   Person 2   yes _____   no _____

   Person 3   yes _____   no _____

2. Have you ever experienced ageism?

   Person 1   yes _____   no _____

   Person 2   yes _____   no _____

   Person 3   yes _____   no _____

3. Tell an experience you had, or someone you know had, that shows ageism.

   Person 1 _____

   _____

   Person 2 _____

   _____

   Person 3 _____

   _____

Lesson 2

Changing Demographics

There are three very strong things that I learned from this program.
First I learned that you should live life to your full extent. Second never
say you are too old for anything. And third that people have to stop being
prejudiced to the elderly people because there are more elderly people
than ever before.

— William, 4th grade

LESSON OVERVIEW

The population of America is changing rapidly. Consider these statistics and predictions from the U.S. Bureau of the Census, 1990 census, which, as of 1997, are continuing to be on target:

- During the twentieth century, the number of persons in the United States under age 65 has tripled, but the number aged 65+ has increased by a factor of 11.
  In 1900 the 65+ age group comprised 1 in every 25 Americans (3.1 million).
  In 1994 they comprised 1 in every 8 Americans (33.2 million).
  The fastest growing group in America is the oldest-old, age 85+.
  In 1997 there were 3.86 million people in this category.
  In 2050 it is predicted there will be 18.2 million.
  In 1997 there were 61,000 people 100+ years old.
  In 2050 it is predicted there will be 834,000 who are 100+ years old.

- The under-18 age group will increase by 26 million by 2050, but its proportion of the total population may never be as large as it is today.

Concerning geographical distribution of this aging population, consider the following statistic taken from Leonard Hayflick's book, *How and Why We Age.*

In 1991, 52 percent of all people 65+ lived in nine states

California	over 3 million
New York	over 2 million
Flordia	over 2 million
Michigan	over 1 million
New Jersey	over 1 million
Illinois	over 1 million
Ohio	over 1 million
Texas	over 1 million
Pennsylvania	over 1 million

Students should understand both the reasons for these changing trends and the effect they will have on society in the future.

Learner Outcomes—Aging Issues
- Students will understand the present demographics of American society.
- Students will understand the future predictions of population demographics.
- Students will hypothesize the implications of those changes on society.

Learner Outcomes—Integration with Academic Curricula
- Students will interpret graphs and charts with mathematical applications.
- Students will form hypotheses.
- Students will identify trends and make predictions.

This lesson integrates with
Math: interpretation and development of graphs; predictions about future trends

Civics: government uses of census data; gathering of census data; government responses to the population it serves

History: how populations have changed through the years

Science: technological advances that contribute to longevity of life, including heart-lung machines, x-ray machines and scans; the role of exercise and good nutrition in maintaining good health; medical advances that have developed, including open-heart surgery, medicines, transplants

GRADE ADJUSTMENTS

This lesson lends itself to significant adjustments for levels of sophistication, but the concept must not be lost for any grade. Demographics is crucial in any sociological understanding of aging.

For lower grades, teachers should develop a simple line graph that depicts the number of older people increasing rapidly and the number of younger people increasing slowly. The lines can eventually cross in about the year 2030. Ask them how old they will be in 2030. Discussion should then focus on why these trends are occurring.

Middle school students can research the numbers in depth and develop different graphs and charts to display. The U.S. Bureau of the Census, Area Agencies on Aging, and AARP are good sources to which they can write or access via the internet for information. Hypotheses and discussions on the effect for the future could include social security concerns for the baby-boom generation and changing direction of U.S. fiscal spending.

TERMS USED

Population   a group of individuals
Census   an official count of population and recording of information

| Trend | to have a general tendency |
| Hypothesis | a principle that is supposed or taken for granted in order to draw a conclusion to prove the point in question |

MATERIALS NEEDED

graphing chart paper
local census form

PROCEDURE

Note: This lesson can be done as a whole class discussion or it can be done as a cooperative learning exercise in which students work in small groups to discuss the chart and try to interpret causes and implications for the future. Groups then come together to discuss each other's interpretations.

1. Discuss what a census is and why it is taken; begin on a local level and then discuss the U.S. census every ten years. Identify the offices responsible for the census taking. Show students a local census form. Discuss why each question is asked. Discuss why a local census is usually taken every year but the U.S. census is only every ten years.
2. Show students the chart below:

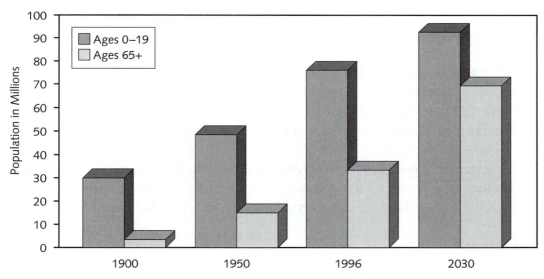

Figure 3–2.1   U.S. Census Data.
Source: U.S. Bureau of the Census, Current Population Reports, series P25-1130, "Population Projections of the U.S. by Age and Sex: 1995–2050." Release date: March 1996.

3. Taking one age group at a time, ask students to describe the trend in the population growth of their own age group and then of the older adult age group.
4. Ask students why they think this is happening in America.

Note: For the trend in the older-adult category, students will probably say that youth and adults are getting older and entering into that category. Accept the validity of that but point out that the death rate should at least equal that. Eventually lead them to realize that older adults are living longer. A discussion of why should include changes in medical technologies, better knowledge of nutrition and exercise for good health, and life satisfaction.

For the trend in the youth category, lead them to realize that the birthrate is declining. For proof of that ask them, by show of hands, how many of their grandparents came from families of five or more. Then ask how many of them come from families of five or more. Discussion should then include the economics of raising large families today, the trend to more working mothers, medical technologies, and changing industrial and agricultural technologies that create less need for large families to work on the farm.

5. Ask students why the changing demographics is important to watch and what it means for the future in their local city/town/community, and what it means to the United States.

Note: Discuss how local towns/cities adjust their spending with changes in population. For example, hiring more teachers, buying supplies and desks, and so on if the student population increases. Speculate how the United States might need to adjust its spending as it watches the number of older adults increase rapidly.

6. Ask students to discuss the importance of the previous lesson on ageism in view of this demographic information.

SUGGESTIONS FOR FURTHER ACTIVITY

1. Arrange a field trip to the local city/town clerk for a presentation about the census-taking procedures and how the results are tabulated and distributed. Students might be able to actually observe or assist in the process.
2. Have students identify problems and postulate solutions associated with taking a census. Example: How do we count the homeless?
3. Have students pretend they are advertising executives trying to come up with a slogan for a new product. Taking demographics into account, what is the slogan, and what is the advertisement/commercial? This can then be acted out and videotaped.

References

U.S. Bureau of the Census. (1992). *Current Population Reports Series.*
Hayflick, L. (1994). *How and Why We Age.* New York: Ballantine Books.
U.S. Bureau of the Census. Available: http://www.census.gov/

Suggested Reading

AARP. (1993). *Aging of the U.S. Population, Economic and Environmental Implication.* Washington, DC.
AARP. (1996). *A Profile of Older Americans.* Washington, DC.

Lesson **3**

How Families Have Changed

A grandmother says to her granddaughter, "I love you. You are a sweet baby. You will grow up to be a great person." She sings the baby to sleep. She hopes when the baby is her age she won't be ignored or be treated like a baby all over again.

— Charlotte, 4th grade

LESSON OVERVIEW

Families in the late twentieth century are no longer as physically close to each other as years ago. In the early part of the twentieth century, the extended family always lived nearby and assistance to family members was offered by that extended family. No longer. High job mobility, easier transportation, and a society that went from being agricultural to industrial to technological has altered that model.

In addition, the individual family structure has changed to include single-parent families; common-gender families; multicultural, interracial, and interreligious families; and multigeneration families. Grandparents raising grandchildren has become relatively common.

This lesson is a continuation of the demographic discussion. The lesson helps students to understand the causality of the changing size and nature of families in general and relate it to their own families. The homework sheet should be assigned prior to the lesson so it is available for discussion.

Learner Outcomes—Aging Issues
• Students will understand the nature of changing families in society.
• Students will understand the implications of those changes for older adults.
• Students will relate this to their own needs as a family.

Learner Outcomes—Integration with Academic Curricula
• Students will identify, through map skills, the location of their own families.
• Students will identify the changes in America from agricultural to technological.
• Students will write about the family.

This lesson integrates with
History: reading and identifying cities on maps; changes in society from agricultural to industrial to technological
Literature: reading trade books that identify the issue

GRADE ADJUSTMENTS

For younger grades, the lesson needs to remain positive. Focus on the strength of the family—whatever form it takes. Have students identify the attributes desired from a family. Then have them identify the people in their lives who provide that attribute. Stress that these people need not be related to them at all. Develop with them a broad definition of the term *family*.

For older grades, the lesson needs to be a recognition of what is occurring in society. Discuss the changing nature of families and allow students to explore and discuss the positive and/or negative implications.

TERMS USED

Paternal   on the father's side of the family
Maternal   on the mother's side of the family

MATERIALS NEEDED

map of the world
markers
prepared chart

PROCEDURE

Day 1
1. Have students do the homework with their parents/guardians.

Day 2
1. Students should individually transfer the first set of data from their homework onto a class map of the world.
2. Discuss with students why they think their families are so scattered or why they have stayed nearby. Discuss what is positive and what is negative about the moves. Be sure not to allow students to place a judgment on any scenario.

   Note: Answers should include jobs, better educational opportunities, and life-satisfaction issues. Positive points involve happiness, whereas negative issues might include being away from family and a support system.
3. Students should then individually transfer the information about family size onto a class chart that is laid out as in Figure 3–3.1.
4. Discuss with students why they think their families have gotten smaller, allowing that there are exceptions to every rule.

   Note: Answers should include a similar discussion to the one on the demographics lesson—the economics of large families, working mothers, technology, and the shift from an agricultural to a technological society. This is a good place for the discussion to focus. If you are in a city environment, ask whether their grandparents were too and trace the change in America as it developed. If you are in a rural setting, discuss why people might choose to stay in such an environment or why they might leave.

Figure 3–3.1 Changes in Family Size.

Number of People in Family for Each Generation

Students' Names	Grandparent	Parent	Student

5. Discuss what all this means for the older adults in society.

   Note: Point out that more older adults live without family nearby than ever before. Also include the discussion of grandparents moving to be in retirement areas such as Florida or Arizona. What does this mean for their old age? For families whose grandparents are nearby, does it or does it not make it easier for old age?

SUGGESTIONS FOR FURTHER ACTIVITY

1. Students can write their feelings about these changes—either in a journal or as an essay.
2. Have students interview older adults who have lived in the neighborhood for many years. Take oral histories and develop them into a book about the neighborhood. Students can discover how the town/city has changed over the years. Students can teach the older adults how to use the computer word processor as they interview them. The final project is a book about the town that can be sold for a fund-raiser or donated to the library.
3. Older students can interview older adults with the intent of discovering how the changes in family structure have affected them in their later years. Have they been able to compensate for the changes that they feel are negative?
4. Have students research maps of the town/city from when it may have been agricultural and discover how it has changed over the years.

5. Take a field trip to the library and research important families from the community, discovering how those families, and their life, differed from today.

Suggested Bibliography for Use with This Lesson

Cooney, B. *Island Boy*. Viking Penguin, 1988.

Ages 5–8. Story of three generations and their life dedicated to family and community and rooted in the island. Achievement, values, and devotion to one's home.

Joosee, B. *Jam Day*. Harper & Row, 1987.

Ages 1–5. Ben and Mama go to visit grandma and grandpa and see all their relatives. Although they are just the two of them at home, Ben finds out that he is part of a big, happy family.

Thomas, J. R. *Saying Goodbye to Grandma*. Clarion Books, 1988.

Ages 5–8. A 7-year-old goes to grandma's funeral. Exploration of death and of families who live far from each other.

Homework

Discovering My Family

Name _____

Answer these questions with your parents or guardian. Do not worry if you cannot answer all the questions; do as much as you can. If the people mentioned have died, just write that on the line.

1. Tell in which city/town and country the following people live

   My maternal grandfather   _____

   My maternal grandmother   _____

   My paternal grandfather   _____

   My paternal grandmother   _____

      _____

   Any aunts and uncles   _____

      _____

      _____

      _____

2. Identify the size of the family of each person listed. Include that person in your count.

   My maternal grandfather's family   _____

   My maternal grandmother's family   _____

   My paternal grandfather's family   _____

   My paternal grandmother's family   _____

      _____

   My mother's family   _____

   My father's family   _____

      _____

   My family   _____

Lesson **4**

Ageism in the Media

From the minute we are born we are on the way to aging. The wrinkles on the face of an older person are the paths they take in their adventures through life. Advertising tries to make everyone look and feel young.

— Katarina, 4th grade

LESSON OVERVIEW

The media is a prime source from which children can make definitive connections to ageism. In this lesson the media includes TV, magazine ads, greeting cards. In the latter case, ageism is quite obvious in the "humor" about aging and old age. The intent is to analyze the media and recognize the prevalence of age-related issues, especially those that are ageist or stereotypic. Then, it is important to determine the extent to which a consumer can make changes.

The materials needed for this lesson could be solicited from the students directly as a homework assignment, but I usually gather them myself so that I am sure they will accomplish the lesson outcomes.

Learner Outcomes—Aging Issues
 • Students will be able to recognize examples of ageism in the various media.
 • Students will recognize the implications of ageism in the media for children.
 • Students will understand how to become activists against ageism.

Learner Outcomes—Integration with Academic Curricula
 • Students will be able to think critically about an issue.
 • Students will hypothesize implications for the future.
 • Students will write letters.
 • Students will develop communication skills.
 • Students will critique the scientific claims of advertisements/commercials.

 This lesson integrates with
 Language arts: written communication
 Science: understanding the cause for signs of old age and evaluating the effectiveness of supposed remedies
 Critical Thinking: being able to evaluate the validity of media claims
 Civics: activism taken to defend consumer rights

GRADE ADJUSTMENTS

This lesson needs little grade adjustment. The benefit for all ages is clear. Younger students could focus more on designing cards that provide a positive message about aging, whereas older students might pursue in greater detail the possibility of becoming activists in their pursuit of eliminating ageism in the media.

TERMS USED

Media   written or electronic communication intended to convey a message or information[*]

Hypothesis   a principle that is supposed or taken for granted in order to draw a conclusion to prove the point in question

MATERIALS NEEDED

about five or six birthday cards that are negative in their view of aging (unfortunately this is easy to find in any greeting card store—look for the "Over the Hill" cards and party accessories) and five or six that are positive

a few magazine ads that advertise "wrinkle-free" creams

any other example of ageism in the media

science books on the skin, describing what causes wrinkles

PROCEDURE

1. Discuss with students what the media is. Be broad in definition and include anything that gets messages out to people—such as the greeting card industry as well as typical media such as TV, radio, magazines, newspapers. Discuss that these messages can be obvious or subtle.
2. Show students the negative birthday cards and ask them to comment on the messages. Contrast it with the birthday cards that have positive messages. Ask for comparisons.
3. Ask students what the negative messages are saying about aging. How do we know they are negative?

   Note: The main issue here is that the messages are negative because society places a low value on the aging process and on older people. Discuss how it would be different if society valued aging or if wrinkles were considered beautiful.
4. Ask students to note the pictures on the cards. Are they stereotypes of old age?
5. Discuss what the person receiving the card must think or feel.

   Note: At this point students always tell me that I have no sense of humor . . . that it is meant to be a joke . . . that they are usually sent to people who are relatively young. The answer I give is that what they are saying is true, but messages can be subtle and can become part of our memories and our beliefs. And even if the people receiving these cards laugh, they also know that they are at an age where people make fun of their age. They are indeed getting older and society will not value them too much longer. That message is hard to erase with a laugh.

---

[*]Author's definition.

6. Ask students why people do not like to tell their age.

   Note: Answers will likely include "they are embarrassed, they don't want to be the object of jokes, they don't want people to think badly of them." Ask students how it would be different if being old was valued. Would people then want to tell their age?

7. Ask students what they can do as consumers to try to eliminate the cards with negative messages about aging.

8. Show students the magazine advertisements; ask for comments on the messages.

9. Ask the students to hypothesize whether they think the claims are accurate or false.

10. Research with them the scientific basis for the claims. Study the skin and why it wrinkles. Then let them decide whether their hypotheses were correct.

11. Discuss the potential of what face-lifts accomplish, and whether that is a temporary or a permanent change in the skin.

12. Ask student what they can do as consumers to try to encourage advertisers to be accurate and value aging.

13. Analyze current TV shows and commercials in the same way as was done with cards and magazine ads. This is a review of the homework assignment.

SUGGESTIONS FOR FURTHER ACTIVITY

1. Have students design birthday cards that talk about aging in a positive way. Be sure they design pictures and text.

2. Students can design a school bulletin board with examples of ageist and nonageist birthday cards, urging students and families to purchase the correct ones. This can also be put into a school newspaper.

3. Have students write to the corporations that produce the examples of negative messages, explaining their aversion to the cards. They can also write editorials and letters to the editor in local newspapers, making the public more aware of the issue.

4. The letter-writing campaign can also be done for local and network TV stations.

Media Alert

Name _____

Watch three TV commercials and one TV show, and find three magazine ads. For each one, answer these four questions:

1. What is the name of the show or the name of the product?
2. What is the age category of the people shown?
3. Was there ageism displayed? If yes, describe it; if no, tell why not.
4. Was there stereotyping? If yes, describe it; if no, tell why not.

TV Commercial

TV Commercial

TV Commercial

TV Show

Magazine Ad

Magazine Ad

Magazine Ad

Lesson 5

Ageism in Literature

*I learned a lot of new things about my grandma when she
was my age. I used to be a little afraid of really old people
(like my great-grandmother who's almost 99), but now I'm not.
I know she was young like me once too.*

—Danielle, 4th grade

LESSON OVERVIEW

Students often believe that what they read in books is true and right. Yet many intergenerational trade books have examples of ageism, stereotyping, and age-related negative attitude portrayals. This lesson will help students to develop critical-thinking skills when reading books and to identify ageist thinking in books. Stress that a book may be sensitive and caring, may provide a wonderful lesson, and may be very enjoyable and still contain ageism or stereotyping. The important point is that ageism and stereotyping are unfortunately integral to our way of life and our thinking, and are, therefore, even reflected in books that provide good reading. As ageism becomes a greater issue in society, this integration into our normal thinking will likely be eliminated.

There is some debate over whether young students should be encouraged to read books that are ageist because they might incorporate that thinking into their normative frame of reference. Nonageist book lists have been compiled. I would rather students read all books and be taught to develop critical-thinking skills that will allow them to assess the books and decide their value. This, of course, is up to individual teachers, and this lesson, although designed to critically assess all books, can be altered to read only books that present older adults or their situations in positive ways.

This lesson accommodates well to a cooperative learning class and is written in that way. But it also does well as a class lesson if you choose to read the books to the class as a whole and then follow it with class discussion.

Learner Outcomes—Aging Issues
- Students will think critically about ageism in trade books.
- Students will recognize the implications of ageism in literature for young children.

Learner Outcomes—Integration with Academic Curricula
- Students will share reading skills in cooperative learning.
- Students will interpret and analyze literature.
- Students will communicate through oral presentations.
- Students will listen to other presentations.
- Students will become critical thinkers.

This lesson integrates with

Literature: reading of books and identifying issues

Critical Thinking: assessment of books for ageist issues; interpretation

Language Arts: oral communication, reading, and listening skills

Art: evaluating illustrations for reality or fantasy

History: comparison of older copyright books with newer ones and the role of the older adult in each—an interpretation that may reflect society's changing roles

GRADE ADJUSTMENTS

The major adjustments for higher or lower grades is in the choice of literature to be read. In addition, the extent of interpretation and analysis can be altered. For grades two and three, teachers may want to provide, or ask the school librarian to choose, intergenerational books that are not only age appropriate, but also limited in their subject to relationship development rather than issues. The choice of books may also focus on stereotypic pictures rather than verbiage. For higher grades, the chapter books can deal with relationships and issues and the extent of analysis can be greater. Older students can also read books intended for younger children (picture books) so that a discussion can occur about influences of books on young children's attitude formation.

TERMS USED

Ageism   discrimination against people on the basis of age

Stereotype an unvarying, fixed, or conventional expression, notion, character, or mental pattern having no individuality

MATERIALS NEEDED

Trade books that are examples of positive age-related issues and relationships or ones that provide examples of negative, ageist thinking. Often these latter books are sensitive and wonderful, but have something in their content or illustration that is stereotypic or ageist. See the bibliography list.

PROCEDURE

1. Divide the class into small reading groups. Provide each group with a book to read aloud by everyone taking turns reading.

   Note: The books I like to use for this exercise are both positive and negative. Examples and include:

   • *My Grandma Has Black Hair,* Mary Hoffman & Joanna Burroughs—ages 5–8
   Obvious example of stereotypes and their comparison to a grandmother who does not fit those stereotypes. One page presents a stereotyped or storybook example of an older person, and the facing page shows the grandparent who

does not fit the stereotype. This allows very young children to easily identify stereotypes and recognize that they often do not apply. Ask children whether the stereotypes in the book apply to an older adult they know.

- *Supergrandpa,* David Schwartz—ages 5–11
Good example of ageism in which an older adult wants to enter a bike race, the Tour of Sweden, and is not even allowed to compete because the judges, and his family, decide he is too old. Students will easily see the injustice because the older man is obviously capable. What makes it so relevant is that it is a true story.

- *The Hundred Penny Box,* Sharon Bell Mathis—ages 8–11
A subtle example of ageism in which an older adult is made to nap even though she is not tired. The stereotype that older people must nap is recognized by the child in the book, who loves his great-great-aunt and feels her pain when she is required to do something against her will. Discuss with the children why the older adult is crying, how she must feel after she is "put to bed" and how adults often treat older adults like children.

- *Wilfred Gordon McDonald Partridge,* Mem Fox—ages 5–8
A sensitive story about a little boy who helps his favorite friend, a probable Alzheimer's victim in the nursing home next to his home, "find" her memories. The problem lies in the pictures that are exaggerated and stereotypic. Although it is the illustrator's stylization, ask students what these pictures say about how older adults look, and what the interpretations of very young children might be.

- *Miss Maggie,* Cynthia Rylant—ages 8–11
A wonderful story of a boy who is scared of the "witch" who lives nearby until his heart conquers his fears. Stereotypes exist in the sensitive pictures and in the text, but they dissolve as the relationship grows.

- *Annie and the Old One,* Miles Miska—ages 8–12
A wonderful story of a Native American girl whose mischievous activity is an attempt to stop the production of a rug after her grandmother predicts her own death when the rug is finished. Grandma helps her understand that death is a normal part of life. A positive example of an older adult as a role model and a productive member of the family who provides a wise and sensitive discussion of the circle of life.

- *Loop the Loop,* Barbara Dugan—ages 8–12
A feisty older woman teaches a young child about the yo-yo and about life. Despite being confined to a wheelchair this woman doesn't fit any stereotypes of old age except biological. Even while confined to a hospital and obviously confused, she presents a positive role model for old age.

2. Ask the groups to discuss the following questions/issues amongst themselves and be prepared to present them to the class. Everyone in the group should have a part in the presentation to the class.

- Give a brief synopsis of the book to the class.
- Explain the examples of ageism or stereotyping you found in the book.
- If your book portrayed the older adult or aging in a positive way, explain how.
- Locate a reading passage, or pictures, that will support your statements.

3. Discuss with the class how, as the groups present their book to the class, the class can be critical listeners and ask pertinent questions. Students should be encouraged to use their own reading experiences to look for the same issues in other books.

4. After all the presentations, students should discuss the books as a class and explore the prevalence of ageist thinking in books.

SUGGESTIONS FOR FURTHER ACTIVITY

1. Students can create a monthly intergenerational newsletter with book reviews that address ageism and stereotypes.

2. Take a field trip to the library and meet with the librarian to discuss the purchase of intergenerational books. Students may be surprised to know the number of books that deal with older and younger people together.

3. Have students take a sampling of trade books and make a graph depicting the number of intergenerational books that deal with death or dying and the number that deal with aging as a productive time in a person's life.

4. Have students write to intergenerational authors and ask them their views on ageism in literature. Ask them their views on aging in society and if they think of that as they write.

5. Have students write an intergenerational book about themselves and an older adult in their life.

6. Invite older adults to the classroom to read some of these books to the children and then to discuss with the children their own feelings about discrimination due to age.

Suggested Reading

Brandt, P. O., & O'Neal, J. I. (1995). *Passing Stories On.* Book Links: Connecting Books, Libraries, and Classrooms.

Hart, A. (1995). *The Young and the Old.* Book Links: Connecting Books, Libraries, and Classrooms.

Hittleman, C. G. (1996, July). *Grandparents and Grandchildren in Children's Literature: Interactions That Enhance Learning.* Paper presented at the International Reading Association World Congress on Reading. Available through ERIC, ED397391.

McGuire, S. L. (1990). *Non-Ageist Picture Books for Young Readers, An Annotated Bibliography for Preschool to Third Grade.* Center for Understanding Aging, University of North Texas, Denton, TX.

Ornstein, S. (1995). *Celebrating Grandparents.* Book Links: Connecting Books, Libraries, and Classrooms.

Pond, M. (1995). *Creating Memories.* Book Links: Connecting Books, Libraries, and Classrooms.

Suggested Bibliography for Use with This Lesson

Dugan, B. *Loop the Loop.* Puffin, 1993.

Ages 8–12. A young girl and an old woman form a relationship that lasts even after the woman enters a nursing home.

Fox, M. *Wilfred Gordon McDonald Partridge.* Kane Miller, 1985.

Ages 5–8. A little boy discovers about memories from residents in a nursing home. Illustrations are stereotypic.

Hoffman, M., & Burroughs, J. *My Grandma Has Black Hair.* Dial, 1988.

Ages 5–8. Stereotypes abound as granddaughter realizes her grandma doesn't fit those stereotypes.

Mathis, S. B. *The Hundred Penny Box.* Viking, 1975.

Ages 8–11. The love of a boy for his great-great-aunt is explored through their games and his protectiveness of her. Treatment of the great-great-aunt by the boy's mother reflects some stereotypes.

Rylant, C. *Miss Maggie.* Dutton, 1983.

Ages 8–11. Miss Maggie appears to be a witch to Nat who is scared of her. When he realizes she has feelings, his stereotypic view disappears and they become friends.

Schwartz, D. *Supergrandpa.* Lothrop, 1991.

Ages 5–11. The true story of an old man disregarding the blatant ageism thrust on him by the judges in the Tour de Sweden bicycle race.

Older Adults in Literature

Name _____

Read five books about older adults and young people. List the books you read and answer the questions.

Books I Read

1. Title _____

   Author _____

2. Title _____

   Author _____

3. Title _____

   Author _____

4. Title _____

   Author _____

5. Title _____

   Author _____

Questions

1. Did any of the books describe or show the older adult in a way that was a stereotype? Was there an example of ageism in the book?

   Book _____

2. Choose one book. Did the story describe or talk about aging, growing old, or dying? How did the characters deal with it? Did they interact?

   Book _____

3. Choose one book. Did the young person in the book always like the older person? How do you know? Did the young person like the older person better at the end of the book than at the beginning? What caused the change?

Book _____

4. Which book did you like best? Why? What did you learn from the book?

Book _____

Lesson 6

Housing Options for Older Adults

This class taught me about relationships between seniors and young people and about stereotypes. No matter how old you are you're still as young as everyone else on the inside, and no one should judge you by your looks.

— Mary Beth, 4th grade

LESSON OVERVIEW

Older adults may want to change their living arrangements later in life for many reasons, and they have many options. Reasons can include the death of a spouse when a large home often seems too hard to handle alone, a desire to live closer to one's children or family, a concern over health-related issues, and a desire to be with people one's own age. The options include congregate housing, assisted-living or managed-care facilities, continuing-care facilities, retirement complexes, and nursing homes. Each has a positive and negative attribute.

Students involved in intergenerational programs may be in families that are making decisions about how to help grandma or grandpa, and a student's suggestions or advice on options can prove valuable. Understanding about these facilities also allows students to get beyond the frightening aspects of them and enables their visits to their grandparent in the facility to be easier and even rewarding.

This lesson does not ask students to understand the housing options to the extent that they can make a decision about their value in society. Frankly unless we have actually lived in a facility we cannot fully understand the ramifications of any particular living arrangement. Instead, the lesson asks students and their families to discuss one of the housing options available and identify what they think would be positive or negative aspects of it. Weighing the benefits and drawbacks of any issue is the way to make good, informed decisions and that is valuable for students to learn. The act of weighing these particular kinds of options with family members, especially older members, allows students to see the value of discussion and the importance of varying perspectives and opinions. Finally, these options must be presented and discussed in a nonjudgmental manner. One option is not better than another. Rather at different stages in life, and with different needs to consider, there are different possibilities.

U.S. Bureau of the Census statistics indicate that in 1990 only 1 percent of those aged 65 to 74 years lived in a nursing facility, but 24 percent aged 85+ lived in nursing homes. With increased age comes increased dependency.

But, the 1993 Census figures on housing indicate that:

In the category aged 65+: 9.3 million live alone
                            16.8 million live with their spouse
                            3.9 million live with other relatives
                            687,000 live with nonrelatives
For those ages 85+:   1.2 million live alone
                            608,000 live with their spouse
                            645,000 live with other relatives
                            85,000 live with nonrelatives

Although dependency increases with age, greater numbers of the oldest-old still live outside of institutionalized settings.

The basic options for housing include

- Living in one's own private home.
- Living with family members in their private home.
- Homesharing. This option allows older adults to stay in their own private home but provides help with finances and housekeeping; it also avoids loneliness by inviting others to share that home with them.
- Accessory apartments. By adding an apartment addition to a private home, older adults can live with others and still remain independent.
- Portable homes. These homes can be placed in the yard of a private home, allowing older adults to live near others but enabling everyone to be entirely independent in living facilities.
- Retirement communities. These are independent living facilities that might be federally subsidized. They are often in village-like settings that are usually for the exclusive rental or purchase of older adults.
- Congregate housing. Usually a large private home or small inn-like facility, this is a residential environment with more shared space than independent space. Residents have their own bedroom units but often share living and kitchen spaces. It is not uncommon to have staff living there to provide support services.
- Assisted-living facilities. These residential group facilities provide private or semiprivate living and assistance with daily activities but no nursing care. They will provide emergency care and a range of related services that differ from one facility to another.
- Continuing-care retirement communities. A full range of living options that allow older adults to remain in one facility and change accommodations to receive added support and care as needed. The accommodations range from totally independent living to assisted living to nursing-home care; meals and activities are available. Residents are under a contractual agreement in this facility.
- Nursing homes. For those whose medical condition requires full time assistance, a nursing home provides that care.

In this lesson only some of these options will be discussed, but certainly each of them warrants exploration if this is of special interest to you and your students.

Learner Outcomes—Aging Issues
- Students will explore the housing options for older adults.
- Students will analyze the pros and cons of housing options.
- Students will hypothesize the effects of housing options on social structures.

Learner Outcomes—Integration with Academic Curricula
- Students will interview older adults and interpret results.
- Students will communicate orally.

This lesson integrates with

Language Arts: interviewing skills, oral communication, listening skills, letter writing

Art: the design of homes for older adults

Math: finances involved in building homes, designs appropriate for older adults and the execution of those designs, measurements

History/Social Studies: neighborhood studies of what is available for older adults in housing opportunities, maps and locations of housing

Literature: reading of books about different housing options, critical evaluation of advantages/disadvantages of each as presented by the author and as evaluated by the students

GRADE ADJUSTMENTS

Teachers of lower elementary grades can use this lesson to refine the development of questions and interviewing techniques. Following the interviews students should report the results to the class. A visit to a local retirement home or nursing home is possible but care must be taken that children are well prepared for what they see. Prior to a visit to a nursing home, children should have some involvement with the well elderly so that the children don't reinforce, rather than change, their stereotypes.

Teachers of middle school students may choose to have students research the numbers of older adults living in various kinds of living facilities in their state (Area Agencies on Aging will be helpful for this information) and graph the results. Implications for how these living facilities affect communities is a relevant discussion. For example, what is the result of a luxurious continuing-care facility that has a bank, grocery store, movie theater, and hair salon located within its own environment? For the older adult, it means never having to leave the house, which results in no interaction with the community or with other generations except grandchildren, if they visit. For the community, it means less revenue for local businesses, no interaction with other generations, and no support of local activities.

TERMS USED

Types of Living Facilities	(see the lesson overview for types and definitions)
Retirement	to withdraw oneself from work

PROCEDURE

Day 1

1. Divide class into small groups. Assign each group a different housing option. If you choose to assign housing options other than those from the list provided in the overview, be sure they represent the kinds of options that will encourage a discussion. A representative sample would be

> living with relatives in a private home
> retirement complexes/villages
> congregate housing
> continuing-care facilities
> nursing homes

2. Homework should be done at this point.

Day 2

1. The small groups convene, discuss the results of their interviews, and prepare a short presentation to the class about their findings.

2. How do the answers of the adults differ from those of the older adults? Does this imply anything about stereotypes of different housing options?

   Note: Most older adults will say they would never want to go into a nursing home, because they have the vision of the older type of nursing facility. Newer ones are trying to break that stereotype and are usually more pleasant than anticipated. This is where a visit to a nursing home would be desirable. Another option is to have a nursing-home director come to visit the classroom. Also, the older adults may have different psychological needs than the younger adult, and that may affect their viewpoint.

3. Discussion about the reports leads to a discovery that there is no one perfect option and that housing is a personal choice.

SUGGESTIONS FOR FURTHER ACTIVITY

1. Arrange a field trip to some of the housing facilities in your area. Prior to your visit, ask the tour guide to discuss with the students the benefits of that type of facility for older adults, as well as the benefits of that particular facility. If they are willing, ask them to also discuss the social problems they encounter with that type of facility. In class have students make a chart depicting the different facilities and their pros and cons.

2. Visit the town/city clerk, board of assessors, or local library and research the number of older adult housing options in your community. Compare this to the demographic information you may have obtained about the community in Lesson 2. Are the number of facilities appropriate to the demographic numbers?

3. Have students make a map of the community and identify the location of the various older adult housing facilities. Are the facilities in the mainstream of the community, or are they located at a distance from the center of the com-

munity? Does this make a difference in the social interactions of different generations?

4. Have students develop pen-pal programs with the residents of the housing facilities. Be aware of the requirements for meaningful programs and note the suggestions about pen-pal programs at the beginning of this chapter.

5. Have students design a living facility that would be welcoming to both older adults and younger generations. This should include physical and social structures.

Suggested Reading

AARP. (1991). *Selecting Retirement Housing.* Washington, DC: AARP Advertising Standards, Publications Division and Consumer Affairs, Program Division.

AARP. (1992). *Your Home Your Choice.* Washington, DC: AARP Consumer Affairs, Program Coordination and Development Department.

AARP. (1992). *Understanding Senior Housing for the 1990s.* Washington, DC: AARP Consumer Affairs Department.

AARP. (1994). *The Do*Able Renewable Home.* Washington, DC: AARP Consumer Affairs, Program Coordination and Development Department.

AARP. (1996). *Housing.* Washington, DC: AARP Consumer Information Series.

U.S. Bureau of the Census. (1992). *Census of Population, General Population Characteristics, U.S.* Washington, DC: U.S. Government Printing Office, CP-1-1.

U.S. Bureau of the Census. (1993). *Nursing Home Population Increase in Every State.* Washington, DC: U.S. Government Printing Office Press Release CB93-117.

Internet access to the U.S. Bureau of the Census: http://www.census.gov/

Suggested Bibliography for Use with This Lesson

Blue, R. *Grandma Didn't Wave Back.* Franklin Watts, 1972.

Ages 8–11. Family deals with grandmother's senility and with granddaughter's anger when the family decides on a nursing home. But grandma helps her granddaughter understand. Also on video from Films for the Humanities, Young People's Specials, 1-800-257-5126.

Brown, M. W. *When the Wind Blew.* Harper & Row, 1977.

Ages 5–8. An old woman lives alone and derives comfort from her 17 cats.

Buck, P. *The Beech Tree.* John Day, 1955.

Ages 8–11. Grandfather comes to live with his family and it is an adjustment.

Bunting, E. *Sunshine Home.* Clarion, 1994.

Ages 5–11. Timmie visits his grandmother who has moved to the nursing home after she broke her hip. He understands that everyone is pretending that nothing is wrong and insists they talk about it.

Caseley, J. *When Grandpa Came to Stay.* Greenwillow, 1986.

Ages 5–11. A widower comes to live with his daughter's family. The grandson visits the cemetery with his grandfather, and they share love for grandma and help grandpa adjust to his new home.

Cleaver, V., & Cleaver, B. *Queen of Hearts.* Lippincott, 1978.

Ages 11–14. A seventy-nine-year-old grandmother cannot live alone without help. Her 12-year-old granddaughter seeks solutions that allow grandmother to remain independent.

Clymer, E. *The Getaway Car.* Dutton, 1978.

Ages 8–11. Maggie and grandma decide to run away together when it is decided to put grandma in a nursing home and Maggie in a good environment.

Cole, N. *The Final Tide.* M. K. McElderry Books, 1990.

Ages 11–14. When the Tennessee Valley Authority builds a dam to bring electricity to the area, everyone moves except grandma who refuses to leave her home.

Delton, J., & Tucker, D. *My Grandma's in a Nursing Home.* Whitman & Co., 1986.

Ages 5–11. Grandson visits his grandmother in a nursing home and with his mother's help discovers it's not so scary and he really can make friends there.

Denker, H. *Horowitz and Mrs. Washington.* Putnam, 1979.

Ages 14+. A 79-year-old independent man makes a decision between going to a nursing home or employing help in his home. His desire to remain in his own home helps him adjust to the independent woman who helps him.

Fine, A. *The Granny Project.* Farrar, Strauss, & Giroux, 1983.

Ages 11+. Four children's efforts to keep grandmother out of a nursing home.

Gaeddert, L. *A Summer Like Turnips.* Holt, 1989.

Ages 11–14. While spending the summer at his grandfather's retirement village, Bruce helps Gramps get over the death of his wife.

Goldman, S. *Grandma Is Somebody Special.* Whitman, 1976.

Ages 1–5. A young girl visits her grandmother in an apartment building in a city.

Green, P. *Mildred Murphy, How Does Your Garden Grow?* Addison-Wesley, 1977.

Ages 8–11. Mildred's loneliness disappears when she befriends a woman living in a condemned garage. Living arrangement can lead to discussion of why older people may be homeless (see Lesson 7 on economics as well).

Greenfield, E. *Grandma's Joy.* Collins, 1980.

Ages 5–8. Grandma is sad because they have to move from their home. Granddaughter reminds her that they still have each other.

Griffith, H. *Georgia Music.* Greenwillow, 1986.

Ages 5–8. Granddaughter spends summer on grandfather's farm in Georgia. When grandfather has to leave, the sounds of Georgia make him feel better.

_____. *Grandaddy's Place.* Greenwillow, 1987.

Prequel to *Georgia Music.* Janetta adjusts to the country with grandpa.

_____. *Grandaddy and Janetta.* Greenwillow, 1993.

Janetta returns to visit after a year's absence.

_____. *Grandaddy's Stars.* Greenwillow, 1995.

Grandaddy leaves Georgia and moves in with Janetta.

Guernsey, J. B. *Journey to Almost There.* Ticknor & Fields, 1985.

Ages 11–14. When grandfather is about to be placed in a nursing home a girl takes him and runs away, but as his health declines difficult decisions are made.

Hamm, D. J. *Grandma Drives a Motor Bed.* Whitman & Co, 1987.

Ages 1–8. Grandson helps grandma who is bed ridden in a hospital bed at home. This book illustrates grandma's frustrations with illness but also expresses love and hope.

Herman, C. *Our Snowman Has Olive Eyes.* Dutton, 1977.

Ages 8–11. A girl shares her room with her grandmother but doesn't mind because grandma is helpful and understanding. Also her granddaughter understands grandma's need to be self-sufficient. The joys and problems of aging are portrayed with great sensitivity.

Hobbie, W. D. *Bloodroot.* Crown, 1991.

Ages 9–12. Lizzie and her grandmother join forces to save the rural New England land they love from the developers who threaten it.

Holl, K. *No Strings Attached.* Atheneum, 1988.

Ages 11–14. A 12-year-old girl's mother is a paid companion to an old man. When they move into his home, the girl experiences an initial resentment. The book illustrates an alternative to older people having to leave their own homes.

Mathis, S. B. *The Hundred Penny Box.* Viking, 1975.

Ages 8–11. Love of a boy for his great-great-aunt. Her move to his home causes problems when his mother tries to get rid of some remaining special possessions. This book illustrates the adjustments that must be made when moving into another's home.

Mazer, N. F. *A Figure of Speech.* Delacorte, 1979.

Ages 11–14. When her family wants to put grandpa in a nursing home, his granddaughter and he run away to his old farm but they find it sad and decrepit. Grandpa gives up and dies.

Myers, W. D. *Won't Know Till I Get There.* Puffin, 1988.

Ages 11–14. A boy and his friends are caught spray painting a subway and are sentenced to work in a nursing home.

Ross, S. *My Visit to the Nursing Home: A Children's Story of Loving and Sharing Between the Generations.* Plantation Distinctive Publishing, 1995.

Ages Preschool–7. This book shows the positive side of sharing time with nursing-home residents.

Ruckman, I. *This Is Your Captain Speaking.* Walker, 1987.

Ages 11–14. Fifteen-year-old Tom, intimidated by his older brother's athletic success, refuses to have anything to do with sports. Instead, he spends time at the nursing home, where his mother is a cook. There he meets a girl and discovers he has a favorite resident who falls seriously ill.

Sarton, M. *As We Are Now.* Norton, 1973.

Ages 14+. A 76-year-old heart attack victim who is put in a nursing home tells of her fight to keep her mind intact and die with dignity.

Schecter, B. *Grandma Remembers.* Harper & Row, 1989.

Ages 1–5. A grandma and grandson tour a beloved old house as they prepare to leave it by saying goodbye to its memories.

Silverman, S. *On Grandmother's Roof.* Macmillan, 1990.

Ages 1–5. Laundry day at grandma's is special because laundry is hung to dry on the roof of the apartment house. While up there, they picnic, dance, and play.

Smith, R. K. *The War with Grandpa*. Dell Yearling, 1984.

Ages 8–11. Upset that he has to give up his room when grandpa moves in, Pete declares war. A nasty trick makes Pete realize he has gone too far and a good compromise is reached.

Snyder, C. *The Great Condominium Rebellion*. Dell, 1983.

Ages 11–14. Thirteen-year-old Stacy and 12-year-old Marc visit their newly retired grandparents in their Florida condominium and find an adventure.

Udry, J. M. *Mary Jo's Grandmother*. Whitman, 1970.

Ages 5–8. Mary Jo visits her grandmother in the country and when grandma falls and there is no telephone in her home, Mary Jo has to go for help. Good discussion of why sometimes it is necessary to move older adults from their homes.

Woodruff, E. *Dear Napolean, I Know You're Dead But...*. Holiday, 1992.

Ages 8–11. Marty sends a letter to Napolean after Gramps tells him about a courier at his nursing home who can deliver messages to the dead. Marty is astounded when he receives a reply to his letter.

Housing Options for Older Adults

Name _____

My assigned housing category is _____

Interview two adults and two older adults. Write their answers in the space provided.

1. What do you think are the benefits of this housing option?

   Adult 1 _____

   _____

   _____

   Adult 2 _____

   _____

   _____

   Older Adult 1 _____

   _____

   _____

   Older Adult 2 _____

   _____

   _____

2. What do you think are the negative things about this housing option?

Adult 1 _____

_____

_____

Adult 2 _____

_____

_____

Older Adult 1 _____

_____

_____

Older Adult 2 _____

_____

_____

Lesson 7

Economics of Living on a Limited Income

I can't wait to meet my pen-pal. From her letters she seems like a very nice and kind person. Since my grandmother just died it is nice that I have someone around her age to talk to and that sounds as nice and kind as my grandmother did and always will.

— Erin, 4th grade

LESSON OVERVIEW

This lesson is a perfect vehicle for both math and aging education lessons. The concept of providing for oneself as one ages, and how to make ends meet on a fixed and often limited income, is important in understanding older adults in our society. But economics is certainly a complex topic, and students need to know at the outset of this lesson that this activity will help them understand only a small part of that topic.

For older students the context of this lesson on budgeting and fixed incomes can be expanded to include an exploration of pensions, social security, savings, and other means of providing financial independence later in life. If that occurs, make clear the distinction between entitlement programs, which are earned benefits, such as social security and medicare, and welfare, which are benefits based on need not earnings. The debate over the possible longevity of the social security system has become a source of generational conflict as some young adults believe they are paying for older adults, but will have no such benefits when they retire.

The U.S. Bureau of the Census in its 1995 Statistical Brief, *Sixty-Five Plus in the United States,* reports that

> The perception of "elderly" and "poor" as practically synonymous has changed in recent years to a view that the noninstitutionalized elderly are better off than other Americans. Both views are simplistic. There is actually great variation among elderly subgroups.

In 1992:

- The poverty rate was 15 percent for those under age 65, 11 percent for those 65 to 74, and 16 percent for those 75 or older.
- Elderly women had a 16 percent poverty rate; elderly men had a 9 percent rate.
- Elderly blacks had a 33 percent poverty rate, elderly Hispanics had a 22 percent rate, and elderly whites had an 11 percent rate.

This lesson will initiate students not only into the complex world of economics, but also to the economic issues surrounding aging in our society.

Learner Outcomes—Aging Issues
- Students will understand the concept of a fixed and limited income.
- Students will investigate concepts such as pensions and social security.
- Students will use current events to recognize the impact of elderly issues on the economy.

Learner Outcomes—Integration with Academic Curricula
- Students will perform basic multiplication and addition exercises.
- Students will draw hypotheses about fixed incomes in a changing financial market.
- Students will explore basic banking and investment strategies.

This lesson integrates with

Math: multiplication in the development of a budget and the evaluation of a predeveloped one, investments and savings accounts, financial markets

Language Arts: interviewing

GRADE ADJUSTMENTS

Lower elementary grade students should remain focused on the simple arithmetic involved in living on a limited, fixed income. Perhaps a simpler budget would need to be developed that would not involve multiplication but would still retain the outcomes of the lesson.

Older students might go beyond the budget and include activities that address the economics of a more global situation. These activities and discussions might include issues such as social security, pension and investment portfolios, and the stock market. An exploration of the newspapers and news magazines would create discussion about the future of the social security system in the light of the aging of the population. In addition, the reason for income disparities among different age subgroups could be a point of discussion and research. Take into consideration age, sex, race, ethnicity, living arrangements, education levels attained, work history, and marital status.

TERMS USED

Economics	the science that deals with the production, distribution, and consumption of wealth and with problems of fiscal issues
Social Security	a system by which a group provides for those of its members in need
Pension	a payment, not wages, made regularly to someone who has fulfilled certain conditions of service
Retirement	to withdraw oneself from a business or professional job
Interest	money paid for the use of money
Dividend	an individual's share of a quantity of money gained through business
Subsidized	financed in part by government

MATERIALS NEEDED

present newspapers listing the sales and costs of typical items used by most people
photocopies of old newspapers (5–10 years ago) listing the costs of same or similar
    items

PROCEDURE

1. Introduce the idea of economics by asking students how they get money, what are the conditions for getting that money, and what they do with their money.
2. Now ask students to explain how their parents/guardians get money and ask them to note the differences.
3. Finally, ask students how they think people who have retired get money and again note the differences. This will introduce the concept of savings and ask them when savings has to begin in order to have money for retirement. Also ask how we can make money work for us, discuss the concept of interest and dividends.
4. Now discuss the cost of items. A good way to do this is to bring in a local newspaper and store circulars and have students make lists of typical items needed and their costs. Repeat with newspapers from 5–10 years ago.
5. Ask students to hypothesize how easy or hard it is for retired adults to live on a fixed income as prices continue to increase.
6. Now have the class do the worksheet on living on a limited income.
7. Treat this as a math lesson and review whatever your class needs to finish the sheet.
    Note: This worksheet has been designed to create a deficit.
8. Ask the students whether their hypotheses were correct. Identify the problems.
9. This can lead to a discussion of delayed gratification or changed expectations.
10. It can also lead to a discussion of the possibility of finding a job to supplement income, which will then lead into a discussion of age discrimination in the workforce.

SUGGESTIONS FOR FURTHER ACTIVITY

1. Younger students can interview an older adult to determine that person's real expenses. They can also draw up a budget for themselves or their family.
2. Older students can research what the social security payments would be for someone who has worked and paid into the plan since age 21. They would need to call the local or state social security office for this information. How do the benefits increase with the cost of living? What are the limits? What determines the benefit?
3. An extension of that research would be to identify the predictions of whether the benefits will expire with the baby-boom generation. Why is social security such a hot political issue?
4. Have students develop a budget based on the expenses of someone they know or interview.

Suggested Reading

AARP. (1994). *Facts About Older Women: Income and Poverty.* Washington, DC: AARP Women's Initiative Fact Sheet.

U.S. Census Bureau. (1997). *Income and Poverty.* Available: http://www.census.gov/

U.S. Census Bureau. (1997). *Sixty-Five Plus in the United States.* Available: http://www.census.gov/

Suggested Bibliography for Use with this Lesson

Gardiner, J. R. *Stone Fox.* Crowell, 1980.

Ages 8–11. Willy is determined to help his grandfather pay off old taxes and harvest the potato crop so his grandfather has a reason to live.

Lasky, K. *A Sea Swan.* Macmillan, 1988.

Ages 5–8. A wonderful story of an active, motivated grandmother, but someone who is quite wealthy and not your typical older adult needing to watch finances.

Economics of Living on a Limited Income

Name _____

Mrs. Smith is an active, healthy, 79-year-old woman. She lives by herself in a subsidized (partly paid for by the government) two-bedroom apartment. The rent includes heat and electric. Figure out whether her budget works. What does this budget leave out?

Income	Yearly Amount
1. Social security check— $260.00 each month	_____
2. Works as clerk to a town board— earns $30.00 every other month	_____
3. Savings account interest is $340.00 each month	_____
4. Summer work in the town library—earns $6.00 each hour; works 10 hours a week, for 8 weeks	_____
Total Income	_____

Expenses	Yearly Amount

Expenses   **Yearly Amount**

1. Telephone bill—$40.00 each month   _____

2. Rent—$300.00 each month   _____

3. Medical expenses
   Yearly checkup—$15.00 (medicare)
   Medication—$8.00 each month   _____

4. Newspaper—$15.00 each month   _____

5. Charity—$5.00 each week   _____

6. Food—$50.00 each week   _____

7. Clothing/cleaning—
   $40.00 each month   _____

8. Internet connection—
   $10.00 each month   _____

9. Car insurance/repairs—
   $100.00 each month   _____

   Total Expenses   _____

Lesson 8

Diversity and Aging

How Does It Feel to Be Old?

I'm sad when people tease me about my wrinkles but I think they look nice.
But sometimes people don't like my opinions or don't listen. It's just not
fair. I think we should have equal rights. We're not so different. We just
have more experiences. If I lived in China I wouldn't be treated this way.
— Joseph, 4th grade

LESSON OVERVIEW

In an attempt to understand the increasingly diverse country in which we live, and the world that appears to get "smaller" each year, we teach respect and celebration of ethnic, racial, and religious diversity. To fully understand the aging population, we must also understand the diversity of attitudes and thoughts that surround that population. Different attitudes about living arrangements, long-term care, death, and dying exist among different cultures. At the same time, no matter what the culture, there are certain attitudes or beliefs that remain the same. An exploration of these differences and similarities can serve as a focus of discussion amongst students in a class—and families around a dinner table.

Also worthy of class time is a discussion of the reasons for age longevity, or lack of it, in minority populations. Consider these statistics from the U.S. Census Bureau in a 1996 report:

Over 65 in 1990

White	28.0 million	
Black	2.5 million	
Other races	0.6 million	(includes Asian & Pacific Islanders, American Indian, Eskimo, and Aleut)
Hispanic origin	1.1 million	

Over 80 in 1990

White	6.3 million
Black	0.5 million
Other races	0.1 million
Hispanic origin:	0.2 million

Over 65 in 2050

White	65.0 million
Black	8.4 million

| Other races | 6.7 million |
| Hispanic origin | 12.5 million |

Over 80 in 2050

White	26.2 million
Black	2.5 million
Other races	2.3 million
Hispanic origin:	4.5 million

In its 1995 Statistical Brief, the U.S. Census Bureau reports that in 1994 one in ten elderly were a race other than white. They predict that in 2050 this should increase to two in ten. The proportion of older adults who are Hispanic is expected to climb from 4 percent in 1994 to 16 percent in 2050.

Learner Outcomes—Aging Issues
- Students will recognize and reflect on how different cultures and societies treat older adults.
- Students will hypothesize why there are differences.
- Students will understand that judgments are not appropriate, but acceptance is.

Learner Outcomes—Integration with Academic Curricula
- Students will refine reading and listening skills.
- Students will learn about different cultures.
- Students will research the field for U.S. population statistics on different cultures.
- Students will form hypotheses.

This lesson integrates with
Reading: students read books aloud
Language Arts: students analyze books and write synopses
Social Studies: studying different cultures and countries
Art: the crafts and clothing of different cultures

GRADE ADJUSTMENTS

Intergenerational trade books present wonderful opportunities for an understanding of the differences among cultures in their beliefs about aging and dying. They also present wonderful opportunities for recognizing the similarities in people's attitudes, health issues, and esteem issues, no matter what the culture. For lower grades, a focus on these books provides all that is necessary for them to benefit from this lesson. For older students, the American Association of Retired Persons and the U.S. Bureau of the Census provide statistics that incorporate diversity issues. Much discussion could result from that information.

MATERIALS NEEDED

trade books that reflect diversity issues

PROCEDURE

1. For this cooperative learning exercise, divide the class into groups and give each group a book that reflects intergenerational diversity issues.
2. Ask students in the groups to take turns reading aloud.
3. Ask students to complete a worksheet that will help them focus on the issues that may be apparent in their book.
4. Have each group report back to the class about the questions presented in the worksheet.
5. Discuss all the books and what they represent in our understanding of different cultures.
6. As a second option, or a second day's activity, focus on the issue of ethnic or cultural traditions that may be presented in the book. Have students share a tradition from their own family that provides an insight into the culture as well. (See number 5 of Suggestions for Further Activity.)

SUGGESTIONS FOR FURTHER ACTIVITY

1. Have students prepare a bulletin board for posters that reflect on diversity issues and are visual reports of the books they have read.
2. Make charts that list different cultures and the similarities between them. Come up with a list of what every human being wants—regardless of culture—that will encourage students to view everyone as equal.
3. Have students research the population of different cultures in the United States and identify on a map the places where there are the greatest concentrations of those cultures. Discuss why that may be so.
4. Have students research health issues that pertain to older adults and discover whether different cultures have different health risks and why.
5. Have students write about their grandparents and what special cultural things they do that preserves their own culture. Celebrate each tradition with a display or a poster.
6. Explore the traditions in families and how they differ. Which traditions are related to culture and which are related to relationship development?

Suggested Reading

AARP. (1995). *A Portrait of Older Minorities.* Washington, DC: AARP Minority Affairs Department.

AARP. (1995). *Health Risks and Preventive Care Among Older Blacks (Pacific/Asian Americans, American Indians and Alaska Natives, and Hispanics).* Washington, DC: AARP Minority Affairs Department.

Labbo, L. D., & Field, S. L. (1996). Bookalogues: Celebrating Culturally Diverse Families. *Language Arts, 73,* 54–62.

U.S. Census Bureau. (1995). *Sixty-Five Plus in the United States.* [On-line]. Available: http://www.census.gov/

Suggested Bibliography for Use with This Lesson

Adler, D. A. *One Yellow Daffodil.* Gulliver, 1995.

Ages 8–14. During Hanukkah, two children help a Holocaust survivor to once again embrace his religious traditions.

Adoff, A. *Black Is Brown Is Tan.* Harper, 1973.

Ages 6–9. Two children with a "chocolate momma," a "white" daddy, and "granny white and grandma black" share the joys of being a family.

Ancona, G. *On Growing Older.* Dutton, 1978.

Ages 8–11. A photographic essay shows the life cycle of people, and a multicultural exploration shows the vibrancy of old age.

Carpenter, F. *Tales of a Chinese Grandmother.* C. E. Tuttle, 1973.

Ages 11–14. An aged Chinese grandmother tells some Chinese folktales and legends to her grandchildren.

Castaneda, O. *Abuela's Weave.* Lee & Low, 1993.

Ages 5–8. Guatemalian culture and crafts are shared by Esperanza and her grandmother. This book also includes the issue of granddaughter accepting grandma's birthmark.

Chase, R. *Grandfather Tales.* Houghton Mifflin, 1948.

Ages 8+. Twenty-five tales from the Appalachians are interspersed with the banter of the teller and his family.

Choi, S. N. *Halmoni and the Picnic.* Houghton Mifflin, 1993.

Ages 6–9. When the class plans a field trip, a classmate invites Yunmi's grandmother to be a chaperone. Yunmi worries about what her classmates will think of her grandmother's Korean ways and foods.

Curtis, C. P. *The Watsons Go to Birmingham.* Delacorte, 1995.

Ages 10+. The Watsons are an African American family from Flint, Michigan. Their 1963 summer visit to grandmother in Alabama changes their lives dramatically.

Daly, N. *Not So Fast Songololo.* Atheneum, 1986.

Ages 1–8. Malusi's grandmother, Gogo, needs help shopping, and they buy him shoes.

Davis, M. S. *Something Magic.* Simon & Schuster, 1991.

Ages 8–11. Through stories of a little girl's summer with her "grammy," a sensitive portrait emerges of a strong, active, kind woman who cherishes her granddaughter. The experiences they share help the child understand her heritage and the special love between the generations.

Delton, J., & Tucker, D. *My Uncle Nikos.* Thomas Crowell, 1983.

Ages 5–8. During the summer, Helena visits her uncle's rustic house in Greece.

DePaola, T. *Watch Out for the Chicken Feet in Your Soup.* Prentice Hall, 1974.

Ages 5–8. Joey is embarrassed by his Italian grandmother but realizes her criticism means special love when he sees how much his friend likes her.

Donehower, B. *Miko: Little Hunter of the North.* Farrar, 1990.

Ages preschool–5. Miko wants grandfather to tell him when the sun will shine again on their frigid Lapland home.

Dorros, A. *Abuela.* Dutton, 1991.

Ages preschool–8. Rosalba imagines that she goes flying over New York City with her adventurous grandma, Abuela.

Flourney, V. *The Patchwork Quilt.* Dial, 1985.

Ages 5–11. Grandmother works on a patchwork quilt of memories. Tanya finishes it when grandma gets sick. This book shows the significance of crafts in cultures.

Ganz, Y. *Me and My Bubby, My Zeidy and Me.* Feldheim Publishers, 1990.

Ages preschool–5. A special relationship between a child and his grandparents is shown by depicting a variety of activities involving Jewish tradition and culture.

Greenfield, E. *Africa Dreams.* Harper, 1989.

Ages preschool–8. A young African American girl dreams about what it would be like to visit her granddaddy's village.

Grifalconi, A. *Osa's Pride.* Little Brown, 1990.

Ages 5–8. Osa's pride keeps her from having friends in their African village. Grandma tells her a story to make her see how foolishly she is behaving.

Hoffman, M. *Amazing Grace.* Dial, 1991.

Ages 5–8. Although classmates say that she cannot play Peter Pan in the school play because she is black and a girl, Grace discovers that she can do anything she sets her mind to do.

Houston, J. *Akavaki: An Eskimo Journey.* Harcourt Brace Jovanovich, 1968.

Ages 8–11. Grandfather and grandson make a journey to fulfill a promise. The wisdom of the old man and the strength of the young boy, and the moral courage of both, make it possible.

Kurtz, J. *Pulling the Lion's Tail.* Simon & Schuster, 1995.

Ages 8–15. Her grandfather finds a clever way to help an impatient young Ethiopian girl to get to know her father's new wife.

Levinson, R. *Our Home Is the Sea.* Dutton, 1988.

Ages preschool–8. A young Chinese boy who lives on a houseboat in Hong Kong harbor looks forward to joining his father on his grandfather's big boat, knowing that he will someday become a fisherman.

Lipsyte, R. *The Brave.* HarperCollins, 1991.

Ages 11+. A 17-year-old Native American boy learns to control his anger by training with a retired boxer.

MacDonald, C. *Secret Lives.* Simon & Schuster, 1995.

Ages 11–15. A 15-year-old Australian boy creates an old character for a school writing project.

Martin Jr., B. *Knots on a Counting Rope.* Holt & Co., 1987.

Ages 5–11. Love and hope develop between a Native American grandfather and his grandson as the old man gives courage to the boy facing his challenges in life as a blind person.

Mathis, S. B. *The Hundred Penny Box.* Viking, 1975.

Ages 8–11. Love of a boy and his great-great-aunt and his protectiveness of her.

Matsuno, M. *A Pair of Red Clogs.* Collins, 1960.

Ages 5–8. Japanese grandmother tells of how she ruined new clogs while playing and almost did something dishonest to get a new pair.

Miles, M. *Annie and the Old One.* Little Brown, 1971.

Ages 8–11. A Navajo grandmother uses the rug she is weaving as a tool to teach her granddaughter that there is a pattern to life and dying is part of that pattern.

Mollel, T. *The Orphan Boy.* Clarion, 1990.

Ages 8–11. An old man accepts an orphan boy as his son and finds it hard to keep a promise he made to the boy. As part of the Masai legend, this story tells how they named the planet Venus, the Orphan Boy. It is a story of youth and age and the trust between them.

Mower, N. A. *I Visit My Tutu and Grandma.* Press Pacifica, 1984.

Ages preschool–5. A little girl is half Hawaiian and half Caucasian. She visits both her grandmothers, speaks with each in their language, and shares each grandmother's customs.

Namioka, L. *April and the Dragon Lady.* Browndeer, 1994.

Ages 10+. A 16-year-old Chinese American girl is torn between her needs and those of her grandmother.

Ness, E. *Josefina February.* Scribner, 1963.

Ages 5–8. Josefina is happy to find a baby burro but unhappy that she can't buy her grandfather a birthday gift because she didn't sell her fruit.

Nye, N. S. *Sitti's Secret.* Four Winds, 1994.

Ages 6–9. An American girl can't speak Arabic, the language of her grandmother, but she remembers that they learned to communicate during the time they spent together in Palestine.

Orr, K. *My Grandpa and the Sea.* CarolRhoda Books, 1990.

Ages 5–8. Lila and Grandpa live in the Caribbean and develop a special relationship as he teacher her the way of the sea and of the heart. Following the sea and his heart he finds a way to make a living even after big industry takes over the fishing trade.

Perkins, M. *The Sunita Experiment.* Joy Street Books, 1993.

Ages 11–14. Thirteen-year-old Sunita learns about her grandparents from India.

Polacco, P. *The Keeping Quilt.* Simon & Schuster, 1988.

Ages 5–10. A quilt made from remnants of clothes from Russia is passed along through four generations. This book would be good to read with *The Patchwork Quilt.*

_____. *Mrs. Katz and Tush.* Bantam, 1992.

Ages 5–11. Larnel and his neighbor, Mrs. Katz, discover the common themes of suffering and triumph that African American history and Jewish heritage share.

Rothenberg, J. *Inside-out Grandma.* Hyperion, 1995.

Ages 6–8. Rosie's grandmother wears her clothes inside-out to remind herself to buy oil for making latkes at Hanukkah. Book includes a recipe for potato latkes.

Ruby, L. *This Old Man.* Houghton Mifflin, 1984.

Ages 11–14. Sixteen-year-old Greta, in a home for girls, is hiding from Hackey, her mother's "old man." Greta meets Wing, a Chinese boy whose "old man" is his 90-year-old grandfather. Drawn into the Chinese culture, she finds the strength and wisdom to deal with life at home and with the other girls.

Russo, M. *A Visit to Oma.* Greenwillow, 1991.

Ages 5–8. Oma doesn't speak English but Celeste makes up stories to fit Oma's facial expressions, and their love allows them to enjoy each other despite language.

Say, A. *Grandfather's Journey.* Houghton Mifflin, 1993.

Ages 8–10. Say tells his own grandfather's story and expresses their mutual love for both Japan and America.

Seabrooke, B. *The Bridges of Summer*. Cobblehill, 1992.

Ages 11–14. Zarah visits her grandmother on Domingo Island and spends a summer without any creature comforts. She learns to treasure life and grandma.

Shea, P. D. *The Whispering Cloth: A Refugee's Story*. Boyds Mills, 1995.

Ages 8–11. Mai practices stitching borders in embroidered story cloths while in a Thai refugee camp with her grandmother. She finds a story within herself so that she, too, can stitch her own *pa'ndau*.

Stock, C. *Emma's Dragon Hunt*. Lothrop, 1984.

Ages 5–8. Grandfather Wong tells Emma all about the ancient dragon myths and teaches her not to be afraid.

Stoltz, M. *Go Fish*. Harper Collins, 1991.

Ages 5–8. After a day of fishing with grandfather, 8-year-old Thomas listens to stories of his African heritage.

Streich, C. *Grandparents' Houses: Poems About Grandparents*. Greenwillow, 1984.

Ages 5–14+. A collection of poems about grandparents of different cultures.

Stroud, V. A. *A Walk to the Great Mystery*. Dial Books, 1995.

Ages 8–11. While exploring the woods with their grandmother, a Cherokee medicine woman, two children learn about the spirit of life that is all around them and within them as well.

Taylor, M. *The Friendship*. Dial, 1987.

Ages 8–11. In 1930s rural Mississippi, four children witness a confrontation when an elderly man calls a white storekeeper by his first name.

Tompert, A. *Grandfather Tang's Story*. Crown, 1990.

Ages 8–11. A story about fox fairies told with tangrams by a grandfather.

Turner, A. *A Hunter Comes Home*. Crown, 1980.

Ages 8–11. Having spent a year in a boarding school learning white man's ways, an Eskimo boy comes home for the summer and learns the old ways from his grandfather.

White Deer of Autumn. *The Great Change*. Beyond Words, 1993.

Ages 8–11. After her grandfather's death, a Native American woman explains the circle of life to her granddaughter.

Wigginton, E. *Foxfire Book Series*. Anchor Press Doubleday, 1972.

Ages 8–11. A collection of folklore, crafts, and memories of Appalachian mountain folk. This book provides knowledge of their roots, heritage and culture.

Williams, V. *A Chair for My Mother*. Mulberry Books, 1982.

Ages 5–8. After a fire destroys their home, a close-knit African American grandma, mother, and daughter save money to buy a big, comfortable chair.

Yep, L. *Child of the Owl*. Harper & Row, 1977.

Ages 8–12. A 12-year-old girl living with her grandmother in San Francisco learns about her Chinese heritage.

Zucker, D. *Uncle Carmello*. Macmillan, 1993.

Ages 5–11. David dreads visiting Uncle Carmello because of all the awful stories he has heard about him. But when David's mom leaves him alone with his uncle, he sees another side of him and bridges the gap of age and culture.

Homework

Diversity and Older Adults

Read the book(s) your teacher has provided for you. For each book answer the questions on this sheet.

The name of the book is _____

1. What does the book say about the relationship of the older person and the younger person? Is the relationship a close one? If yes, why is it close and how do you know?

2. In what way does the culture play a part in the story? How does it differ from your own culture?

3. Does the older person in the story tell about a tradition that is passed on to the young person? What is that tradition and why is it important in the story?

4. What do the older and the younger person want in their life that is the same for everyone no matter what culture they belong to?

Lesson 9

Violence Against Young and Old

Making new friends that are not my age was the best part of the intergenerational program. I also made a new friend with my next door neighbor who is 83. I visit her house every week.

— Kimberly, 4th grade

LESSON OVERVIEW

The sense of vulnerability to violence and the fear of violence in our society are important issues to everyone. We need only to examine a political campaign and realize that when candidates talk about "restoring law and order," "taking a hard stand on crime," or "reforming our criminal justice system," they do so because surveys show that violence and crime are major concerns of Americans. Vulnerability and fear are especially apparent in both children and older adults.

Older adults remember a lifestyle that was simpler and crime that seemed less frequent and less violent. Even during wars and eras associated with violence, people had a sense that violence was limited to the underworld or to battlefields and that it wouldn't reach neighborhoods. Older adults' age and their circumstances, often create the sense of vulnerability they feel today. Today violence is not limited to inner cities or battlefields; it reaches everyone.

Young children are also subject to violence and crime because of their age and their circumstances. Very young children are now taught not to talk to strangers, to come directly home after school, and to stay in the house if they live in projects and not play in the fresh air.

The forms of violence and how they affect each of us are important to discuss here. A sharing of the fear or the concerns helps alleviate them.

Learner Outcomes—Aging Issues
• Students will understand and empathize with older adult safety issues.
• Students will generate a list of violence and crimes against the elderly.
• Students will take some form of action to address violence issues.

Learner Outcomes—Integration with Academic Curricula
• Students will interview and hold discussions with others.
• Students will create charts to elucidate the issues.
• Students will evaluate their own communities.
• Students will problem solve within the parameters of their communities.

This lesson integrates with
Language Arts: interviewing skills, analysis of situations, community outreach

Critical Thinking: problem solving for violence issues

Social Studies/Civics: distinctions between violence and crime, mediation skills

GRADE ADJUSTMENTS

This lesson carries strong potential for follow-up activities that are highly multi-cultural and intergenerational and that provide service to the community. For all grades, the lesson enables its participants to work together as a group and brain-storm ideas that are feasible for local action. The lesson is relatively simple and should remain the same for all grades. Yet for different grade levels the discussion should be different and the resulting activity should be different. The teacher must remain the realist about feasibility, without hindering creativity or enthusiasm.

Inviting a police officer to the class to be part of the discussions is an excellent idea. He/she can provide insight into curbing violence in the community, or avoiding scams through vulnerability, as well as provide a reference point for what the law actually is concerning crime. If your community takes part in a TRIAD (community policing initiative between seniors, law enforcement, and service providers) program in which older adults work directly with law enforcement agencies to monitor their own safety and to make the entire community safer, that is a wonderful opportunity for infusing intergenerational programming into the existing programs. TRIAD groups nationwide are recognizing the similarities in vulnerability between young and old and the subsequent value of joining these age groups.

TERMS USED

Vulnerability	can be wounded or physically injured
Violence	a use of force to cause injury or damage
Crime	an act committed in violation of a law prohibiting it

PROCEDURE

1. Older adults are invited to the class for this lesson. The number should be deter-mined by the class size—two older adults in each group of four or five students is a good ratio. The best places to recruit older adults are senior centers, local retirement villages, or an Area Agency on Aging. For the older classes, try to locate older adults who are politically active.

2. Divide the class into groups and pair one older adult with each group. Have the groups do the following exercise to help make everyone feel comfortable with each other and to help identify each group. Find something each of them has in common, such as birthday month, favorite ice cream, favorite TV show, pet, color of eyes, best wish, whether they can curl their tongues, or common initials in their names. When that is decided, they should choose a name for the group using that commonality. The name of the group can be silly or serious and should be noted on the worksheet.

3. Discuss with the whole class the definitions of violence and crime. Talk about different forms and levels of violence. Ask if the following are examples of violence and/or crime:

kicking	name-calling, put-downs	hitting
teasing	pushing, shoving	cutting in line
grabbing someone's purse and running		selling drugs to youth
child abuse, elder abuse		

Ask students to come up with other examples. Discuss the difference between violence and crime. Ask the students to come up with a list of crimes to young and old. Distinguish between violent crimes and crimes that take advantage of people.

Note: Examples of the latter would be fraud concerning retirement estates or business opportunities, laboratory tests, miracle cures, home repairs, or used-car sales. Discuss vulnerability with the whole class. Ask everyone to describe what makes them feel vulnerable.

4. Each group should then complete the worksheet. Tell the groups that after they work together they will be asked to present their ideas to the class and then lead a discussion to elicit ideas and constructive criticism. Take a break sometime—this lesson can be difficult. Snacks are a good idea!

Note: Older adults should be part of the group with equal input with students. They should not feel they are in charge of leading the group.

5. After the worksheet has been completed, have the class get together and allow each group to present its ideas. Other groups should be involved in questioning the small groups so that the ideas are refined.

Note: Some examples of ideas are noted in Suggestions For Further Activity.

6. You may decide that the class should work on only one idea or on many.

SUGGESTIONS FOR FURTHER ACTIVITY

1. Older grades might decide to develop a list of questions people can ask when faced with salespeople or vulnerable situations, and they can distribute the list in town to help people avoid difficult situations.
2. Older grades might try to work with local law enforcement agencies to assist them in neighborhood watch or TRIAD programs.
3. Older grades could work with older adults to develop antiviolence bills to present to state legislators and request sponsorship. The legislative process, as well as the issue of violence itself, is learned. (This suggestion is taken from the Dade County Public Schools and Florida's Department of Elder Affairs Intergenerational Program titled, "The Youth and Elderly Against Crime Program.")
4. Younger grades could develop a school bulletin board showing words and actions that are violent and should not be used in school. The bulletin board should include words that reflect issues for older adults, too.

5. Younger grades might draw pictures of violent and corresponding nonviolent techniques to handle different situations.

Suggested Reading

Dade County Public Schools. *Youth and Elderly Against Crime Program.* Dade County Public Schools' Intergenerational Programs, 1450 Northeast Second Avenue, Miami, FL 33132.

Dade County Public Schools. *Intergenerational Law Advocacy Program.* Silver-Haired Legislative Junior Aide Project, Dade County Public Schools, 1450 Northeast Second Avenue, Miami, FL 33132.

TRIAD, Association of AARP, International Association of Chiefs of Police, and National Sheriffs' Association, Triad at NSA, 1450 Duke Street, Alexandria, VA 22314.

University of New Mexico. (1986). *An Intergenerational Advocacy Program.* University of New Mexico School of Law, Albuquerque, NM 87131.

Suggested Bibliography for Use with This Lesson

Bryant, D. *Miss Giardino.* Ata Books, 1978.

Ages 14+. A retired teacher is mugged and through flashbacks tells the story of her life. Readers learn how the world changes and realize one is never too old to change or begin again.

Denker, H. *Horowitz and Mrs. Washington.* Putnam, 1979.

Ages 14+. A 79-year-old independent man is mugged and suffers a paralyzing stroke. Rather than going to a nursing home, he chooses to remain at home with a woman who is equally independent.

Violence Against Young and Old

Names in our group are _____

Name of our group is _____

1. How does violence make us feel?

2. Why and when do we feel vulnerable?

   Why do older adults feel vulnerable?

   Why do young people feel vulnerable?

   What do older people and younger people have in common that often makes them the target of criminals?

3. What are examples of violence or crimes committed against the young?

4. What are examples of violence or crimes committed against older adults?

5. What can young and old do to help themselves or help others help them?

6. What can we do to help make the community a safer and happier place to live?

Chapter **Four**

Psychological Aspects of Aging

CHAPTER OVERVIEW

T his chapter will help students recognize that being an older adult is no different than being any other age. All ages have both positive and negative attributes. The recognition in Chapter 3 that society generally paints a negative picture of aging needs to be countered with examples of how aging can be good and even fun. The impact of our individual attitudes must be seen as crucial to the development of a healthy ego and a healthy adjustment to old age. Students should be encouraged to share these lessons with grandparents so that they too can remain positive in the face of possible difficult situations.

INTERGENERATIONAL PROGRAM SUGGESTIONS

Friendly Visiting in Nursing Homes or for Home-Bound Older Adults

Program: Similar to the friendly visiting program outlined in Chapter 3, this program involves visiting specifically in nursing homes, assisted-living facilities, or with home-bound older adults where the older adults are often grateful for visitors and where psychological needs are great. Students, with or without other well older adults, would visit on a regular basis and spend time in structured activities or in informal talk. If the program takes place during school hours and is an integral part of the school curriculum, the psychological ramifications of giving up one's independence is an important component for discussion.

Mutuality and Ongoing: The ideal situation would be for the program to last as long as the school year. A commitment of that magnitude results in significant relationship building and can be extremely meaningful to those involved. Activities should be planned that allow each partner to receive equal benefit from the interaction. Oral histories, for example, are good vehicles for this. (For a full discussion of oral history programs, see Chapter 5.)

Many of the programs suggested in Chapter 3 can be used here as well. While addressing sociological issues in society we are often simultaneously addressing psychological issues for the individual as well. Especially successful are theater programs in which shared feelings are acted out and written into scripts, storytelling in which generations share stories of age-related feelings, and dance productions in which people allow movement to express their emotions.

Suggested Reading

Seefeldt, C. (1987). The Effects of Preschoolers' Visits to a Nursing Home. *Gerontologist, 27* (2), 228–232.

Smilow, P. (1993). How Would You Like to Visit a Nursing Home? *Equity and Excellence in Education, 26* (2), 22–26.

Lesson 1

Adjustments at Any Age

I think if you have a good attitude about being a senior, then you'll have a lot of activities to do and you won't have time to feel sad. But if you sit around all day in a chair or bed, you'd probably feel old and weak, because you're not doing anything. A lot of people think old people need to be taken care of because of that.

— Caroline, 4th grade

LESSON OVERVIEW

Individual life events always seem catastrophic when we are young. Students need to realize that life is a constant series of adjustments to major and minor life events that occur at all ages. The way we respond to those events often determines whether those events become catastrophic. The life event known as aging is no exception.

This lesson provides an overview of the many adjustments in life. It does not ask students to solve, or even to understand, the dilemmas of any one age. It asks only that they identify possible dilemmas. The understanding that every age is faced with different dilemmas gives students a sense that they are not alone in their own adjustments and that their adjustments are no more or less difficult than the adjustments being made at any other age. Students will begin to see beyond themselves and learn to reach out to or empathize with others.

Learner Outcomes—Aging Issues
  • Students will recognize that every age faces its own set of adjustments.
  • Students will understand that old age may be unlike other stages, but still requires the same adjustment techniques.

Learner Outcomes—Integration with Academic Curricula
  • Students will develop lists that compare and contrast.
  • Students will critically evaluate different roles in a lifetime.

  This lesson integrates with
  Language Arts: comparing and contrasting, evaluating, theater exercises
  Critical Thinking: evaluating roles in a lifetime
  Psychology: understanding responsibilities, stresses, changes, attitude development, role playing

GRADE ADJUSTMENTS

I have done this lesson with different grades and find it is equally appropriate. The level of the answers given is what will differ with age and grade.

MATERIALS NEEDED

chart paper
magazine or newspaper articles about people who appear to be positive about life
(optional)

PROCEDURE

1. This lesson works well as a cooperative learning exercise. Divide the class into small groups. Depending on the size of your class, one or more groups will be working on each category. Assign the groups to these four categories:

   • children—birth to age 12
   • teenagers—age 13 to 20
   • adults—age 21 to 60
   • older adults—age 61+

2. For each category, ask the students to write the things that this age group has to adjust to that the other age groups do not usually have to adjust to.

   Note: The answers will require generalizations about activities for the different age groups. There will certainly be some overlap and also examples of people who have learned, or done things out of the "normal" sequence. You may want to explain the reasons for generalizations. Ask students to write adjustments that most often occur in their age group. For example, a child has to learn to walk, feed itself, be toilet trained, learn to make friends, begin school, do homework, and learn to read and write. No other age group usually needs to make those particular adjustments. Teenagers most often must adjust to dating, peer pressure, going away to school, doing one's own laundry, cooking, and learning to earn money. Adults have to adjust to marriage and raising a family, developing a career, and learning to save money and plan for retirement, all adjustments that usually occur when one is an adult. Finally, older adults usually have to adjust to retirement, living on a fixed income, and facing the death of friends and spouse. These are limited lists, but they are the answers most often given by students. Older students may probe more into the psychological adjustments to each life event.

3. Ask groups to report their lists to the class and you write a chart, or ask groups to write their statements directly on a class chart for the different age groups. Allow the class to add to or question the lists developed by each small group.

4. Have students then examine the entire chart and evaluate what allows some people to make these adjustments easily whereas others struggle to do so.

   Note: Answers will probably range from self-esteem issues to having supportive people in their lives to religion. All answers are obviously correct, and discussion as to how they help should occur. Be sure, however, that having a good, positive attitude toward life is part of that list.

5. Ask students how a positive outlook on life can help make those adjustments easier.

6. Ask students to role play—for the class—one situation in which an older adult has a positive attitude toward life and one in which an older adult has a negative attitude.

   Note: Two simple examples: An older person living alone and celebrating an 80th birthday who sits in her home all day and says, "Oh, I'm so old, I will probably die soon," as opposed to someone who says, "Oh, I can't believe I am 80 years old, but I feel good and so I am going to go to the movies with my friends now and then invite them to my house for cake and ice cream." Or an older person who says, "I'm so old, I can't try new things and there is so much I never got to do in my life," as opposed to one who says, "You know, I've always wanted to learn how to swim so I think I will celebrate my birthday by giving myself swimming lessons at the local YMCA."

7. Ask students to discuss in which scenario the person will be the happiest? Why?
8. Follow this lesson with the homework assignment on "Attitudes" and discuss it at the next class.

SUGGESTIONS FOR FURTHER ACTIVITY

1. Have students make a collage from magazine pictures of older adults engaging in activities that appear to indicate that the older adults have a positive attitude about life.
2. Have students make a collage of positive words.
3. Ask students to read stories that indicate positive attitudes about aging and about life.
4. Have students research the Internet or write to organizations that provide insight into older adults in active, positive roles. Discuss older adults who volunteer in the community and what they do and what important role they serve.

Resources

Elderhostel, 75 Federal Street, Boston, MA 02110
Elderhostel Institute Network, 125 Technology Drive, Durham, NH 03824-4724
Eldercorps, 19 Harrison Avenue, Cambridge, MA 02140
Adult Health and Development Program, University of Maryland, HHP Building, College Park, MD 20742

Suggested Bibliography for Use with This Lesson

Abrams, S. *Gray-Haired Grins & Giggles Guess What—Grammy & Grandy Have a Sense of Humor Too!* Borough Books, 1995.
   Ages 11+. Forty-five older adult authors tell 160 humorous true tales: anecdotes, stories, and essays about the lighter side of life from childhood through retirement.
Ackerman, K. *Song and Dance Man.* Knopf, 1988.
   Ages 5–8. Up in the attic grandpa pulls out props from an old trunk and is transformed into a vaudevillian again. Grandchildren see him in a new, vital way.

Andrews, J. *The Auction.* Macmillan, 1991.

Ages 5–8. A boy and his grandfather come to terms with the sale of the family farm in this moving story. Grandfather shares treasured memories of life on that farm.

Auch, M. J. *Glass Slippers Give You Blisters.* Holiday House, 1989.

Ages 11–14. Junior high student Kelly gets involved in a school play. Encouraged by her artist grandmother but discouraged by her mother, the two have a confrontation and Kelly discovers her talents.

Bauer, M. D. *When I Go Camping with Grandma.* Bridgewater, 1995.

Ages 5–8. When a girl camps with her grandma, it's always an adventure and a celebration of nature.

Bryant, D. *Miss Giardino.* Ata Books, 1978.

Ages 14+. A retired teacher is mugged and through flashbacks tells the story of her life. Readers learn how the world changes and realize one is never too old to change or begin again.

Buck, P. *The Beech Tree.* John Day, 1955.

Ages 8–11. Grandfather comes to live with his family and it is an adjustment. MaryLou explains he is like a beech tree giving life to the little trees around it.

Burch, R. *Two That Were Tough.* Viking, 1976.

Ages 5–8. An independent old man plans to move to the city to live with his daughter. He sees himself in the fierce independence of a wild chicken, and he wants to take it with him but decides not to risk its life.

Carlson, N. *A Visit to Grandma's.* Viking, 1991.

Ages 5–8. A Thanksgiving visit to grandma in her new condo in Florida is a big surprise. Grandma is different and so is the Thanksgiving celebration.

Caseley, J. *When Grandpa Came to Stay.* Greenwillow, 1986.

Ages 5–8. A widower comes to live with his daughter's family. The grandson visits the cemetery with his grandfather and they share their love for grandma.

Clifford, E. *The Rocking Chair Rebellion.* Houghton Mifflin, 1978.

Ages 11–14. Opie volunteers in a nursing home and finds himself involved in a rocking chair rebellion.

Cole, B. *The Trouble with Gran.* Putnam, 1987.

Ages 1–5. Fantasy about a fun grandmother who is a secret alien and is very lively.

Cooney, B. *Miss Rumphius.* Viking, 1982.

Ages 5–8. Alice tells her grandfather she wants to travel. He agrees but says she must do something to make the world more beautiful. She does and passes the message on.

Douglas, B. *The Great Town and Country Bicycle Balloon Chase.* Lothrop, Lee and Shepard, 1984.

Ages 5–8. A grandfather and granddaughter join a bicycle race to reach a hot air balloon.

Dyjak, E. *I Should Have Listened to the Moon.* Houghton Mifflin, 1990.

Ages 11–14. A 12-year-old girl comes to terms with growing up and growing old when her best friend develops an interest in boys and her confused grandmother moves in to share her room.

Farber, N. *How Does It Feel to Be Old?* Dutton, 1979.

Ages 5–14. When granddaughter asks the question, grandmother shares all her feelings about the frustrations and joys of aging.

Henkes, K. *Grandpa and Bo.* Greenwillow, 1986.

Ages 5–8. Grandfather and Bo celebrate Christmas in summer, and when they see a shooting star, their wishes are the same.

Hest, A. *The Midnight Eaters.* Four Winds, 1989.

Ages 5–8. Samantha and Nana sneak downstairs at midnight to eat ice cream sundaes. They share a special relationship, and even though Nana confides it's not easy to grow old, Sam knows they will share more midnight eating again.

Hoff, S. *Barkley.* Harper & Row, 1975.

Ages 8–11. When he gets too old to perform in his act in the circus, Barkley tries to find something else to do.

Hurd, E. *I Dance in My Red Pajamas.* Harper & Row, 1982.

Ages 1–5. Mother and father tell Jenny not to make noise when visiting grandma, but she knows better; they create noise and activity.

Jarrow, G. *If Phyllis Were Here.* Avon Paper, 1989.

Ages 10–14. Libby, age 11, has to learn to adjust to living without her best friend—her grandmother—who moves to Florida.

Khasa, D. K. *Tales of a Gambling Grandma.* Clarkson Potter, 1986.

Ages 8–11. A girl and her grandma are best friends, and grandma tells her stories of her life and her adventures.

Klein, L. *How Old Is Old?* Harvey House, 1967.

Ages 5–8. Lessons about how old age is relative and that it depends on how one feels.

Knox-Wagner, E. *My Grandpa Retired Today.* Whitman & Co., 1982.

Ages 1–8. When grandpa retires from his barbershop, it is an adjustment for him and his granddaughter. Soon they realize that life is just beginning again.

MacLachlan, P. *Arthur, For the Very First Time.* Harper & Row, 1980.

Ages 8–11. A 10-year-old boy spends the summer with his great-aunt and great-uncle and discovers a new way of seeing things.

Mitchell, M. K. *Uncle Jed's Barbershop.* Simon & Schuster, 1993.

Ages 9–12. Uncle Jed refuses to let racial prejudice and economic setbacks keep him from realizing his dream.

Okimoto, J. *Take a Chance Gramps!* Little Brown, 1990.

Ages 11–14. Jane worries about beginning a new school without her best friend, and Gramp's needs encouragement to go to a senior citizen dance to meet new friends. This story illustrates adjustments for both ages.

Patterson, K. *The Flip Flop Girl.* Viking, 1994.

Ages 9–12. Father's death is hard enough to cope with, but moving to a new place, living with grandmother, and dealing with poverty make life even more difficult.

Pomerantz, C. *Buffy and Albert.* Greenwillow, 1982.

Ages 5–8. Growing old presents problems for a grandfather and his two cats. This story is humorous, serious, and realistic.

Radley, G. *The Golden Days.* Macmillan, 1991.

Ages 11–14. Eleven-year-old Cory and 75-year-old Carlotta struggle over feelings of belonging and family. He is in a foster home and she is in a nursing home; they both must make adjustments.

Reeder, C. *Grandpa's Mountain*. Macmillan, 1991.

Ages 11–14. Eleven-year-old Carrie watches as her grandpa fights to save his land from becoming a national park. She learns about struggling against the odds and about the human spirit and the nature of life.

Schwartz, D. *Supergrandpa*. Lothrop, 1991.

Ages 5–11. Gustaf looks like an old man but doesn't feel or act like one, and he enters the Tour de Sweden and wins.

Simpson, C. *Everything You Need to Know When Living with a Grandparent or Other Relatives*. Rosen Publishing Group, 1994.

Ages 11+. An updated guide to coping with the sudden change of a live-in relative.

Smith, R. K. *The War with Grandpa*. Dell Yearling, 1984.

Ages 8–11. Upset that he has to give up his room for grandpa, Pete declares war in an attempt to get it back. This story illustrates making adjustments to living together.

Stevenson, J. *Could Be Worse*. Greenwillow, 1977.

Ages 5–8. Things at grandpa's house are the same, but a fantasy story of adventure occurs in which children use grandpa's words, "could be worse."

Talbot, T. *Dear Greta Garbo*. Putnam & Sons, 1978.

Ages 11–14. Miranda and her grandmother face similar needs and struggles for independence as grandma adjusts after her husband dies and Miranda grows up.

Van Zwanenberg, F. *Caring for the Aged*. Danbury Franklin Watts, 1989.

Ages 14+. A book about the many needs that older adults have and how to care for them.

Waddell, M. *My Great Grandpa*. Putnam & Sons, 1990.

Ages 5–8. A girl describes special times with her great-grandfather who may be slow and weak but still travels to places in his mind.

Homework

Attitudes

Name _____

1. What do you think about this statement: Education is for young people; work is for adults; leisure is for old people. Tell why you think it is true or not true.

2. What do you think makes someone "young"? What makes someone "old"? Can a person who is 80 be young? Explain.

3. What worries you most about being over 65?

4. What do you look forward to when you are over 65?

Lesson 2

Achievers at Any Age

A hush falls in the hospital as the baby is born. Everyone is happy about the new arrival. Everybody is happy when she is seven years old. Old, old, old. How does it feel to be old? What is it like? How will I look? Will it be fun? "I can't answer those questions for you," her mother said. "You have to answer those questions when you are old." When she was old, she thought hey, this isn't so bad after all.
— Leah, 4th grade

LESSON OVERVIEW

Achievement can be measured through great or small accomplishments. Students should recognize that we each achieve success in our own way and that our self-esteem is fed by our ability to overcome our own small obstacles and meet our own needs. Because aging sometimes diminishes abilities, it can create a certain sense of loss; therefore, the nurturing of self-esteem is often critical as we age. In this lesson students will realize that achievement is not limited by age or physical abilities and that the human spirit and a positive attitude can make a difference.

Learner Outcomes—Aging Issues
• Students will recognize that success is measured within ourselves.
• Students will understand that achievement is possible at any age.

Learner Outcomes—Integration with Academic Curricula
• Students will refine interviewing techniques.
• Students will develop questions that address an issue.

This lesson integrates with
Language Arts: interviewing, communication skills, evaluation, analyses
Psychology: self-esteem and achievement issues

GRADE ADJUSTMENTS

This lesson is appropriate for any age. Self-esteem issues and individual achievement are important points of discussion for any age.

TERMS USED

Self-Esteem   belief or pride in oneself
Achievement   to effect a desired result especially by skill, work or courage

MATERIALS NEEDED

magazine or newspaper articles that focus on individual achievements of older adults (This can be assigned to students to look for and bring in.)

PROCEDURE

Day 1

1. Ask students to discuss the relationship between self-esteem and achievement.
2. Ask students to identify at what age self-esteem and a sense of achievement is needed.

   Note: Students should realize that this is true of any age. The concept of not having to do anything when one is older because a lot was achieved when one was younger is fallacious and needs to be discussed. Self-esteem grows and is always important.

3. Present to the students the following examples:

   A 56-year old woman founded *Dancin' Grannies,* a video aerobic exercise program for older women.

   A 75-year-old woman ran the James Joyce Ramble in Massachusetts.

   A 106-year-old woman attended her alumnae reunion from Mount Holyoke College, class of 1908.

   A 70-year-old woman attained her solo pilot's license.

   Ten percent of all Peace Corps volunteers are over 50.

   John A. Kelley ran the Boston Marathon 61 times. He finished 58 times: he won it twice, he came in second 7 times, and he placed in the first ten 18 times. He ran his last marathon when he was 85 years old.

   And from *The People's Almanac Presents the Book of Lists: The 90s Edition* by David Wallechinsky and Amy Wallace (1993) comes the following:

   David Ray, a 99-year-old man from Tennessee, first learned to read.

   Beatrice Wood, 98 years old, exhibited her ceramic art.

   Martin Miller, at 97 years old, worked full-time as a lobbyist for older adults in Indiana.

   Martha Graham, at 95 years old, worked with her dance troupe.

   George Burns, at 94 years old, performed at Proctor's Theater in Schenectady.

   George Spangler, at 92 years old, completed his 14th marathon.

   Hulda Crooks, at 91 years old, climbed Mount Whitney.

4. Ask the students if they know of any older adults who accomplished something important to them in their older years. Remind them that the significance might be to them alone but it is still important.
5. Introduce the homework assignment to interview older adults about their sense of achievement in their lives. Develop with students questions they will ask that

encourage older adults to realize that achievements are valid no matter how small. Discuss the need to look at many things as achievements.

Note: Many older adults will say they are just ordinary people who have not done anything extraordinary in their lives. It may be up to the students to seek that accomplishment by having the older adult tell them about their life.

Day 2

1. Discuss the interviews in class. Perhaps make a chart of the age and the accomplishment.
2. Ask students to evaluate what constituted an achievement in the lives of those they interviewed.

SUGGESTIONS FOR FURTHER ACTIVITY

1. Have students look through magazines and newspapers for examples of older adults and their achievements. Many newspapers now have columns written about and by older adults.
2. Prepare a bulletin board that identifies different older adults, their age, and their accomplishments. Place the bulletin board in a prominent spot in the school as a way of recognizing the older adults who may volunteer (a good way to say thank you) in the school or as a way of promoting self-esteem.
3. Have students make a list of their greatest achievements to date and why it was an important accomplishment to them. Or have students write an essay about it.
4. Have students sponsor an essay contest that promotes the idea of self-esteem at any age or asks participants to use the essay to nominate an older adult they know who has achieved much. Have a ceremony to honor the winners of the contest.

References

Wallechinsky, D., Wallace, D., & Wallace, A. (1993). *The People's Almanac Presents the Book of Lists: The '90s Edition.* New York: Little Brown & Co.

Suggested Bibliography for Use with This Lesson

Byars, B. *Trouble River.* Avon, 1978.

Ages 8–11. A boy takes his grandmother down river to escape the Indians. With her wise advice they avoid wolves, enemies, and the rapids. This book illustrates a philosophy of not giving up, a sense of achievement, and family love.

Girion, B. *Joshua, the Czar and the Chicken Bone Wish.* Scribner, 1978.

Ages 8–11. Joshua is the klutz of the fourth grade. But new friends and a special friend at the nursing home praise his good qualities. New self-confidence allows him to take charge in an emergency on a class field trip.

Hoffman, M. *Amazing Grace.* Dial, 1991.

Ages 5–8. When Grace is told by classmates that she can't be Peter Pan in the class play because she's black and a girl, she proves otherwise.

Houston, G. *My Great-Aunt Arizona.* Harper, 1992.

Ages 5–11. A portrait of a remarkable Appalachian schoolteacher at the turn of the century.

Lasky, K. *Sea Swan.* Macmillan, 1988.

Ages 5–11. Grandma decides at the age of 75 to learn to swim.

Kesselman, W. *Emma.* Doubleday, 1980.

Ages 11–14. Motivated by a birthday gift, a 72-year-old woman begins to paint.

Homework

Achievement and Self-Esteem

Name _____

Interview an older adult about his/her achievements since he/she has been an older adult. Use over 65 as a general range. The person you interview can be a grandparent, neighbor, friend of the family, or a friend's older adult friend. The questions you ask are the ones you have developed with your class. Write the questions and the answers on this paper.

Lesson 3

What Does It Feel Like to Be Old?

These two student statements refer to the caption accompanying the picture of four generations that is pictured at the end of this lesson. I often ask the students to tell me about a picture that I present or make up a story to explain the picture.

I think it is a good poem. It means that everyone is the same. Even if you are old you are just as beautiful. No matter the age you are still the same person inside. I like the way it shows the aging process. Kids should always remember that an older person was once a child too.

— Daniel, 4th grade

When you get older you are no less beautiful than when you were younger. For example, when you are a baby people think you are very cute and beautiful. But as you get older, they think you get less and less cute and beautiful. But inside, you are the same beautiful person you were 30 years ago.

— Kate, 4th grade

LESSON OVERVIEW

Children's, especially young children's, perception of aging is that all old people are lonely or sad or are in poor health. The lessons on achievers and on attitudes will have begun to dispel these common perceptions. They need to realize that old age can be a time of opportunity, excitement, and new beginnings; that older people are mostly busy, happy, and in good health.

In this lesson students will try to empathize with older adults and try to see aging from an older adult's perspective. What are the frustrations and fears and what are the joys of aging? The writing exercises provided for classwork and homework will allow students the opportunity to imagine the feelings of aging and to project those feelings through offering advice to people their age or interpreting pictures.

This lesson has strong value in its introspection. It should allow students to express their fears and their concerns as well as what they see as terrific about being old. It also allows them to recognize that every age has both good and bad things about it and that our happiness as we age depends on our attitudes.

Learner Outcomes—Aging Issues
• Students will try to understand feelings attached to aging.

- Students will recognize various aspects of aging that are good and bad.
- Students will see every age with both positive and negative attributes.

Learner Outcomes—Integration with Academic Curricula
- Students will write about feelings.
- Students will use metaphors, comparisons, and descriptives.
- Students will use poetry to express themselves.

This lesson integrates with
Language Arts: writing, poetry, exploration of feelings

GRADE ADJUSTMENTS

This is an opportunity to integrate poetry into an aging lesson. If the students have had some exposure to poetry already, allow them to write a poem to complete the lesson. Younger children will probably try to make everything rhyme and because that may be difficult, either discuss how to write a poem without rhyme or have them write an expository piece. Older students may be able to express feelings succinctly through poetry without rhyme. This can also be used as a writing exercise in formats of the teacher's choosing—essay, expository writing, journal entries, creative writing. In any case, the recognition of the feelings attached to aging is important for this lesson.

MATERIALS NEEDED

a picture(s) of a young and an old person together (It can be from any source—possibly in magazines, on greeting cards, or in newspaper ads—but the picture should show some kind of intergenerational interaction; or use the picture, with the caption, provided in this lesson.)

PROCEDURE

1. Ask students to make a list, either on their own or as a class, of what they think is really terrific about being old.

   Note: Students will come up with anything from discounts to the movies to not having to go to school to having free time to exploring interests. All answers are valid, but try to guide the discussion to feelings as well as facts. For example, feeling bold and able to express themselves without restraint, or feeling free from overwhelming responsibility and able to pursue interests.
2. Now ask students to make a list of what they think is not terrific about being old. Again guide them to anticipate feelings as well as factual things about aging.
3. Ask students what they think older people feel about aging. Have them use a familiar older adult as a reference point because that will be easier. Ask them to defend their position with examples of why they might feel that.

4. Have students look at the picture you present, or use the one presented in this lesson. Ask students to write about what they think the older person is saying to the young person in the picture or what is happening in the picture. If you use the picture provided in this lesson, ask them to write about what the picture and the caption means.
5. Have students share their writing with the class. Allow other students to comment.
6. Assign the accompanying homework assignment. Allow sharing of writing the next day in class.

SUGGESTIONS FOR FURTHER ACTIVITY

1. Have students explore the world of feelings about aging through key words. Develop a chart or bulletin board that indicates the words and explains them. They can be categorized under "terrific things" or "not such terrific things."
2. Students can interview older adults and ask them their feelings about aging. They need to be careful to separate feelings from facts here.
3. Students can interview other students their age to determine feelings about growing older—what gets better, what becomes more difficult? What is terrific about being 10, what is not so terrific? This will allow students to realize that every age has good things and not so good things about it. Do the same with parents, teachers, or teenagers.

Suggested Bibliography for Use with This Lesson

Anders, R. *A Look at Aging.* Lerner, 1976.

Ages 8–11. Photographs showing joys, problems, contributions, and physical changes in elderly.

Cartwright, P. *What Is It Like to Be Old?* Rainforest, 1988.

Ages 5–11. Two young girls ask their grandparents what it's like to be old. With colorful drawings, this book examines old age and how people feel emotionally and physically as they age.

Farber, N. *How Does It Feel to Be Old?* Dutton, 1979.

Ages 5–14. When granddaughter asks the question, grandmother tells her all the good and bad things about growing older. Frustrations and joys of aging are mixed with the reality that this is part of the normal course of life. An excellent book to read in conjunction with this class.

Geras, A. *My Grandmother's Stories.* Knopf, 1990.

Ages 11–14. Short stories about a grandmother and about aging.

Hadley, I. *The Lility Summer.* Feminist Press, 1979.

Ages 8–11. A girl becomes a companion to a 77-year-old woman, and the two learn from each other about loneliness and love. This book illustrates looking at life from an older person's perspective.

Hughes, S. *The Snow Lady.* Lothrop, 1990.

Ages 5–11. Samantha lives next door to Mrs. Dean but doesn't like her because she seems mean to the neighborhood children. Yet when something is done to hurt Mrs. Dean's feelings, Sam makes sure Mrs. Dean doesn't see it.

McConnell, N. P. *Young and Old Alike.* Current, 1984.

Ages 8–11. This book explains the aging process, the advantages and problems of being old, and the many things the old and young have in common.

Nystrum, C. *Jenny and Grandpa, What Is It Like to Grow Old?* Elgin Lion Publishing, 1988.

Ages 14+. An examination of all aspects of growing old.

Sanders, P. *What It's Like to Be Old.* Gloucester Press, 1992.

Ages 8–11. An introduction to what it's like to be old, physically and mentally, describing the joys and challenges of old age.

Schulman, L. M. *Autumn Light; Illuminations of Age.* Crowell, 1978.

Ages 14+. A collection of short stories about the problems of aging.

Shanks, A. Z. *Old Is What You Get; Dialogues on Aging by the Old and the Young.* Viking, 1976.

Ages 9+. With photos and commentary on the aspects of aging, this book examines realities but few joys.

Stewart, G. B. *The Elderly.* Lucent Books, 1996.

Ages 11+. An in-depth look at the reality of growing older.

Wild, M. *Our Granny.* Ticknor & Fields, 1994.

Ages 1–5. To the children who love her, this granny is perfect. A celebration of grandmothers and all they are and can be. A modern, nonageist view of possibilities.

The Sun Setting Is No Less Beautiful Than the Sun Rising

Figure 4–3.1 Faces of Aging.
Source: Courtesy of Life Care Centers of America. Reproduction of photograph is subject to a revocable license.

What do you think this picture and these words mean?

What Does It Feel Like to Be Old?

Name _____

How do you think it feels to be 80 or even 90 years old? Write a poem, a story, or an essay about what you think it feels like. Use a lot of comparisons, descriptions, and emotions.

Chapter Five

Historical Perspectives of Aging

CHAPTER OVERVIEW

T his chapter discusses aging on a more personal level. Until now we have dealt with older people in society, how society responds to this group of people, and the concept of aging in our society. With this chapter we personalize older people and encourage students to believe that remaining in touch with the older adults in our own lives can enrich and benefit us.

Children are fascinated by life before they were born. I believe that much of the "magic" that happens between young and old revolves around the fact that they can share experiences that are similar but at the same time so very different. Perhaps the "stories" that are told by older adults seem so unbelievable to students that they often appear to be fiction. For whatever reason, students often gain from these oral histories a sense of historical perspective that they do not receive in the same way through texts. Although it may not be immediately evident, that perspective provides a continuity and relevance to history that has staying power. Some of the most powerful intergenerational programs I have witnessed have occurred when students, figuratively speaking, become part of the older adult's life by hearing their life stories. The empathy and excitement of sharing is visibly evident in the young; for the older adults the experience of sharing may provide a further sense of validity to one's life as life experiences are passed on, or perhaps it provides an outlet for memories to be revived and intimacies shared, or maybe it is simply having someone to listen. It is an important lesson and a shared joy.

The interconnectedness among politics, economics, historical events, and demographic changes can be developed in this chapter. It is most likely to be obvious in Lesson 2 on immigration. It is something educators should keep in mind as the different lessons are presented.

INTERGENERATIONAL PROGRAM SUGGESTIONS

Oral Histories

Program: Students develop questions to ask older adults who not only answer the questions but can provide further insight into the topic being explored. Guidelines for oral histories should include:

- Choosing an older adult who has memories of the topic being discussed. Asking someone who grew up in Europe what school was like in America in the 1930s is not relevant.
- Making a list of questions that are relevant to the topic under discussion or the goal of the classroom project. Questions should be open-ended to encourage the telling of stories. Doing some background research about the topic is often helpful, so that follow-up questions will be easier to ask and impromptu stories surrounding the question can be better understood.
- Being flexible and open to other memories and stories that occur when the initial question is asked. Although reminding the older adult to answer each question is good, allowing further exploration of the topic by listening to the stories that may evolve is also important. Be sure the interview is relaxed and fun rather than requiring a specific outcome.
- Being sensitive to possible lapses in memory. If the older adult does not remember the answer to one question, students should be prepared to redirect the question or move on to the next one.
- Recognizing that the information and stories are precious and understanding their value and the value of the person providing the insight.
- Knowing what the final product will be. What will be done with the information obtained? Taking oral histories for the sheer beauty and fun of it is certainly valuable; but if we are to recognize its value, then we should also recognize the need to preserve the information.

Mutual Benefits and Ongoing: When the histories are complete, the program should not end. Students and older adults should work together on publishing the book, writing the play, sharing the stories, and so on. If the final product is to be a book, for example, and the writing will be done on a word processor, have the student teach the older adult how to use the computer (if they do not already know). Encourage collaborative writing. Learn together publishing techniques and the art of bookmaking by designing book jackets, binding the book, and illustrating it. Create marketing strategies together—will it go into the school library or local senior center? be distributed throughout town? be presented to the town governing body in a formal presentation? be sold to raise money for another intergenerational project? There are infinite possibilities and potential for oral histories. For further guidelines, see Lesson 4 in this chapter.

Project Fair

Program: Choose an era of history and create small research groups of students and older adults to work together on researching a particular phase of that historical era. For example, the Roaring Twenties: Zany Fads, Day-to-Day Living for Parents and Children, Transportation, Entertainment, Sports, Dance and Music, Clothing Styles, the Economy, What Things Cost, and World Affairs. Other eras could be World War II or the Depression. Groups should develop a presentation of their research to be presented to the community at large at a Project Fair. Wonderful resources for this type of program are

This Fabulous Century, Time Life Books, 1969–70, Volumes 1–8.

America Awakes, A New Appraisal of the Twenties, Jan Farrington, Westover Publishing Co., 1971.

American Destiny, An Illustrated History of the US, Henry Steele, Ed., Orbis, 1986, Volumes 1–20.

American Decades, Matthew L. Bruccoli, Richard Layman, Gale Research, Eds., 1996, Volumes 1–9.

Mutual Benefits and Ongoing: As stated, the gain for each is in the mutual accomplishment of the task and the presentation as a team. Again there can be marketing and publicity of the program. The presentation can be as individual projects to be viewed or presented as a skit or show. This program can be simple or get more sophisticated as the grade levels increase.

Suggested Reading

Cohen, C. (1983). Building Multicultural and Intergenerational Networks Through Oral History. *Frontiers, 7* (1), 98–102.

Lawrence, J. H. (1981). Oral History and the Motivation to Learn: An Exploratory Study. *Educational Gerontology, 7,* 135–149.

Lesson 1

Exploring My Family History

I enjoyed the family tree and how my grandparents and great-grandparents came to America. Mostly I enjoyed learning about the olden days from my grandparents. It's hard to imagine the way they lived. My favorite part was all the treasures found and talked about. The treasures build memories of life enjoyed to take into old age and pass down to young children like me.

— Katarina, 4th grade

LESSON OVERVIEW

This lesson will begin taking the concepts of aging from a global to a very personal level. Who are the people in my own life who are older? How do I relate to them and what is the purpose of knowing them and remembering them? It will also give students a sense of how family is connected despite geographic mobility.

The information gathered in this lesson will directly lead to the next lesson. Both are trying to explore the early years of immigration in the late 1800s and early 1900s. Although many of the students will not have living relatives who actually immigrated during those years, the understanding of how immigration has drastically changed over the years and what that enormous early wave of immigration meant to America is a valid objective. It also provides students with a sense of humility if a comparison is drawn between life for early twentieth-century immigrants and life today.

Learner Outcomes—Aging Issues
- Students will understand about family lineage and history.
- Students will appreciate the reasons for immigration.
- Students will understand why America is as multicultural as it is.

Learner Outcomes—Integration with Academic Curricula
- Students will create an abbreviated genealogical chart.
- Students will do research on their family.
- Students will understand the validity of genealogy as a science.
- Students will work on map skills.
- Students will increase geographical knowledge.

This lesson integrates with
Geography: map skills and identification of countries and continents
Math: determination of percentages of class ancestors that are immigrants
Critical Analysis: the diversity of America and benefits gained from that diversity
Literature: trade books that explore diversity and immigration
History: immigration

GRADE ADJUSTMENTS

Younger grade students should focus on the relationship of themselves to their ancestors and realize that they may be descendants of immigrants. This connection to immigrants and to the contribution of America as a "melting pot" should be emphasized. Further it should be stressed that most of us have immigrant ancestors and that we need to empathize with today's immigrants.

For fourth graders and older, the concept of genealogy as a science is a valuable activity. The abbreviated chart in this lesson could be made more sophisticated by adding siblings. The questions following the genealogical chart could also be more sophisticated by asking for more specific information. Researching what was happening in the identified countries at the time of greatest emigration and what kind of work/activity was done when arriving in the United States are two aspects that warrant extra attention.

TERMS USED

Immigrant   a person who comes into a new country to settle there
Genealogy   a recorded history of the descent of a person from an ancestor

MATERIALS NEEDED

an actual genealogical chart (optional)
map of the world
pushpins or markers
chart paper, magic markers

PROCEDURE

Day 1
1. The homework should be assigned and completed prior to the lesson.
    Note: Be sure students know that the person does not have to be alive to be included in the chart. The students may not know all the answers but should be as complete and specific as possible. They do not need to know details; for example, knowing an ancestor was born in Poland is important, but knowing exactly which city in Poland is unimportant; knowing an ancestor was born in 1908 is important, but knowing their exact birthday is unimportant. Also you may need to make decisions or allowances about adoption or divorce situations.

Day 2
1. Ask students to look at their charts and answer the following questions with a show of hands.
    How many of you are immigrants? Have class note how many hands went up.
    How many of your parents are immigrants? Note numbers.

How many of your grandparents are/were immigrants? Note numbers.

How many of your great-grandparents are/were immigrants? Note numbers.

2. Ask students to explain why more hands went up each time we went further back into our family lineage.

3. Ask students to again look at their charts, and for those relatives who are immigrants to America, answer the following questions. As the answers are given someone should be marking or using pushpins on a map at the front of the class to identify the locations.

In what country were you born?

In what country(ies) were your parents born?

In what country(ies) were your grandparents born?

In what country(ies) were your great-grandparents born?

Determine how many countries and how many continents are represented by one class.

4. Ask students to explain why America is called a melting pot. How is America enriched by having such a diverse lineage?

5. Ask students to consult Part II of their charts. Discuss how the immigrants in the students' families got to America, why they immigrated, and under what circumstances. Ideally this information should be recorded in chart form for use in the next lesson.

6. Finally, ask students to describe the kind of work the immigrants performed when they came to America. This discussion provides an introduction to the next lesson and a vehicle for understanding that education years ago was a luxury not everyone had the option to obtain.

Note: Do not dwell on questions 5 and 6 at this time, because it will be discussed in detail in the next lesson.

SUGGESTIONS FOR FURTHER ACTIVITY

1. Take the students on a field trip to a U.S. Center for Immigration, or have them search the Internet for information on the wave of early twentieth-century immigration.

2. Create a map that uses pictures of the students and lines connecting them to the locations of their ancestors. It will help visualize that America is a melting pot.

Suggested Bibliography for Use with This Lesson

Addy, S. H. *A Visit with Great-Grandma.* Whitman & Co., 1989.

Ages preschool–5. Barbara visits her great-grandma and they cook together and look at the family album. Even though great-grandma doesn't speak English well they understand each other because they talk with their hearts.

Cornish, S. *Grandmother's Pictures.* Bradbury Press, 1976.

Ages 5–8. A youngster expresses his special feelings about his grandmother and the family pictures she shares with him.

Doherty, B. *Granny Was a Buffer Girl.* Orchard, 1988.

Ages 11+. As Jess gets ready to leave for college she pieces together the history of her family. Stories of her grandparents are the fabric for a loyal family.

Feder, P. K. *The Feather-Bed Journey.* Albert Whitman & Co., 1995.

Ages 11–14. As she rescues the insides of a torn feather pillow, grandma tells about her childhood in Poland, the Nazi persecution of Jews during World War II, and the origin of this special pillow.

Finkelstein, R. *We're So Lucky! A Book about Our Bubbies and Zaidies.* Ruth Finkelstein, 1996.

Ages preschool–5. This book illustrates sharing information about grandmas and grandpas.

Ganz, Y. *Me and My Bubby, My Zeidy and Me.* Feldheim Publishers, 1990.

Ages preschool–5. This book depicts the special relationship that children share with their grandparents by showing them participating in a variety of activities involving Jewish tradition and culture.

Johnson, A. *Tell Me a Story, Mama.* Orchard, 1989.

Ages 5–8. Mama tells her daughter stories about when she was young and living with her mama.

McMillan, B. *Grandfather's Trolley.* Candlewick Press, 1995.

Ages 6–8. This story takes readers back to the trolley days of the early 1900s as a little girl hops aboard a trolley car motored by her grandfather. She feels the breeze and sway as the trolley rolls, and she gets to help her grandfather motor it home. Captures tender rapport between grandparents and grandchildren through beautiful photos.

Rylant, C. *The Relatives Came.* Bradbury, 1985.

Ages 5–11. The story of a family reunion in rural Virginia.

Schertle, A. *William and Grandpa.* Lothrop, 1981.

Ages 5–8. A boy visits his grandfather in Florida and they talk about continuity through the generations.

Showers, P. *Me and My Family Tree.* Crowell, 1978.

Ages 5–8. Nonfiction briefly discusses the principles of genetics as illustrated by a child's family tree.

Waddell, M. *Grandma's Bill.* Orchard, 1990.

Ages preschool–5. Bill asks his grandma who is in a picture. The answer is an afternoon of discovery and memories as Bill and his grandmother talk about Bill's grandfather and parents.

Homework

Exploring My Family History

Name _____

With your parent's or guardian's help, develop a simple family tree by completing the following chart. For each person listed, there are three empty lines. They are for the person's name, year of birth, and place of birth. If you don't know an answer, leave it blank. Be as specific as possible.

PART I

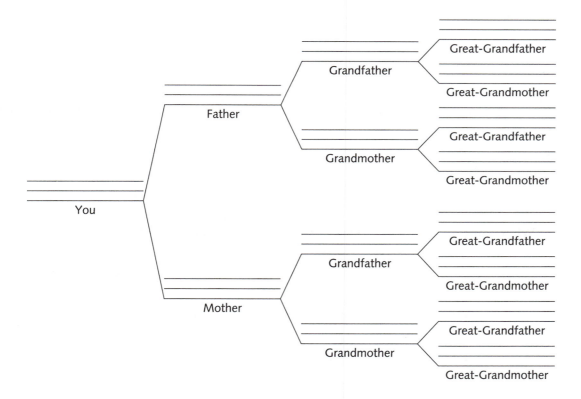

PART II

If anyone on your family tree was *born* outside of America but came to America to live, answer these next questions:

1. Why did the person(s) want to come to America?

2. How did the person(s) get to America?

3. What work did the person(s) do when he/she got to America?

Lesson 2

Immigration Then and Now

Seniors can be very helpful. You could ask them what it was like when they were kids; they'll give you a full report!

— Katie, 4th grade

LESSON OVERVIEW

To be used as a cooperative learning exercise, this lesson explores immigration through Ellis Island in the early twentieth century and compares and contrasts it to today's immigration procedures. Presented as a puzzle in which each student group has a piece of that puzzle, the puzzle only becomes complete when the groups have reported to the class in the correct order that enables the "story" of immigration to make sense. The values of cooperation and dependability are integral to this group lesson.

Although this lesson is certainly easier for those classes in which immigration is part of the social studies curriculum, it is still important and valuable for those who may not have a greater context in which to place it. I have tried to provide ample Note sections for educators, so that the intent of the group work and the objectives sought are easier to discern. I have provided some pictures that illustrate the points being made in each group work but more should be provided if possible. The two books I highly recommend for all ages, but for younger students in particular, are *Immigrant Kids,* for its wonderful photographs and clearly presented story, and *If Your Name Was Changed at Ellis Island,* for the question-and-answer format that helps students conceptualize the process. Both books are listed in the Suggested Reading section.

Learner Outcomes—Aging Issues
 • Students will understand the anxiety that coupled with joy for early immigrants.
 • Students will understand the difficulties immigrant ancestors had in America.
 • Students will appreciate the adjustments that needed to be made.

Learner Outcomes—Integration with Academic Curricula
 • Students will work cooperatively.
 • Students will hypothesize about the feelings of immigrants.
 • Students will evaluate pictures and verbalize the content.
 • Students will sequence events.
 • Students will compare and contrast.

 This lesson integrates with
 Social Studies: immigration in the early 1900s, study of different nationalities and their homeland

Language Arts: reading, evaluating pictures, comparing and contrasting
Critical Thinking: recognition of the problematic nature of immigration
Arts: study of the culture and art of immigrant peoples
Math: measure the size and structure of the Statue of Liberty, determine how it was put together

GRADE ADJUSTMENTS

Younger grades will be stretched a bit with this lesson. It can be made easier if it is done as a whole class and the "story" is told through the pictures presented by the teacher. If possible, invite an immigrant who went through Ellis Island, or one whose parents immigrated through Ellis Island and knows all the "stories," to the class to tell the story. The class should prepare questions to ask. Unfortunately, as the next century approaches, the likelihood of this is becoming less plausible. If it is possible, videotapes or oral histories should certainly be taken so as to preserve these wonderful accounts. If it is not possible, a good option is to read aloud to the class trade books about immigration.

The fourth grade, for which this lesson was developed, has no trouble with the concept or with evaluating the pictures and/or captions to elucidate and sequence the story. However, the events themselves are hard for them to imagine, and they may need assistance in conceptualizing reasons for them. This understanding can be accomplished with adult assistance during the cooperative work or as a class as the information is presented.

Older grades could continue this lesson by examining immigration during the late nineteenth and early twentieth centuries and comparing world events to overall immigration patterns. They should recognize that the numbers of immigrants increases when worldwide events occur that cause people to leave their native countries. For example, during the 1840s a potato famine hit Ireland and in the 1860s 2.5 million new immigrants came to America; in the late 1800s and early 1900s, Jews were being persecuted in Russia and from 1901 to 1910, 9 million new immigrants arrived in the United States. Although not all the new immigrants were Irish or Jewish, they probably represented a significant number, which swelled the overall immigration statistics. In more modern examples, students may examine the influx of Vietnamese following the Vietnam War, the Haitians escaping their own country to arrive in Florida, or the large numbers of foreign students at today's colleges. War, poverty, or political persecution, the thirst for American education, and other reasons for immigration are important topics for discussion.

This connection of immigration to politics, economics, historical events, and demographic changes is a valuable understanding to pursue for any age group. Students may discover that the reasons for immigration today hardly vary from the early 1900s.

TERMS USED

Trachoma   a contagious form of conjunctivitis causing inflammatory granulations on the inner eyelid (it is more dangerous than conjunctivitis because it could cause blindness)

Buttonhook   a tool used to examine for trachoma; it resembles a crochet hook[*]

MATERIALS NEEDED

copies of pictures that show the process of immigration through Ellis Island (Captions and/or paragraphs in explanation should be included with the pictures.)

copies of questions to use as guides for students as they piece the story together

PROCEDURE

Day 1

1. Divide the class into small groups and present each group with a packet that contains a list of questions, pictures, and text to support the questions.

2. Explain that the group's job is to look at the pictures, figure out what is happening in each picture, and try to put them into a sequence or find a unifying theme to all of them. By reading the captions and explanations, students should be able to sequence the events.

   Note: Using your knowledge of your class and your judgment about the amount of explanation needed, provide suitable amounts of captions and explanations. Also, the source you use for the pictures and explanations should fit the level of sophistication desired. The three books I have found most helpful for students are listed in the Suggested Reading section at the end of this lesson. Sections of these books could be part of the reading material to help students piece together the story. You may also need to actually work with each group as they attempt to do this, because it does require some conceptualization skills. The questions listed for each group contain specific notes for the teacher as well.

3. Students must then answer the provided questions and come up with a story to fit their piece of the puzzle. They should decide how their information will be presented to the class.

   Note: The last question for each group is to decide how the immigrants felt at this stage of the process. It is not necessary to provide text for this. The objective is to have students use their own intuitive feelings to decide how they would feel in such a situation. This question is important because it allows students to take a concept and personalize it.

4. When all the groups have completed their work—and this might take two days depending on how much time you can allow for the lesson—the groups need to

---

[*]Author's explanation.

present to the class in one or two sentences the basic topic for their puzzle piece. The class then should decide the order of presentation of the groups.

5. Presentations to the class should include a review of the pictures as they describe what is happening. The questions can be read or used as a guideline for the presentation.

Group I

Pictures/explanations used should depict
> steerage class on a boat
> a crowded boat (Figure 5–2.1)
> items used to carry belongings (Figure 5–2.2)
> examples of what people brought with them to America

Note: This piece of the puzzle tells of the passage to America. Students should deduct from the pictures that the passage was difficult, crowded, and took quite a while because ships were not as fast or as luxurious as they are now. In addition, they need to surmise why people would leave their own country to come to a new, foreign one and to imagine what kinds of belongings would be important enough to take.

Questions in this group's packet:

1. Why did people want to leave their own country to come to America?
2. What kinds of things did people take with them to America?
3. What kind of luggage did people use to carry their possessions?
4. How did people immigrating to America get to America? Was it a pleasant journey?
5. How do you think immigrants felt as they journeyed to America?

Group II

Pictures/explanations used should depict
> large families with numbered tags on their clothing
> immigration officers examining immigrant's eyes (Figure 5–2.3)
> hospital rooms on Ellis Island
> dormitories on Ellis Island

Note: The second piece of the puzzle is the landing at Ellis Island and the medical tests performed in order to be accepted into the country. There was significant tension for immigrants who did not speak the language, yet they knew from fellow immigrants that they could potentially be sent back to their old country if they were found to have a contagious disease such as trachoma. Families, often quite large, were marked with numbers to keep them together. Inspectors also marked immigrants' clothing with chalk letters as they passed from one test to the next to indicate their medical status. The medical exams were indeed a traumatic event. Those who did not initially pass the exams because of minor sickness were detained in the hospital on the island while their family members stayed in the dormitories.

Questions in this group's packet:

1. Where did most immigrants land when they arrived in America?
2. After landing, what was the first thing that the immigrants had to go through? Why?
3. What happened if one child of a large family was sick? What if the sickness was highly contagious?
4. Why did the immigration officers put chalk letters on the immigrants' clothing?
5. How do you think the immigrants felt as they went through these medical examinations?

Group III

Pictures/explanations used should depict
registry room (Figure 5–2.4)
immigration officer interrogating an immigrant (Figure 5–2.5)
examples of the kinds of questions asked by immigration officers

Note: The third phase of this story involves the long waiting in lines for the interrogation by inspectors. Immigrants were asked if they had somewhere to go, if they had enough money to start a new life and not be a burden on an already overcrowded New York, and if they had a criminal record. There were interpreters for most languages, but not all; the immigrant's names were difficult for officers to pronounce and/or spell and so they often got changed to a simpler form; and money was scarce because families had often spent all they had to book passage to America. This, too, was a stressful moment for families.

Questions in this group's packet:
1. Where did the immigrants go after their medical examinations? Why?
2. What did the Registry Room look like?
3. What kinds of questions did the immigration officers ask the immigrants? What purpose did asking those kind of questions serve?
4. Do you think it was really possible that people's names got changed when they were in the Registry Room? Why?
5. How do you think you would feel if your name got changed?
6. How do you think the immigrants felt as they went through the Registry Room?

Group IV

Pictures/explanations used should depict

immigrants waiting to go on a boat to Manhattan (Figure 5–2.2)
tenement homes and crowded conditions
crowded New York City streets
children playing and working in crowded cities

Note: Once on the ferry to New York, immigrants were relieved and pleased. Yet the difficulties in being in America, and assimilating, were often just beginning. Life in New York was hard, yet families either stayed permanently or worked to save the money needed to move. Tenement homes and apartments were often crowded and poorly kept by landlords, yet there was running water and inside toilets and the immigrants were grateful to be here.

Questions in this group's packet:

1. After leaving Ellis Island where did most immigrants go?
2. What determined how long they stayed before moving to where they actually wanted to live?
3. What were many immigrants' homes like when they arrived in America? What were some of the "modern" home conveniences they had here that they didn't have in their old country?
4. What do you notice about the numbers of people in the cities?
5. How do you think the immigrants felt as they started their life in America?

Group V

Pictures/explanations used should depict
immigrant men and women at work in factories or on farms
immigrant children at work—"newsies"
schools in the early 1900s

Note: The final part of the story is the adjustment to America. Work was mostly as laborers—tailors, store clerks, chefs, carpenters, housemaids—because immigrants rarely had a higher education. Work, in the sweatshops of New York was legendary for the cruel working conditions. Child-labor laws were nonexistent and families worked long days. Yet there was a resilience and satisfaction to life in America. It was better than what they left.

Questions in this group's packet:

1. How did immigrant children learn to speak English? How did adults learn English?
2. How were schools different than yours are today?
3. Why did children work as well as go to school? How old do you think they were and what kind of work did they do?
4. What kind of jobs did adults have? What were the working conditions like?
5. How do you think immigrants felt as they worked and went to school in America?

Figure 5–2.1 Immigrants on Atlantic Liner, S.S. Patricia, December 10, 1906. Levick Edwin, Photographer. *Source:* Ellis Island and Immigration Collection, Prints and Photographs Division, LC-USZ62-11202, Library of Congress.

Figure 5–2.2 Waiting for Ellis Island Ferry, October 30, 1912. Photographed by Underwood and Underwood. *Source:* Ellis Island and Immigration Collection, Prints and Photographs Division, LC-USZ62-11203, Library of Congress.

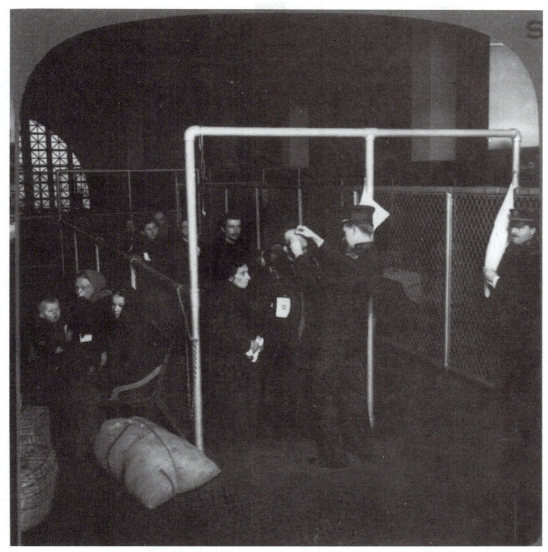

Figure 5–2.3   Eye Examination at Ellis Island. Photograph copyrighted 1913 by Underwood and Underwood.
Source: Ellis Island and Immigration Collection, Prints and Photographs Division, LC-USZ62-7386, Library of Congress.

Figure 5–2.4 Examination Hall, Ellis Island. Photograph copyrighted 1913 by Underwood and Underwood.
Source: Ellis Island and Immigration Collection, Prints and Photographs Division, LC-USZ62-15539, Library of Congress.

Figure 5–3.1   Immigrants at Ellis Island, ca. 1912. Photographed by Bain News Service (Lot 7172). *Source:* Ellis Island and Immigration Collection, Prints and Photographs Division, LC-USZ62-26543, Library of Congress.

Day 2

1. Once the puzzle about immigration through Ellis Island is complete, students need to examine immigration today to be able to compare and contrast the process.

2. If you have a student in your class who is a recent immigrant, ask him/her to answer questions about the experience. If not, invite a parent or someone from the neighborhood to discuss the issue. If no one is available, contact an immigration officer or call the airport immigration services to get some answers.

3. Make a class chart that lists the salient points of the immigration process in the early 1990s including

   - why the immigrants came to America
   - how they got here
   - the processing in of immigrants at Ellis Island
   - the difficulties encountered during assimilation to American life

4. In another column or a separate chart, list the salient points of the immigration process today after asking questions of the guest or student in the class. The list should include

   - why the immigrant (or family) came to America
   - how they got here
   - the processing in procedure
   - the difficulties encountered during assimilation to American life

5. Ask students to compare and contrast the experiences.

SUGGESTIONS FOR FURTHER ACTIVITY

1. As a current affairs project, ask older students to research current immigration laws and determine how those laws would have affected the millions of immigrants coming to America at the turn of the century.

2. Have students construct a picture collage to tell the story of immigration.

3. Writing exercises could include topics such as "How Does an Immigrant Feel?" or "If I Had to Pack in One Suitcase, What Would I Take with Me?"

4. Have students write an autobiography of themselves as an immigrant. Assign each child a "new identity"—a name and a country in which they were born. They must research why they want to leave their country to come to America and tell about their life as an immigrant.

5. Have students study the Statue of Liberty. A study such as this can integrate with math—its dimensions are 151 feet, 1 inch from the base to the tip of the torch. Ask students to give it a comparable equivalent, such as how many football fields it is high.

   History—why was it given to us as a gift, under what circumstances and to commemorate what event?

Literature—read the poem written by Emma Lazarus on a plaque on the wall inside the pedestal.

Critical analysis—what is the meaning of the Statue of Liberty as a symbol?

Suggested Reading

Allen, L. (1985). *Liberty, The Statue and the American Dream.* New York: The Statue of Liberty—Ellis Island Foundation, Inc., Distributed by Summit Books, a division of Simon & Schuster, Inc.

Freedman, R. (1980). *Immigrant Kids.* New York: Scholastic.

Levine, E. (1993). *If Your Name Was Changed at Ellis Island.* New York: Scholastic.

Suggested Bibliography for Use with This Lesson

Bales, C. A. *Tales of the Elders: A Memory Book of Men and Women Who Came to America as Immigrants, 1900–1930.* Follett, 1977.

Ages 8–14. Stories of twelve naturalized Americans.

Freedman, R. *Immigrant Kids.* Dutton/Scholastic, 1980.

Ages 5+. Photographs plus text are used in this book to describe the immigrant experience through Ellis Island. It is a good source of photos to use with this lesson.

Langer, N. *Freddy, My Grandfather.* Four Winds, 1979.

Ages 5–8. A girl tells of her immigrant grandfather who leads a busy life.

Levinson, R. *Watch the Stars Come Out.* Dutton, 1985.

Ages 5–8. Grandma tells about her grandma and how she took the long journey to America. Some sad tales, some wonderful.

Lesson 3

Scavenger Hunt for Treasures

Mrs. Friedman gave awesome homework assignments like the scavenger hunt which was fun too.

— Jessica, 4th grade

LESSON OVERVIEW

Of all the lessons I have ever taught, by far this is the most successful. I think it is because it allows students to be with an older adult in a setting that takes them to another place in time and allows them the privacy of sharing that space in a special way. Memories of older adults provide vehicles for children to see history in a personal way. This sharing allows for a very important kind of interaction that is different than and can go beyond the programmatic tutoring or mentoring often associated with intergenerational programs. This is where the magic occurs, and it often occurs privately!

This lesson and Lesson 4 are inextricably linked. In fact, if I decide to do Lesson 4 as a homework assignment, I often give both homework assignments together so that the student can explore memorabilia and interview at the same time—an easier logistical situation. For purposes here, I will present them separately so that I am able to stress different ideas.

It is a good idea to discuss with students where people keep "treasures." Stress that any place where memories are stored is fine—it might be an attic or a basement in a big old house, but treasures might also be found in photo albums, a trunk, a scrapbook, a drawer, or a box on a shelf. Where do they keep their treasures? The lesson is simple in execution yet powerful in its message.

Some community and city museums have trunks filled with artifacts from other cultures and time periods that they often loan to teachers or use with outreach programs. Having students explore these trunks is a good follow-up to this lesson. A local historical museum might also be an opportunity for a field trip.

Learner Outcomes—Aging Issues
- Students will gain an historical perspective of life before them.
- Students will empathize with life during difficult times.
- Students will understand that society changes.
- Students will experience, through artifacts, historical change.
- Students will learn to value the older generation.

Learner Outcomes—Integration with Academic Curricula
- Students will refine interviewing techniques.
- Students will communicate through public speaking.

- Students will become good listeners.
- Students will become critical thinkers.

   This lesson integrates with
   Social Studies: examination of memorabilia of past times and cultures
   Language Arts: communication, listening, and interviewing skills
   Art: recognizing craftsmanship of past years
   Critical Thinking: recognize why people save and how artifacts provide historical perspectives

GRADE ADJUSTMENTS

For younger students, this show-and-tell lesson is an age-appropriate experience. The emphasis will be on the sharing and the objects themselves. The discussion that surrounds the sharing will allow students to see the artifacts as part of a person's life story.

For older students it is also a valid lesson, but needs to be presented in a context of age-appropriate sharing. The emphasis should be twofold: first on the feelings that the search evoked in the students as well as the feelings that resulted as the older person relived the memories; and second on the investigation of history through the artifacts found. The discussion that occurs should reflect on the historical perspectives students can obtain by sharing the artifacts with those who have lived in that era.

Discussion surrounding the presentations should be channeled so that the older adults share with students the fact that the world has changed significantly and that the older adults of today often exhibited great strength as they went through some challenging times.

TERMS USED

Artifacts   any object made by human work

PROCEDURE

1. The accompanying homework assignment must be completed prior to the lesson. Discuss with the students what artifacts are. Tell the students that the purpose of the lesson is to share memories and time with an older adult. It doesn't matter what they choose to share with the class—that it can be anything that is special to them and/or to the older adult. Discuss what a scavenger hunt is and that they will be hunting for special treasures.
2. Invite one or two older adults to the classroom for this lesson. Explain that they will be asked to share their memories about the objects presented and about anything they believe relevant to that time period. Share the need to be as specific and descriptive as possible when working with young students and to keep answers relatively short.

Note: Older adults do not always know about child development, and it is important to share this information so that the time together is rewarding for each of them. It may seem as if they should know this and you are being condescending to tell them, but that is not so, and if presented as a way of helping to make the lesson special, it will be accepted and welcomed by the older adult.

3. Introduce the older adult to the class and explain that he/she is here to share his/her memories and that the artifacts the children present will be the spark for those memories. Place the older adult in a circle with the students or in front of a close cluster of students on the floor. Everyone must be sitting close to each other for ease of looking at the objects, and for a feeling of closeness and of sharing.

4. Students will each have a chance to present their objects. The presentation should include

> what the object is
> who it belonged to
> what its significance is
> what makes it so special that it was saved

5. Call on students one by one to share. After the student has presented, the older adult should be allowed to comment and share his/her memories. If nothing comes to mind, you can "lead" the older adult into a discussion with questions or just move on to the next student.

Note: Typically the objects shared might include World War II memorabilia such as medals, ration stamps, posters, pictures, uniforms; kitchen utensils; clothing and jewelry; old photos. Anything is fine but obviously some items will create greater opportunities for discussion. For example:

- If a photo is shown, comment on the clothing or hairstyles in the photo and ask the older adult about the styles of that era or what he/she wore to school (no jeans or sneakers).
- If World War II memorabilia is shown, discussion could be on the war itself but also on the people left at home and how they managed and sacrificed. For older students, the concepts of war is a valuable discussion, especially if the visiting older adult had been in the war and can discuss the negative aspects of it. The older adult might be valuable in discussing why people were "eager" to fight in World War II and whether that would happen now and under what circumstances.
- If jewelry is brought in, ask the older adult to comment on the handicrafts of an earlier era and about the effect of industrialization on our crafts.
- If kitchen utensils are presented, discuss how kitchens were different and ask the older adult what those differences were. Ask the older adult to recall when he/she was little and when his/her parents were little. Use the photo in this lesson as an example of the differences in appliances then and now—ice boxes that required visits from the iceman compared with refrigerators now.

Figure 5–2.5 An Iceman. Photographer: Lewis W. Hine. *Source:* Courtesy George Eastman House.

SUGGESTIONS FOR FURTHER ACTIVITY

1. Students can write about what they learned from the activity and/or write thank-you letters to the older adult(s). They can also write about their feelings about the older person who came in to share or the older person with whom they did the homework assignment.
2. A book about their shared objects, with illustrations, can be presented to the library.
3. Arrange a field trip to the local historical society or library to view objects or photos about the town years ago.
4. Have the students research the town history and write about the changes through the years.

Suggested Bibliography for Use with This Lesson

Ackerman, K. *Song and Dance Man.* Knopf, 1988.

Ages 5–8. Up in the attic grandpa pulls out props from an old trunk and is transformed into a vaudevillian again. Grandchildren are enthralled and they see their grandpa in a way that makes him seem vital and in an important role.

Adler, C. S. *The Silver Coach.* Coward, McCann, 1979.

Ages 11–14. Twelve-year-old Chris finds a tiny silver coach when she explores grandma's treasures during a summer visit following her parent's divorce. Grandma tells her about it, and Chris finds grandma is a good person to be with.

Bonners, S. *The Wooden Doll.* Lothrop, 1991.

Ages 5–8. Visiting her grandpa's house, Stephanie learns the origin of grandpa' beautiful doll.

Howard, E. F. *Aunt Flossie's Hats.* Clarion, 1991.

Ages 5–8. Sunday afternoons are special because Sarah and Susan get to visit great-great-aunt Flossie and hear the stories about her wonderful hat collection.

Homework

Scavenger Hunt for Treasures

Name _____

With an older adult, spend time looking through that person's old treasures. Discuss the objects you find and why they are important to that person. List four items that you found that seem important or special and tell why they are important. Then, with permission, bring one of those items to class on the day for sharing. If the older adult would rather you didn't bring it in, you can draw a picture of it, make a photocopy of it, or simply plan on describing it to the class. Remember to treat all the objects with care and respect—they are someone's treasures!

Item One:

Item Two:

Item Three:

Item Four:

Lesson 4

Living History

I never thought I would be friends with a senior. I know more about seniors and my own grandparents. It was amazing how much they had to go through during a war. And when I asked the questions what their clothing looked like I couldn't believe how much it has changed since then.

— Elise, 4th grade

LESSON OVERVIEW

Learning history through the memories of those who have lived it makes the lesson relevant and allows our historical imaginations to flourish. This is certainly not new to any teacher who has encouraged experiential education. It becomes obvious as one observes the avid attention paid by students to the information imparted by the older adults.

Because this is an oral history lesson, it can be altered to reflect any one era of history, an area of class interest, or an extension of a preexisting curriculum topic. Because oral histories provide such an unending list of possibilities, this lesson should be made relevant to the already existing curricula or special project. I do hope that during the fiftieth anniversary year of World War II, many teachers, during social studies or history classes, encouraged oral histories with older adults who had fought in the war. Recognizing that these people are mostly in their 70s, we must document their memories now! But don't wait for a milestone to document the past. Everyday is a milestone.

To make the oral history especially relevant and to activate interest, encourage students to structure interviews to their own concerns as well as to the goals of the class lesson. For example, if a school is about to embark on its seventy-fifth anniversary and the sixth grades decide to interview older adults who may have attended that school when it first opened, it is obviously important to structure the questions about how the school and the neighborhood have changed. But it is also valid for the students to ask questions that reflect their interest in that time. Older students may be interested in parent involvement in the school: they may choose to explore the differences in our societies from years ago when it was assumed that the women would be providing the cookies and staffing the bake sales. This is in contrast to today's parent–teacher organizations in which fathers are equally active and fundraising can be on a more sophisticated scale. Or students may be interested in exploring the concept of children's heros then and now, comparing the kinds of people or the attributes that children admired then and who they admire now. Or students might develop questions about sports and the possible differences in the level of competition, or what sports meant to the community then and what it means now.

In developing questions for interviews be sure students create open-ended questions. Questions that are answered with either yes or no do not allow for stories to be told. So rather than ask, "When you were in school, did you play games at recess?" students should ask, "When you were in school, what games did you play at recess?"

In any oral history you should predetermine what you will be doing with the information once attained. Culminating activities are important for closure and for the recognition that this information is worth sharing in some way. There are many options for this, and I have discussed them in the Suggestions for Further Activity section of this lesson.

As mentioned in Lesson 3, these two lessons are easily linked together, and this one can also be accomplished as an in-class exercise rather than as a homework assignment.

Learner Outcomes—Aging Issues
- Students will understand how society has changed.
- Students will appreciate the older adult adjusting to those changes.
- Students will understand the difficulties inherent in change.
- Students will compare and contrast society then and now.

Learner Outcomes—Integration with Academic Curricula
- Students will create questions relevant to the issue.
- Students will interview older adults.
- Students will compile and evaluate information.
- Students will communicate information verbally or in writing.
- Students will critically evaluate contrasting societies.
- Students will create a culminating document.

This lesson integrates with
Language Arts: interviewing, communication, listening skills
Critical Thinking: comparing and contrasting life of different generations
Social Studies: analysis of different eras of history, effects of different cultures on America
Math: comparing the costs of items through the years, how economies have changed

GRADE ADJUSTMENTS

This lesson is wonderful for all ages, but the level of questioning and the depth of understanding will depend on the grade level. Younger grades should focus on questions that are relevant to them and that they can easily comprehend—clothing styles, kitchen appliances, differences in the physicality of schools and the routine of the school day, going to the movies then and now. Older students, in addition to those topics, which are interesting for any age, might also focus on questions that provide insight into a changing society—roles of men and women in family life and career orientation, the effects of current events such as wars and the changing roles of men and women in those events, the changing economy, slang sayings and the evolution of language, changes in school in relation to education reform ideas.

For this lesson, questions will be geared toward determining how life has changed over the years. I have listed some questions that I have found to be fun for students to explore, but they should be considered only a starting point. The questions you use must be relevant and accomplish the goal of the individual class lesson.

PROCEDURE

1. Have the students do the accompanying assignment prior to the class discussion, or, invite enough older adults into the classroom to provide a group setting of one older adult for every four or five students. In either case, students will interview an older adult by asking the questions in the exercise.

   Note: Be sure students realize that either they or the older adult may elaborate on the questions asked during the interview. The beauty of oral histories is that they often uncover memories or information that could not be anticipated by predetermined questions. If the older adult answers the proposed question and then says, "That reminds me of . . . ," encourage the students to listen and ask follow-up questions. Role-playing exercises as a way of practicing interviewing techniques are beneficial.

   Note: You may choose to have some books available to help older adults illustrate what they are describing or to help spark memories. This may or may not be easy to do depending on the topic under consideration and the questions. The Project Fair program suggestion at the beginning of this chapter has a list of possible books that may help.

2. Once the interviews have been completed, class discussion should focus on what was asked and the answers. Sharing the information is valuable because one older adult may remember more, less, or different issues than another.

3. Decide with the students and older adults (if they were present in the classroom), what they want to do with this information. Will it be turned into a book, presented as a play, or shared with other classes and groups? Complete that project.

SUGGESTIONS FOR FURTHER ACTIVITY

1. Have students write a play based on the information obtained through the oral histories and perform it for local older adult groups, for parents, and/or for the school. I would encourage the play to be intergenerational!

2. Have students and their older adult partners write a book based on the interviews and present it to the local senior center as well as the school library/media center. Actually getting the librarian involved in the process is another source of academic integration as students learn about accessioning a new book into a

library collection. Be sure to have the intergenerational teams work on the final product together; use a computer word processor (have students teach the older adults how to use it if they don't know how) to put the book into correct typed form, illustrate it, create a cover, bind it, and present it.

3. Have a culminating, thank-you party when the project is complete. It is a way to say thank you to the older adults for sharing and a way for the older adults to thank the students for including them in an important project.

Suggested Bibliography for Use with This Lesson

Cherry, M. *Josephine.* Pocahontas Press, 1995.

Ages 11+. The author recounts the life and adventures of her grandmother as a young girl struggling to survive on her own during and after the Civil War.

Cross, V. *Great-Grandmother Tells of Threshing Day.* Morton Grove, 1992.

Ages 11+. A narrative by a great-grandmother recreates the life of American farm children on threshing day in Missouri. The story is about a little girl and her brother helping out on threshing day in the early 1900s as the neighbor men arrive to thresh the family's wheat and bring it to the mill and the neighbor women assist with the huge midday meal.

Fancher, B. *Our Favorite Things Way Back Then & Now.* Fancher & Associates, 1995.

Ages 8–14. The story is a cooperative effort between a 65-year-old grandfather and a 12-year-old grandson that presents a format for communicating between a pre–World War II generation and modern youth.

Johnson, A. *Tell Me a Story, Mama.* Orchard, 1989.

Ages 5–8. Mama tells her daughter stories about when she was young and living with her mama.

Johnson, H. L. *Picture the Past: 1900–1915.* Lothrop, 1975.

Ages 11–14. This book illustrates everyday life of children growing up in the early twentieth century.

Ketner, A. G. *Ganzy Remembers.* Atheneum, 1991.

Ages 5–8. Great-granddaughter visits Ganzy in the nursing home and loves to hear the stories she remembers about her childhood when she was called Daphne, not Ganzy.

Kumin, M. *When Great-Grandmother Was Young.* Putnam & Sons, 1971.

Ages 8–11. Story of a great-grandmother's life on an island in Canada before cars and TV.

Lasky, K. *The Night Journey.* Warne, 1981.

Ages 8–11. Rachel ignores her parent's wishes and persuades her great-grandmother to tell the story of her escape from Czarist Russia.

McDonald, M. *The Potato Man,* Orchard Books, 1991.

Ages 5–11. Grandpa shares a story about when he was young and how he knew a man who sold potatoes from a wagon. The man taught young grandpa an important lesson.

Moore, F. *I Gave Thomas Edison My Sandwich.* Albert Whitman, 1995.

Ages 1–5. A story based on the author's memories of a field trip during which he met the inventor of the lightbulb, Thomas Edison. Shows the value of oral histories.

Sobol, H. L. *Grandpa, A Young Man Grown Old.* Coward, McCann & Geoghegan, 1980.

Ages 11+. A 17-year-old's views of her grandfather are juxtaposed with his descriptions of his life.

Homework

History That Talks

Name _____

Name of older adult interviewed _____

Interview an older adult. It can be your grandparent, a friend, or a neighbor. Ask the questions below and write the answers in the space provided. Think of other questions about things you would like to know and write down the questions you asked and his/her answer.

1. What was it like to go to the movies when you were my age? How much did it cost? What did you see besides the feature presentation?

2. What were the clothing fashions of the day when you were my age? What did you usually wear to school?

3. Do you remember any slang sayings you used when you were my age or a teenager?

4. Tell me three things you remember about what it was like to live during a war. How do you think World War II was different from any wars there have been since?

5. Describe your elementary school. What made it different from my school today?

6. Other questions I asked:

Lesson **5**

Stories About My Family Traditions

The questions that were asked really made me think about older people and how they feel and how they live. Some of the assignments were especially interesting because I had the chance to talk with my grandfather in Florida and my nana in Belmont. I got a special chance to be with my nana and see some of her old treasures. It was really neat for just me *to be with her. In March my grandfather died of a stroke. I feel special that just before he died I got to talk with him about his work, his parents, the cars back then, and slang. If I didn't have this program I would never have known these things because to tell you the truth I would never have asked.*
— Elizabeth, 4th grade

LESSON OVERVIEW

Family traditions and their origins are a good way to enable students to see themselves as part of an historical continuum. Stories about family traditions are usually passed down from one generation to the next, so the art of storytelling becomes an integral part of this historical context. In this lesson students can speak with either their parents or grandparents and then share their stories and traditions with the class. If students are unable to identify any family traditions, they should try to describe their family's present-day rituals and recognize that these will become the traditions of their descendants.

Chapter 3, Lesson 8, Diversity and Aging, makes reference to traditions but in a cultural context. This lesson will focus on tradition for its historic value.

Learner Outcomes—Aging Issues
• Students will recognize the value of passing information to new generations.
• Students will understand the relationship between traditions and history.
• Students will link traditions to their everyday lives.

Learner Outcomes—Integration with Academic Curricula
• Students will become storytellers.
• Students will communicate verbally.

This lesson integrates with
Language Arts: verbal communication, interviewing skills, storytelling
History: transmission of information between generations

GRADE ADJUSTMENTS

Younger students may want to tell their stories by bringing in pictures taken during a family celebration, holiday, or other tradition and describing what is happening in the picture. Older students will be able to tell their stories and should try to incorporate storytelling tips into their presentations.

TERMS USED

Tradition   the handing down orally of customs from generation to generation; a long-established custom that has the effect of an unwritten law

Storytelling   a series of connected events, true or fictitious, that is written or told with the intent of entertaining

PROCEDURE

Day 1
1. Students should do the homework assignment prior to Day 2 class. Ask younger students to bring in a picture to accompany their story.
2. Discuss traditions and what they are. Describe events that often become traditions.
    Note: Students may suggest things such as birthday celebrations, holidays, specific foods on specific days, family reunions, outings or vacations, and specific stories told.
3. Discuss things that families do today that students think might become a tradition. Why do they think that will become a tradition?
4. Discuss storytelling. Ask students what attributes make a good story for them. List these on the board or on a chart. Discuss how to tell a story so that the audience stays interested and attentive.
5. Practice storytelling techniques by pairing students and having them practice on each other—any story will do.
6. Discuss with students what questions they may need to ask of their parents or grandparents in order to be able to tell a good story to their class.

Day 2
1. Ask students to tell their stories. This can be done in front of the class or in small groups.
2. Ask students what benefit is derived from discovering where traditions began and how they are perpetuated through the years.
3. Discuss the feelings they have knowing that this has happened over and over again and will likely continue. Is it boring? Does it make them feel secure? Does it bring pleasure?
4. Hypothesize with the students why they think so many older adults like to tell stories about their children and/or family traditions.

SUGGESTIONS FOR FURTHER ACTIVITY

1. Younger students can either bring in pictures or draw pictures of different family traditions and make a mobile out of the drawings. A picture of themselves could be at the top, or a picture of an older adult who may have started the tradition.

2. Make a scrapbook of class traditions with an indication of where the tradition started and by whom. Determine whether older adults play important roles in these traditions.

Suggested Reading

Family Traditions, Curriculum. The Norman Rockwell Museum, Stockbridge, MA.

Suggested Bibliography for Use with This Lesson

DiSalvo-Ryan, D. *Uncle Willie and the Soup Kitchen.* Morrow Junior Books, 1991.

Ages preschool–5. A boy spends the day with Uncle Willie in the soup kitchen where he works preparing and serving food for the hungry.

Ganz, Y. *Me and My Bubby, My Zeidy and Me.* Feldheim Publishers, 1990.

Ages preschool–5. This book illustrates a special relationship with grandparents and a variety of activities involving Jewish customs.

My Family Traditions

Name _____

Ask your parent, guardian, or grandparent the following questions. Ask them to choose one family tradition they like the best and to tell you a story about it. Be sure you understand the story well so that you can share it in class.

1. How were family birthdays and holidays celebrated? Was anything the same about the celebrations of these events year after year?

2. Is there a special tradition that you love the most? Why do you love it? How did it begin? Why do you think it continues?

3. Is there a special place that family members go to all the time? Why?

4. If you could create a family tradition now, what would it be? Why did you choose that one?

5. Tell me a story about a special tradition or about something that happened during that special event.

Lesson 6

Consider the Changes

I like this program a lot because we got to do activities that we wouldn't usually do in class. We learned a lot about olden days when there was no technology which today there is like computers and heat! And I got to teach my grandma something.

— Chris, 4th grade

LESSON OVERVIEW

When my grandmother was well into her 70s she and I would sit and talk about the "olden days." It always amazed me how she adjusted to so many changes in her life (although, in truth, she never really adjusted to anything even resembling technology). But what she witnessed and experienced were things I had only read about, so I always sat in awe and listened attentively.

I now realize that I too have been witness to many events and changes that young children might only read about. And as we think about history evolving so quickly it is good to think about what we are experiencing now that may be significant in the future. This lesson allows students to recognize these moments.

Learner Outcomes—Aging Issues
• Students will gain an appreciation of the experiences of older adults.
• Students will recognize the vast changes that have occurred in this century.

Learner Outcomes—Integration with Academic Curricula
• Students will understand that history is also what is happening now.
• Students will identify current events as potentially significant in history.
• Students will examine the concept of "time capsules."

This lesson integrates with

History: formation of a time capsule; predicting events of future historical significance

Arts: examining old masters and modern artists; drawing pictures of objects that represented the past and represent the present

Language Arts: writing about feelings associated with the passage of time; writing about a particular event and why it may be significant

Science: recognizing the advances in medicine and technology

GRADE ADJUSTMENTS

I believe this lesson is appropriate for any age. Younger children may struggle a little with the past/present concept, because their years are limited. They certainly can understand "today" and they can be asked to imagine "tomorrow." An interesting exercise is to have them use the Internet to identify events, discoveries, or inventions that have occurred since they were born. The depth of research and subsequent discussion on any one topic may be adjusted for grade levels.

TERMS USED

Time Capsule   a storage of present-day memorabilia to be retrieved at a later date
Survivors   a person who continues to live after something

MATERIALS NEEDED

a time capsule container
collection of objects deemed important to represent the present
library books or high school history texts that identify key historical events/issues
      since approximately 1945

PROCEDURE

The Past

1. Provide small groups of students with a research book of inventions and events prior to about 1950.
2. Ask the student groups to look through the books to identify significant events and make a list of them.
3. Then have groups come together and make a class list of items on their individual lists. This list represents the changes and inventions in the world that older adults have experienced. They do not always have to be serious.

   Note: The identified changes can include

television	penicillin	polio shots
frozen food	copy machines	fax machines
disposable contact lenses	frisbees	jet planes, Concorde
radar	credit cards	laser beams
ballpoint pens	dishwashers	microwaves
air conditioners	clothes dryers	washing machines
designer jeans	fast food	Man on the Moon
computer dating	tape decks	CDs
illegal drugs	artificial hearts	men wearing earrings

The Present

1. Ask students to go back into their small groups and to think about changes in the world that they can remember. Have them make a list of these.

2. Then have groups come together and develop a class list of changes and events in their lives.

   Note: The list generated will depend on the age of the students, and younger students may not be able to generate a list beyond their immediate sphere of experiences. It is not necessary for the answers to be of great significance, but it is necessary for the students to see that changes are constantly occurring. The list might include

space stations	Berlin wall down	AIDS
Apartheid gone	turn of the century	laptop computers
cellular phones and beepers	war on drugs	medical technology
Air Jordan sneakers	sneakers with lights	
HMO health groups	Internet	

3. Have students compare and contrast the kind of events/changes between the two lists.

   Note: Obviously the older adult list will be significantly longer, but focus instead on the kinds of events and changes. For example, whereas years ago the medical advances centered on vaccinations and medicines, today's focus includes technological advances such as CAT scans and ultrasounds. Include in the list events or changes that may not seem significant now, but in the future might be. Ask students to defend why they think that event might become significant.

4. Ask students what they think best represents today's world. Explain that the class will be making a time capsule to be found years from now and that the artifacts inside must be representative of today. Decide with the class what the container of the capsule should be, when the capsule should be opened, and where it should be placed until then.

5. Have students collect the objects chosen for the time capsule (this may take a few days to do), place them in the container (see number 2 under The Future), and put them in the designated location. This can be done in ceremonial fashion with invited guests.

The Future

1. Ask students to return once more to their small groups and to hypothesize, or fantasize, about what the world may be like in the year 2050. What changes do they predict will happen? What events do they think will occur that will be significant?

2. Develop a class list when the groups have come together. Decide whether those predictions should be part of the time capsule.

SUGGESTIONS FOR FURTHER ACTIVITY

1. Students can write essays, poems, or expository pieces about what makes "today" significant.

2. Students can draw pictures of items that represented the past, that represent the present, and perhaps that will be part of the future. Make a mobile out of these.
3. Have students write about what life will be like years from now. Have them write about what it might have been like to live without any one particular event/object.
4. Have students study paintings from many years ago and those of present-day artists. What are some of the differences? How has painting changed? Invite a modern artist to class.
5. Students can study science and the difference technology has made in the world of medicine. Invite a scientist to class to discuss these changes.

Suggested Bibliography for Use with This Lesson

Johnson, A. *When I Am Old with You.* Orchard, 1990.

Ages 5–8. Grandson thinks of all the things he will do with his grandpa when they are old together. As long as granddaddy is next to him it will be perfect. Good discussion about how things change even when we don't want them to.

Chapter **Six**

The Biology of Aging

CHAPTER OVERVIEW

As the demographics of the world rapidly change, the need for scientists and physicians to enter the field of biogerontology increases. But lay people also must understand the biology of aging so that they can prepare for their own aging and care for their aging loved ones. This field is growing exponentially, and although this manual is not meant to be a treatise on biogerontology, nor am I qualified to present it as one, students must understand the basic tenets of this important field.

What is aging and why does it happen? This chapter provides a basic understanding of the *process* of aging and the crucial difference between normal aging and disease. Actually the term *normal aging* is a misnomer because aging *is* normal; it is more accurate to describe aging that is free of disease in comparison with aging that results from the effects of disease.

This chapter also addresses the issue of death and dying. Many trade books deal with this issue in a sensitive and empathic way, but the overabundance of these books implies a certain insistence that if we are to read about older adults, we will need to read about death and dying. Instead death and dying must be viewed as part of the aging *process*, which has no fixed points but is a continuum that begins at birth and ends at death. Death does not begin to be an issue at a specific age.

Finally, this chapter encourages critical-thinking skills as students evaluate the many "antiaging," "increased longevity" myths that exist and the reasons for them. Nutrition, exercise, life satisfaction in living a long life, and the acceptance of the aging process are important for healthy individuals.

INTERGENERATIONAL PROGRAM SUGGESTIONS

Students' and Older Adults' Health Days

Program: This program suggestion is patterned after the University of Maryland Adult Health and Development Program (AHDP), which is the model for the National Network for Intergenerational Health (NNIH). The NNIH proliferation has created AHDP programs in university settings nationwide and internationally.

In addition, AHDP received a U.S. Department of Education Grant (1990–1993) to provide AHDP-associated research. AHDP trains college students to work with institutionalized and noninstitutionalized older adults, one-to-one, in a program of physical fitness and health education. In the process, social well-being is also achieved. I believe a modified program can be accomplished on the elementary and middle school level. A basic outline follows.

Each student is paired with one older adult in the community and is required to meet once a week for some combined physical activity. This can occur in the school setting and be held during the students' gym class (this is a good chance to allow integration between a classroom teacher and the gym teacher), during recess if you have no specific gym classes, or after school or on Saturdays on the student's own time. The activity can be bowling, walking, jogging, bicycling, working out in a gym, low-impact aerobics classes (or more limited fitness classes, possibly programmed and available in nursing or assisted-living facilities), or any other form of physical exercise. The only requirement is that it be enjoyable for both and noncompetitive or nonthreatening. Students and older adults will also meet with the entire class and their partners a predetermined number of times (probably four to five times for younger students and up to twice a month for older students) during the span of the program to learn together about good nutrition and the benefits of exercise. This can be taught by the gym teacher, health teacher, classroom teacher, science teacher, a senior center director, or town health officer.

Mutual Benefits and Ongoing: The program should ideally last the entire year, but lacking that possibility, it should at least last a semester. Meeting once a week for a minimum of 16 to 20 weeks allows both students and the older adults to develop an important relationship and experience some physical benefits. The goals for all are to develop a social relationship that may be a mentoring one or simply a friendship, to gain an education about health and fitness, and to actually practice physical fitness and recognize that everyone can be active.

A final culminating activity occurs at the end of the year and should be related to the physical theme of the program—for example, a picnic with lawn games such as croquet or old-fashioned relay races, a day at the beach with long walks to collect shells, a day at an amusement park, a leisurely hike to a scenic spot, a day or evening of dancing.

For more information about the University of Maryland program contact, Dr. Dan Leviton, Director, Adult Health and Development Program, HHP Building, College Park, MD 20742, 301-405-2528.

Sharing Gym Class

Program: This simple program is similar to Health Days but is not as structured and health classes are optional here. The program involves inviting older adults to be part of the students' gym class or physical fitness program. If your school does not have such a program, some structured form of physical activity should be planned and can be accomplished as a recess program. (If this is what will be done, all parties involved—teacher, students, and older adults—can decide together on the kind of physical activity done at recess.)

Students are paired with an older adult on a one-to-one basis or in teams of four to five students for each adult. The older adults come to the school once a week for the length of the program. A commitment by both generations to do some form of physical activity at least four other times during the week is part of the program. Students and older adults keep a "fitness journal" to record what activity they did and when it was done and then to write about how they feel about themselves, how they feel physically, and how they feel about the participation in this program. Journal entries can be shared during time together if desired or can be private. The program can be accompanied by student health classes if there is a desire to expand the program. The role of exercise for good health should be stressed.

Mutual Benefits and Ongoing: This program should last as long as possible. The full year is ideal, but if this is being done in conjunction with a gym class, it may not fit into a gym teacher's curricula. In that case some of the time may be spent in gym and other shared time can be during recess. Each generation is gaining recognition that activity is important and improving overall physical health.

Let's Build a Fitness Trail

Program: This is an excellent example of young and old working together to benefit the entire community and an excellent example of academic and social integration. It is probably more appropriate for middle school students, but I would not discount the possibility that upper elementary students could do it as well. It will integrate with the academic disciplines of science, math, environmental studies, language arts, industrial arts technology, health, and physical fitness. It will also be interdepartmental within a community in that a recreation department, a department of public works, and a youth commission could be involved. The concept is that a class and older adults—approximately one for every four students would be ideal—would spend time together researching the idea of building a fitness trail in the community. Because everyone, at every age, benefits from physical activity, the community at large is being served. In this case the first and third generations in town would generate the initiative.

The research would involve locating an appropriate site with the recreation or public works department, investigating environmental issues about the site, determining what kinds of activity would benefit what parts of the body, designing the apparatus using math and industrial arts technology, and developing a proposal. The proposal would then need to be presented, through both written and oral communication, to the community, city, or town governance body for approval. Finally the actual building and installing of the trail would require the assistance of local departments.

Mutual Benefits and Ongoing: When both generations are working together for the benefit of a larger population, the personal benefits are inherent in the actual work. Because this is obviously a large project, it would take the better part of a year and so the ongoing nature of this is also inherent in the project.

Friendly Visiting with a Medical Purpose

Program: This is similar to a typical friendly visiting program (see the list of suggested programs in Chapter 3), but with a purpose beyond visiting. It usually occurs in the homes of older adults who are managing without nursing facilities but are in need of visiting nurse/medical services. Initiated because visiting nurses were unable to physically reach everyone they needed to in a single day, this program is appropriate for older students. Students are trained to notice physical or emotional signs of distress and to determine whether the older adult they visit is in need of some kind of medical services. Following the visit, the student calls whatever medical agency oversees the program and reports on the condition of the older adult.

Note: Although this obviously cannot replace medical treatment and insurance and liability issues need to be addressed, it is a way for responsible students to be invaluable in the national attempt to allow older adults to remain in their homes as long as possible. The partnership with a medical agency or visiting nurses agency is mandatory.

Mutuality and Ongoing: Although the youth is obviously serving the older adult in this program prototype, there is always room for the older adult to reciprocate in some way that is meaningful to both. This may take the form of oral history, sharing stories, teaching a craft, cooking together, tutoring, or mentoring. The program needs to be long term so that the student knows the older adult well enough to recognize medical changes.

Lesson 1

Signs of Aging

Most people think seniors are elephants old and grey
But most are happy all day.
I used to think they had no fun
But now I know all the things they get done.
I used to be afraid of them
But now I know they can be lots of fun.
So don't make such a fuss
Because seniors are the same as us!

— Cailin, 4th grade

LESSON OVERVIEW

The study of aging has become more relevant as the large numbers of baby boomers approach and reach old age. Although much has been learned, much is unknown about the aging process. Some biogerontologists, studying the aging process, have noted that the greatest advances in this field recently are attitudinal rather than biological—the realization that aging is not a death sentence and that loss of mental capacity with age is not inevitable. Geriatricians, studying the diseases associated with the aging process, have been aided in their research by increased technology and by resources available to study individual body systems.

What follows is a lesson that helps students understand what changes occur in the body as we age and why they happen.

Learner Outcomes—Aging Issues
- Students will understand that aging is a normal process that is part of life.
- Students will compare and contrast aging with illness.
- Students will evaluate and critically determine the effectiveness of antiaging advertisements and suggestions.
- Students will experience some effects of aging.

Learner Outcomes—Integration with Academic Curricula
- Students will understand biological reasons for body changes.
- Students will conduct research.
- Students will evaluate and think critically about effective advertising.

This lesson integrates with
Science: understanding the changes associated with the aging process
Language Arts: write feelings about aging in journals or conduct interviews with older adults or scientists

Math: collect data and graph the frequency or prevalence of physical signs of aging in older adults

Health: discussions of puberty as a sign of the normal aging process

GRADE ADJUSTMENTS

The amount and depth of information provided and the amount of research required (or desired) will depend on the age of the students. For young students a discussion of the signs of aging and the basic reason for them, with an emphasis on the normalcy of the process, may be enough. Younger students usually identify aging with death, and this is an excellent opportunity to dispel that myth. They also are eager to share stories about the health status of their own family members, trying to understand more clearly what has happened to them or why they have changed, or how aging seems not to have changed their lifestyles.

For older students an exploration of how the systems in the body work and change with age can be a long-term study. It can include individual and class research, interviews with or surveys of biogerontologists and older adults, and a study of the role technology has played in medicine and scientific research. Visits to research facilities or classroom visits by research scientists can add a strong dimension to an understanding of the science (see Suggestions for Further Activity at the end of this lesson).

All age groups should be introduced to the basic reasons for the normal signs of aging.

TERMS USED

Gerontology	the study of aging in all living things, including issues such as psychological and sociological issues of aging[*]
Biogerontologist	biologists in the field of aging[*]
Geriatrics	the branch of medicine that deals with old age

MATERIALS NEEDED

enough cotton balls for two for each student
popcorn kernels
plastic wrap
straws for each student
a few Ace bandages
adhesive bandages or tape

---

[*]These definitions are taken from the book *How and Why We Age* by Leonard Hayflick, Ph.D.

PROCEDURE

1. Ask students to place a cotton ball in each ear, a bandage or tape on the index finger knuckle of the hand that they use to write, and some popcorn kernels in their shoes. Ask students who wear glasses to place some plastic wrap over their glasses. For students who volunteer (number depends on how many Ace bandages you have), have them wrap their elbows with the bandages. Ask students to breathe through straws that they keep in their mouths (do this for only a short time).

   Note: This will simulate some of the normal signs of aging, including hearing loss, the effects of arthritis on joints, the loss of body fat on the soles of the feet, cataracts, and decreased lung capacity. Please be sure students understand that these physical conditions are NOT limited to aging only, that they do NOT automatically occur as one ages, and that they are NOT experienced by all older adults.

2. Tell students you will now carry on with class and they should try not to notice these accessory items. Tell them to be sure to take some notes; younger students should try to write sometime during the class.

3. Ask students to picture an older adult in their mind. Ask them how they would know that person is old. Elicit a list of descriptive words to describe an old person and write them on a chart or the board.

   Note: Students might be reluctant to use words that appear stereotypic but explain that if the words describe the reality of someone, it is fine to use them. Because some older adults will obviously display these signs of aging, use in this lesson is not stereotypic.

   Note: Be sure to tell students you want only words that describe a person in physical appearance or action—you do not want a list of diseases or things that are not associated with most older people, only normal signs of aging. The list should resemble this:

   wrinkles
   grey or white hair or bald
   short in stature or bent over
   walking slowly
   hearing loss
   out of breath after walking fast or up stairs

4. Acknowledge this list and keep it for reference throughout the class. Ask students what the smallest living part of our body is. The answer is a cell because it has the ability to reproduce itself. Explain that in our bodies, cells are dying and new cells are "born" to take their place. This happens from birth to death. But cells in young people reproduce more often and more regularly than those in adults. As we age, some cells die and do not get replaced. This causes changes in the functioning of systems in our bodies.

5. Have students close their eyes and pretend they are flying over a big city and it is nighttime. Lights are on all over the city. As it gets later and later lights go off and the city "sleeps." But lights still remain on because some activities are

occurring—janitors cleaning, night clubs and restaurants, hospitals that are open all night, and so on. Explain that the cells in our bodies are like the lights in the city. The cells in our bodies that are dying are like the lights going off in the city—some go out, new ones come on, but as it gets later at night (as we get older), not as many new lights come on (new cells are reproduced). That does not mean the building (or the body) is ever without any new lights (cells). And stress that a big city has millions of lights and we have millions of cells.

6. The rest of the class is a discussion of each item in the list generated by the students and an explanation of why these things happen. Each change is due, in part, to the loss of cells as demonstrated in the analogy of the city lights.

7. **The Skin**

The second layer of skin, the dermis, changes as the number of cells in that layer declines. The elastic fibers in that layer of skin are replaced by thicker tubules, and there is a loss of collagen, a protein that forms the connective tissue in the dermis. The resiliency of youthful skin is gone and wrinkles form. Another protein, elastin, increases as we age, and that protein contributes to the wrinkling of the skin as well. Finally, what some scientists believe is the main cause of wrinkled skin is the excessive exposure to the effects of ultraviolet light from the sun. This is called photoaging and causes the "age lines" on the skin.

Note: A discussion can occur here about why wrinkles are considered "bad" and why media advertisements advocate antiaging or wrinkle-free skin creams. The most stereotypes associated with aging focus on this organ of our body, and the most attitudinal devaluation of a person results from the appearance of skin.

Note: A discussion can also occur here about how environmental factors such as a decrease in the ozone layer is a cause for concern in relation to photoaging.

Exercise: Have students pinch the skin on the back of their hand for several seconds. Then, measure the amount of seconds it takes for the skin to return to its original look. As we age that time increases. This is a measure of the loss of elasticity of the skin. Students may want to compare their skin with that of an older adult.

8. **The Hair**

Grey hair is caused by the loss of cells that produce melanin, a pigment that gives hair its color. The color is gone when the cell is gone. Baldness is most often associated with men and is genetically determined. As one ages, hair loss over most of the body is common in both sexes.

9. **The Musculoskeletal System**

Normal aging includes loss of bone tissue cells. It can happen quickly in some people and slowly in others. Bone is made of a collagen matrix and the presence of calcium and phosphorus. The cells that make bone are called osteoblasts, and their rate of activity often depends on the demands the body makes for bone support. For example, in a sedentary person who exhibits minimal weight-bearing activity, unneeded calcium is excreted in the urine, the osteoblasts are inactive, and less bone is produced. The more active a person is, the greater will be their bone mass. Young girls have less bone mass than young boys and that remains true as they age. The loss of bone cells can result in fractures. It can also cause the collapse of a vertebra, which is known as osteoporosis. The result of osteoporosis is the recognizable bent over or curved back.

Height: When the cells of the connective tissue between the vertebra die, the space between lessens. This spinal disk deterioration is one of the causes of loss of height during the aging process. Other factors noted include water loss, weaker muscles, postural changes, and osteoporosis. The loss of height is quite small and begins at approximately the age of 40. It increases in rate as one ages.

Note: Although arthritis is a disease, not a normal sign of aging, its prevalence to some degree in many older adults and its ease in simulating it, make it worth noting at this point. Arthritis is an inflammation of the joints and has nothing to do with the loss of bone mass.

10. **The Cardiovascular System**
Two factors here change with age—the heart and the arteries.

Heart: The heart increases in size as we age but that is not an ideal situation. As the cells of the cardiac muscle die, they are replaced by fat and connective tissue. When this happens, the heart's ability to contract and relax is lessened. The heart becomes less forceful in its ability to pump and this occurs at about 1 percent each year after age 30. As cells receive less oxygen from the red blood cells, they are less able to work efficiently resulting in slower activity levels.

Arteries: Arteries slowly change in thickness as we age. This is due to collagen deposits resulting in the artery becoming rigid and unable to contract in response to the pumping of the heart. There are three layers in the arterial vessels, and when the innermost layer thickens in this way, it lessens the space available for blood to flow. This is a normal condition, but when other factors, such as cholesterol deposits, are also present, heart attacks or strokes can occur.

11. **The Respiratory System**
The lungs are affected by the loss of cells in the muscle of the chest and the diaphragm and the buildup of collagen. Under these circumstances, the lungs become less elastic and are unable to totally inflate or deflate. Also the chest wall is more rigid and it is harder to breathe deeply. This normal change often accounts for greater loss of breath as we age. Breathing through a straw can simulate decreased lung capacity.

12. **The Senses**
Hearing: The loss of nerve cells that conduct sounds to the brain to be interpreted results in a loss of hearing. This is known as presbycusis, age-related decline in hearing, and is a normal result of aging. It usually affects high-pitched sounds. About one-third of people over 65 are hearing impaired to some degree.

Sight: The lens of the eye becomes less elastic and thicker as we age and can prevent the ability to change focus or allow light transmission. Most people in middle age usually require reading glasses to correct this. The formation of cataracts is considered a disease but occurs so frequently that it appears to be a normal sign of aging. It is caused by a change in the protein structure of the lens of the eye.

Note: This is a good example of the use of technology in treating conditions of aging, because cataracts are now removed from the lens of the eye with lasers.

Taste: Although the number of taste buds does not seem to decline with age, the cells that make up the taste bud show degenerative changes. This results in a lessened ability to detect subtle flavors.

Smell: A possible degeneration in the cells of the nose, or the degeneration of brain cells that interpret the smells, is the cause of the gradual decline in the ability to detect odors as we age.

13. When the discussion about the causes of the normal signs of aging is complete, ask students to discuss how the simulations of these conditions caused them discomfort, anxiety, or frustration. Encourage empathy of aging conditions from a physical and a psychological point of view.

14. Discuss how aging differs from illness. Point out that what has happened to the body in all of the previous examples is due to normal changes within the body itself, rather than being caused by an outside agent such as a bacteria or virus— the cause of most illnesses that we know about today.

SUGGESTIONS FOR FURTHER ACTIVITY

1. For older students, invite a biogerontologist to class to discuss aging issues in greater detail. Or invite an older adult to class who may not be shy about sharing changes they are experiencing. This can include psychological and sociological changes as well as physical.

2. Have students conduct surveys among older adults to determine the prevalence and extent of signs of aging. Once the data is collected, graphs can be made to present the differences.

3. Ask students to compare and contrast the stereotyped physical signs of youth and older adults. Make charts of comparison by listing the body system in the center and then how the body changes at puberty compared to old age. This will create a recognition that our bodies go through major changes twice in a lifetime, and it provides another connection and sharing of experiences between young and old.

4. Have students do a physical activity with an older adult, such as have a picnic and play lawn games. Have children notice the older adult's strengths and limitations, and then discuss and write about it in class afterwards.

5. Ask older adults to be part of a book written about physical changes as we age, starting at birth and continuing until death. Allow students to interview older adults and do research with them (many older adults may not know why these things are happening to them!).

6. Have students bring in pictures of themselves through the years. Ask them to note what physical changes occurred and what was noticeable. Have students make charts of their own growth in height and weight at different ages. This allows them to witness their own aging.

Suggested Reading

Aging-Related Changes. Ohio Aging Network Education Project, Western Reserve Geriatric Education Center.

Barrow, G. (1996). *Aging, the Individual, and Society.* (6th ed.). St Paul, MN: West Publishing Company.

Healthy Aging, Why We Get Old. (1992, October). Harvard Health Letter, presented in Social Issues Resources Series, Aging, Vol. 4, Art. 40, pp. 9–12.

Hayflick, L. (1994). *How and Why We Age.* New York: Ballantine Books.

Suggested Bibliography for Use with This Lesson

Sanders, P. *What It's Like to Be Old.* Gloucester Press, 1992.

Ages preschool–5. An introduction to what it's like to be old, physically and mentally. This book describes the joys and challenges of old age.

Sinclair-House, E. *Advanced Years.* Steck-Vaughn Library, 1991.

Ages 8+. This book describes the aging process, physically and mentally.

Lesson 2

The Role of Good Nutrition in Aging

The Senior's Rap

My name is Jill and I'm eighty-five; I may be old but at least I am alive
I got grey hair but I don't care, you see that's the look for us seniors here.
I don't sit down on my lazy chair, I go outside and see what's out there.
I run, I jog, sometimes I even skip. I may not be you're age but I'm still hip!
Being old is great you're more loving and kind, So if you think old is bad get it
OUT OF YOUR MIND!

— Jillian, 4th grade

LESSON OVERVIEW

Americans are responding to the information available about proper nutrition. One needs only to see the increased number of magazines about cooking, healthy eating, and light fare to know this is true. Many restaurants have heart healthy, vegetarian, or diet choices on their menus and chefs are advocating lower fat cooking. In addition supermarket items now have nutritional labels attached and consumers are reading about dietary fat.

The role of good nutrition in the aging process, and its importance in healthy lives, is of significance not just for the already older person, but for the young person as he/she ages. Being healthy and active when young makes for a healthier older adult.

Learner Outcomes—Aging Issues
• Students will understand how good nutrition contributes to a healthy old age.
• Students will research which foods are good for you and which are not and determine why.
• Students will determine why some older adults may have poor eating habits.

Learner Outcomes—Integration with Academic Curricula
• Students will make hypotheses.
• Students will make deductions from observations and collection of data.
• Students will assess choices and make a self-determination.

This lesson integrates with
Health: discovering which foods are good for us and why

Science: the role of nutrition in building strong bodies; especially the role of nutrition in the normal aging process

Life Skills: cooking a healthy meal

Math: measuring and determining amounts for cooking

Language Arts: writing about the reasons to eat healthy foods

GRADE ADJUSTMENTS

This lesson has two parts—the sequences that occur in class and involve using available visual materials might be enough to do with lower elementary grade students. You might choose to list on the board first, or have available in chart form, foods that are important for healthy eating. They can either do research to determine why these foods are important, or you can tell them. This would eliminate the need for young students being required to read articles in magazines that may be too advanced for them. The sequences that employ direct observations, interviews, and collection of data outside the classroom might be easier for the upper elementary and middle school students. In either case a good understanding will result.

TERMS USED

Nutrition   taking in and assimilating food for the purpose of growth

MATERIALS NEEDED

a supply of food magazines promoting healthy eating (be sure the magazines have information inside about healthy foods)

paper, markers, and an easel for making charts

PROCEDURE

Sequence One

1. Divide the class into small groups. Each group will be given a few magazines.
2. Ask students to read the magazines to see whether they suggest people eat any particular foods to stay healthy. After a short time, ask groups to share that list with the class and write the recommended foods on a chart in column one.
3. Students should then determine what part of the growth of our bodies benefits from which foods. This will require some minimal research; it might be in the article in the magazine, or you might want to have available a list of what is required for healthy bones, good eyesight, and so on. Write the benefit received in column two on the chart.
4. Now compare the information about what happens to our bodies as we age (from Lesson 1) with the foods the students have determined are important. Write the benefit for healthy aging in column three on the chart.

Note: For example, students will say milk is important for strong bones. They should then note that as they are aging their bones need to grow and get stronger, and then as we continue to age and become older adults, some of that bone mass is lost. Because bones require calcium for good growth and to help prevent osteoporosis, and because milk contains calcium, therefore, milk or dairy products with calcium are suggested for healthy aging.

5. When the chart is complete, students should evaluate it and determine what one should eat to remain healthy as we all age.

Sequence Two

1. Ask students to do the following homework assignment asking two older adults what their daily diet is like. Have students choose older adults that display differing living styles. Try to identify adults in as many living arrangements as possible. For example, one older adult may live with his/her son and family and eat meals with them; another may live in his/her own home or in a retirement village and cook for him/herself; a third may live in an assisted-living facility and go to the dining room where he/she can choose items from a menu, and a fourth may live in a nursing facility where foods may be preprepared. Students should hypothesize what the dietary and nutritional results will be under varying living conditions.

   Note: Be sure students understand that we are not trying to reinforce any preconceived ideas or stereotypes about older people being taken care of well or poorly. The purpose is to evaluate what we eat, and if we have choices, are they good ones. This is important for any age, not simply older adults.

2. The next day have students work in small groups that are formed around the kind of living arrangement in which the person they interviewed lived. Students should compile data in their small groups and develop a sample menu of what a day in the life of an older adult in this living facility is like.

3. Have the students share the results with the class and allow the class to determine how the living arrangement of the older adult might affect his/her food intake and nutritional value. Were their hypotheses correct?

4. Ask students to fill in the same assigned chart for themselves and hypothesize whether it would change if they were in charge of all their own meal choices. Do we always choose what is best?

SUGGESTIONS FOR FURTHER ACTIVITY

1. Students can research the effects of low-fat diets on longevity or interview a doctor to discuss this issue.

2. Divide the class in half and have each group plan a part of a healthy, balanced meal. Let each group also develop a shopping list for that part of the meal. If possible, have students shop for the items and then actually cook the meal.

3. Repeat the planning of a meal, but this time determine how ethnic foods fit into the guidelines for healthy eating. Why might some parts of the world reflect different eating patterns? Are the aged in some parts of the world healthier than in others? Why?

4. Students may choose to publish their findings (without names) and submit them to the local older adult living facilities with the caveat that it is to be used privately and for education purposes only.

Eating to Stay Healthy as We Age

Name _____

Interview two older adults from different types of living arrangements. Ask them what they ate in one day and write down the answers by putting the foods into the categories of food types. The older adult's name is optional.

First Older Adult

Name (Optional) _____

Living Situation _____

Breakfast

Protein	Fruits/Vegetables	Breads/Grains	Dairy Products	Fats

Lunch

Protein	Fruits/Vegetables	Breads/Grains	Dairy Products	Fats

Dinner

Protein	Fruits/Vegetables	Breads/Grains	Dairy Products	Fats

Second Older Adult

Name (Optional) _____

Living Situation _____

Breakfast

Protein   *Fruits/Vegetables*   *Breads/Grains*   *Dairy Products*   *Fats*

Lunch

Protein   *Fruits/Vegetables*   *Breads/Grains*   *Dairy Products*   *Fats*

Dinner

Protein   *Fruits/Vegetables*   *Breads/Grains*   *Dairy Products*   *Fats*

Lesson 3

The Role of Exercise in Aging

I am retired now and I have days to relax. To be old is as if everyone thinks you can't do much. I'm playing my grandson's sports! I feel young and full of pep. I tell stories and myths. It feels good to be wise. I'm fishing and catching more than ever before. It feels great to be old (If I am!).

— Justin, 4th grade

LESSON OVERVIEW

The role of exercise in our lives has become as important as eating well. Indeed, the two are inextricably linked for good health. Students often assume that as people age their need for activity decreases and their actual activity level decreases. That is not true and the myth needs to be corrected.

This lesson will provide an opportunity for many critical and evaluative thinking skills as students attempt to identify exercises they may do, modify those exercises for older adults, and determine why a modification may be necessary. The important point is that the exercise is still crucial, but the execution of that exercise may alter as we age.

Students must also recognize that people who begin a form of exercise when they are young, and continue it regularly as they age, may not require a modification of it at all. They may find their performance level changes slightly but their body is accustomed to the exercise. Examples include many runners who compete in marathons well into their 70s or even 80s.

Learner Outcomes—Aging Issues
- Students will understand that aging may require certain adaptations in lifestyle.
- Students will identify exercises that are age appropriate.
- Students will evaluate and determine appropriate modifications to exercise for older adults.

Learner Outcomes—Integration with Academic Curricula
- Students will understand the importance of exercise in our lives.
- Students will understand the effects of exercise on good health.

This lesson integrates with
Health: understanding the role of exercise in good health
Science: how exercise keeps bone and muscle healthy
Critical Thinking: making modifications, evaluation
Math: determining angles in relation to stress

GRADE ADJUSTMENTS

Students in lower grades may need to work with gym teachers and actually try different exercises to show how they may change. Also the need for physiological reasons for the adjustments may not be necessary. A discussion about exercise for the handicapped may be included, but this would include all ages of those who have special needs, not simply the older adult.

Older grades may choose to investigate the reasons for the modifications in more detail. Consultation with an exercise physiologist or an exercise specialist at a senior retirement or exercise class may be of value as well.

TERMS USED

Quadriceps	the large muscle at the front of the thigh that extends the leg when contracted
Gluteus Muscle	the muscles that form the buttocks and extend, abduct, and rotate the thigh
Hamstring Muscle	one of the great tendons at the back of the knee
Cardiovascular	pertaining to the heart and vessels of the heart of the bloodstream
Neuromuscular	pertaining to the nerve and muscular system
Aerobic Exercise	exercise that increases the heart rate and allows it to use more oxygen

PROCEDURE

1. Have students list some normal, age-related, physical changes that occur in the body and that would be associated with exercise and write them on a chart.

    Note: The list can include decrease in physical endurance, decrease in flexibility, changes in actual strength, increase in injuries due to loss of bone mass. Younger students might describe the changes as not being able to run or walk as fast, not being able to jump as easily, not being as strong, and so on.

2. Now, have students identify exercises that might use those kinds of physical requirements and write them on the chart.

    Note: The list might include jumping jacks for endurance or for strength of bones in legs, touching one's toes for flexibility, and lifting heavy weights for strength.

3. Discuss with students that there are certain concerns for older adults as they exercise that have to do with changes in the body as we age. Tell students you will list a few of these concerns and then they will need to identify an exercise that would normally involve that concern, and then decide how to modify the exercise so that the same benefits result but the danger for injury is reduced.

    Note: You may want to do this in chart form.

Principle 1: Older adults should not put undue stress on knees and joints.

Exercises that involve this principle could be: jumping jacks, running, walking up stairs or using a stairmaster machine, regular walking or using a treadmill, squats.

Modification of exercise: reduce the weight-bearing aspect of the exercise by doing standing jacks instead of jumping, walking on flat surfaces at a slower pace, and doing squats by leaning against a wall for support and decreasing the angle by bending knees to about 45 degrees instead of a full 90 degrees. The benefit to the gluteus and quadriceps muscle and to the hamstrings is still there but the exercise is modified.

Principle 2: Stretching is important to increase flexibility.

Exercises that involve this principle could be: touching one's toes, pushing against a wall and stretching legs back. For youth stretching is usually done before and after the exercise period.

Modification of exercise: instead of standing where one's back is not supported and reaching to touch one's toes the older adult could sit and reach the toes, or lean against a wall to support the back, or in a sitting position put a large elastic band around the feet and pull back on it. For older adults it is wise to stretch between repetitions, and between different exercises within the same exercise period.

Principle 3: Cardiovascular and aerobic exercise is important.

Exercises that involve this principle could be: anything that increases the heart rate and keeps it steady for an extended period such as bike riding, skating, aerobic and step aerobic classes, running, fast walking, swimming, rowing.

Modification of exercise: Doing the same thing but less of it is a good rule of thumb to follow when modifying aerobic exercise. Keep in mind Principle 1 as well because some aerobic exercise might affect stress on knees. Thus running is probably not good, but walking is; high-impact aerobic classes may not be good, but low-impact or step aerobics are; swimming laps in competition with a 20-year-old is not good, but relaxed swimming is; bike riding on a bike that forces you to hunch over is not good, but riding on a recumbent bike that supports the back is.

4. Discuss with students how this forced changed in exercise routine may affect older adults psychologically and why it is so hard to accept for some people.

   Note: An example might be a man who played football in college and in an over-20 league for many years but at the age of 55 was told by his doctor not to play anymore. A good alternative for him would be to coach football.

SUGGESTIONS FOR FURTHER ACTIVITY

1. Have students research manuals and fitness magazines for other types of exercises, determine what type of exercise is needed for good health, and ascertain why that exercise is important.

2. Students can invite older adults to their gym classes or for a walk during recess. This can become a regular event. (For further information, see suggestions at the beginning of this chapter.)
3. Make a class bulletin board with each child's name listed and have each of them write what form of exercise they did each day—a class effort to eliminate "couch potatoes."

Suggested Reading

Berg, R., & Cassells, J. (Eds.). (1990). *The Second Fifty Years: Promoting Health and Preventing Disability.* Washington, DC: National Academy Press.

Carter, W., McKenna, M., Martin, M., & Andresen, E. (1989). *Health Education: Special Issue for Older Adults, 13,* 117–131.

FallCreek, S., & Mettler, M. (1984). *A Healthy Old Age: A Sourcebook for Health Promotion with Older Adults.* New York: Haworth Press.

Fretz, B. (1979). College Students as Paraprofessionals with Children and the Aged. *American Journal of Community Psychology, 7,* 357–360.

Leviton, D. (1991). From Theory to Practice: The Adult Health and Development Program and Theories of Children's Love and Peace Behaviors. In D. Leviton (Ed.), *Horrendous Death and Health: Toward Action* (pp. 245–260). New York: Hemisphere Publishing.

Leviton, D. (1992). The Adult Health and Development Program: More Than Just Fitness. In S. Harris, R. Harris, & W. S. Harris (Eds.), *Physical Activity, Aging and Sports: Volume II: Practice, Program and Policy* (pp. 232–250). Albany: Center for the Study of Aging.

Leviton, D. (1993). Adult Health and Development Programs Spreading Throughout the United States. *Aging Network News, 10*(12).

Leviton, D., Kennedy, J., & Woodruff, R. (1992). *ADHP Manual for Staffers.* College Park, MD: University of Maryland.

Living Healthy, The Magazine for Blue Cross and Blue Shield Members. (Fall 1995) Boston, MA: Blue Cross and Blue Shield of Massachusetts.

Suggested Bibliography for Use with This Lesson

Lasky, K. *Sea Swan.* Macmillan, 1988.
Ages 5–11. Grandma misses her grandchildren after a visit and decides to cheer herself by taking swimming lessons.

Lesson 4

Illness and Aging

Being old is not so bad, as long as you're not an old grump
Being old is not quite the fad, but I'm definitely not an old mump,
I may have wrinkles and crinkles, but why does it bother you?
It may make me look ugly and bugly,
Why it matters I haven't a clue!
I like reading and pets, writing and sports, growing plants, seeing
family and friends,
I have memories that go back to the past and before, philosophies
that go off on all ends.
I have some arthritis, but it's not going to bite us
I'm your grandpa, I'm sweet, and I love you.

— William, 4th grade

LESSON OVERVIEW

Sometimes our attitudes about aging automatically associate old age with illness. Demographics shows this is not true and people are living longer and are healthier. Yet even the children's literature about aging is replete with stories about older adults being sick or dying. In recent years this has begun to change and there are wonderful children's books that depict aging as a vital, exciting stage of life.

This lesson explores aging and illness and allows students to understand the difference. The teacher and students should recognize that illness is certainly a greater factor as we age, but that one is not automatically associated with the other. In this lesson students will often want to share the psychological traumas of grandparents' illnesses, and that kind of sharing can highlight the need to be empathic and caring.

Learner Outcomes—Aging Issues
- Students will understand the difference between aging and illness.
- Students will understand the difference between aging and illness in relation to the changes in one's life.
- Students will be able to empathize with the psychological needs of the characters in the children's literature on illness.

Learner Outcomes—Integration with Academic Curricula
- Students will think critically about aging and its relationship to illness.
- Students will make comparisons and evaluations.

This lesson integrates with
Language Arts: recognizing positive and negative nouns and adjectives, reading and sharing ideas in literature, writing

Critical Thinking: evaluation of aging/illness on life, comparing two lists, identifying societal attitudes with aging/illness

GRADE ADJUSTMENTS

The critical evaluation of the differences between aging and illness is an assessment that should be made by all ages. For older students, however, there can be a greater focus on the emotions that center around illness and the psychological impact of illness on family members. This will allow them to be more empathic and to understand family members as they may experience the illness of loved ones.

The value for all ages of a discussion such as this is that it allows children to discuss their fears and to share their concerns about illness. This and the lesson on death are important in providing an outlet for children to understand the facts and clear up any misperceptions.

TERMS USED

Illness   an unhealthy condition of the body or mind
Aging   to grow old or mature

MATERIALS NEEDED

either chart paper or a blackboard

PROCEDURE

1. Create two charts on paper or the blackboard. Label one "Illness" and the other "Aging." (Based on the information already provided, to write "normal aging" would be inaccurate because aging *is* normal. But I often find I need to write "normal aging" so that younger students in particular can make the distinction more easily.)
2. Ask students to provide words that are associated with these two headings. Remind students that you want single words or small word phrases, that the words should represent both physical conditions and emotions (either theirs or people's in general) associated with the words, and that the words can be the same in both lists if they feel that is appropriate. Write these words under the headings on each chart.
   Note: You will probably get words for "Aging" such as grey hair, wrinkles, canes, and then words that reflect attitudes such as happy, sad, lonely, busy, and so on. For "Illness" you may get answers such as sick, dying, sad, Alzheimer's, heart attack, cancer, and so on.
3. Ask students to look at the two lists and decide which words are negative, which ones are positive, and which words are the same for both lists. Discuss the reasons for the choices of words.

Note: You should have positive words for aging and more negative ones for illness. But depending on when you do this lesson in relation to the ongoing intergenerational program you are conducting, students may still have negative attitudes about aging in general, which may be reflected in their choice of words. If that happens, discuss why we think of aging as negative (see Chapter 1). If you get a lot of words that are on both lists, discuss with students why they think aging and illness are the same. Point out the effect society has on our attitude that illness is automatically associated with old age.

4. Now ask students to decide whether aging changes one's life. If the answers are yes, ask students to evaluate how important they think those changes really are. This will be a critical-thinking exercise on what really is important in life.

   Note: You may get answers that reflect changes in the way people look or the things they can no longer do. This lesson will help students to realize that there are other good things to do and that the way people look is irrelevant to their being valuable citizens.

5. Ask the same question about illness changing one's life. The answers should be yes, and a discussion can follow about how and why that may change one's life.

   Note: Be careful not to make it seem that illness equals death. Students should realize that older people can get sick and can recover. A good point of discussion here is how modern technology and medicines have made recovery so much greater and living so much healthier.

SUGGESTIONS FOR FURTHER ACTIVITY

1. Students can research various illnesses and the advances medicine has made in curing or treating these illnesses.
2. Classroom discussions may have revealed that there is an illness that has affected many of the student's families. The class may decide to have a fund-raiser of some sort to raise money for a donation to that cause.
3. Students may choose to interview older adults who have recovered from a serious illness and find out what moderations have been made, if any, to their daily lives as a result of that illness. Older adults are sometimes reticent to discuss a personal illness with children for fear they will frighten or "harm" them in some way. But if their recovery is complete and if they are happy and productive people now, they should be made to understand that they represent a good role model for students.
4. In programs that involve nursing homes, students can observe older adults and see the results of various illnesses. Empathy about why the older adults are there is a positive outcome.

   Note: I would not do this with very young children, and I would only do it at all if children have interacted with well older adults first. It is important to allow children to see the difficult part of aging, as long as they already know the positive part. If not, then the nursing home resident will become their normative frame of reference and this could augment any existing stereotypic attitudes. Seefeldt (1987) suggested caution in the design and implementation of programs with frail elders only.

Reference

Seefeldt, C. (1987). The Effects of Preschoolers' Visits to a Nursing Home. *Gerontologist, 27* (2), 228–232.

Suggested Reading

Seefeldt, C. (1987). The Effects of Preschoolers' Visits to a Nursing Home. *Gerontologist, 27* (2), 228–232.

Toufexis, A. (1988, February 22). Older—But Coming on Strong. *Time* pp. 76–79.

Suggested Bibliography for Use with This Lesson

Ackerman, K. *Just Like Max.* Knopf, 1990.

Ages 4–8. When great-uncle Max, the tailor, becomes sick and can no longer sew, his nephew Aaron becomes his "hands" and makes something special.

Bahr, M. *The Memory Box.* Albert Whitman, 1992.

Ages 5–8. When Gramps realizes he has Alzheimer's disease, he and his grandson start filling a memory box. Stored in a place of honor, no matter what happens to Gramps, the memories are saved forever.

Blue, R. *Grandma Didn't Wave Back.* Franklin Watts, 1972.

Ages 8–11. A family deals with grandmother's senility and with granddaughter's anger when the family decides on a nursing home for grandma. Also on video from Films for the Humanities, Young People's Specials, 1-800-257-5126.

Brancato, R. *Sweet Bells Jangle Out of Tune.* Knopf, 1982.

Ages 11–14. Ellen's grandma has become senile and her eccentric behavior is the source of teasing. Ellen faces the reality of what has happened to her grandmother and helps save her life.

DePaola, T. *Now One Foot, Now the Other.* Putnam, 1981.

Ages preschool–5. Grandfather teaches his grandson how to walk, and when, years later, the grandfather suffers a stroke, his grandson teaches him how to walk again. Very sensitive.

Donnelly, E. *Offbeat Friends.* Crown, 1979.

Ages 11–14. A friendship develops between an old resident of a mental hospital and an 11-year-old girl. When the woman runs away from the hospital, Mari knows she must help.

Duffy, J. *Uncle Shamus.* Scribner, 1992.

Ages 8–14. Ten-year-old Akers befriends an elderly blind man and begins the adventure of his life.

Dugan, B. *Loop the Loop.* Greenwillow Books, 1992.

Ages 5–11. A young girl and an old woman form a relationship that lasts even though the older woman is frequently forgetful and even after she enters a nursing home.

Ellis, E. T. *Hugo and the Princess Nena.* Atheneum, 1983.

Ages 11–14. Nena learns to live with Hugo, her poet grandfather. In the process she accepts the fact that his health is failing.

Flourney, V. *The Patchwork Quilt.* Dial, 1985.

Ages 5–11. Grandmother works on a patchwork quilt of memories. When grandma gets sick, Tanya continues the work. This book shows trust and sharing between a young girl and her beloved grandmother.

Gold, S. *Alzheimer's Disease.* Silver Burdett Press, 1995.

Ages 9+. Through color photos and large print, this book offers the reader insight to the realities of Alzheimer's disease and discusses coping mechanisms.

Green P. *The Empty Seat.* Elsevier/Nelson, 1980.

Ages 11–14. Eleven-year-old Michael must ride alone the tandem bike he and his grandmother used to ride together. This summer grandma seems to be keeping to herself.

Guthrie, D. *Grandpa Doesn't Know It's Me.* Human Science Press, 1986.

Ages 5–11. A girl tells about her grandfather's fight with Alzheimer's disease and how she deals with it.

Henroid, L. *Gramma's Wheelchair.* Whitman, 1982.

Ages preschool–5. Four-year-old Thomas spends his mornings helping grandma in her wheelchair.

Johnston, T. *Grandpa's Song.* Dial, 1991.

Ages 6–8. When a girl's grandfather becomes forgetful, her love for him motivates her to help him by singing their favorite song.

Karkowsky, N. *Grandma's Soup.* Kar Ben Copies, Inc.

Ages 5–8. Grandma makes the best chicken soup but when she begins to forget, the soup tastes bad and her granddaughter gets sad. Introduction to Alzheimer's disease.

Keller, H. *The Best Present.* Greenwillow, 1989.

Ages 5–8. A girl wants to visit her grandmother in the hospital, but when she sees it is against the rules she lets her flowers speak for her.

Kibbey M. *My Grammy.* CarolRhoda Books, 1988.

Ages 8–11. Grandma has Alzheimer's disease and moves into Amy's room. Amy is impatient with her until Dad explains what Alzheimer's is. Now Amy and grandma are good friends, and Amy is patient and loving.

Kirk, B. *Grandpa, Me and Our House in the Tree.* Macmillan, 1978.

Ages preschool–5. Grandfather and grandson build a tree house and share its joys. They also share a special relationship despite the man's illness.

Lexau, J. *Benjie On His Own.* Dial, 1970.

Ages 5–8. Benjie doesn't want his grandma to walk him to and from school, but when she doesn't show up one day he worries. After making his way home alone, he finds his grandma sick and he has to take charge.

Luenn, N. *Nessa's Fish.* Atheneum, 1990.

Ages 5–8. In the Arctic, Nessa and her grandmother fish inland. During the night grandma gets sick and Nessa protects her and their fish from wild animals until help arrives.

Lundgren, M. *Matt's Grandfather.* Putnam & Sons, 1972.

Ages 5–8. Story of a little boy visiting his grandfather in a nursing home on his 85th birthday and learning a special secret.

MacLachlan, P. *Through Grandpa's Eyes.* Harper & Row, 1980.

Ages preschool–5. Boy tries to see the world through the eyes of his blind grandfather. He listens, smells, and feels things. Sensitive drawings.

Nelson, V. M. *Always Grandma.* Putnam, 1988.

Ages 5–8. Grandma and her granddaughter are good friends and do many things together. When grandma gets Alzheimer's disease and goes to a nursing home, her granddaughter visits and remembers her just the same.

Pearson, S. *Happy Birthday, Grampie.* Dial, 1987.

Ages 5–8. A family visits their blind grandpa in a nursing home on his birthday. His granddaughter makes him a card that he can "read" by feeling. Will he like it? When grandpa smiles and hugs her, she knows.

Rappaport, D. *But She's Still My Grandma.* Human Sciences Press, 1982.

Ages 8–11. Jessica wants to visit her grandma who has Alzheimer's disease and is in a nursing home. She is devastated at first and disappointed that grandma doesn't know her, but discovers they still share love.

Sakai, K. *Sachiko Means Happiness.* Children's Book Press, 1990.

Ages 4–8. Although 5-year-old Sachiko is upset when her grandmother no longer recognizes her, she grows to understand that they can still be happy together.

Sarton, M. *As We Are Now.* Norton, 1973.

Ages 14+. A first-person account by a 76-year-old heart attack victim who is put in a rest home, this book tells of her fight to keep her mind intact and die with dignity.

Schick, E. *Peter and Mr. Brandon.* Macmillan, 1973.

Ages preschool–5. Peter stays with his neighbor while his parents visit his sick grandma. Mr. Brandon takes Peter into the city to help sell his special birds and Peter forgets his sadness.

Skurzynski, G. *Dangerous Ground.* Macmillan, 1989.

Ages 8–11. Angela lives part-time with her 78-year-old grandmother and is afraid she has Alzheimer's disease.

Sonneborn, R. *I Love Gram.* Viking, 1971.

Ages 5–8. When her gramma is hospitalized, a little girl discovers how much her gramma really means to her.

Strangis, J. *Grandfather's Rock.* Houghton Mifflin, 1993.

Ages 8–14. Based on a traditional Italian folktale, this story explores the timeless problem of treatment of older adults when the family decides it's time for grandpa to go to a nursing home but the children say no.

Talbert, M. *A Sunburned Prayer.* Simon & Schuster, 1995.

Ages 8–12. Eloy determines to go alone on a pilgrimage to save his grandmother who is dying of cancer.

Tolan, S. *Grandpa and Me.* Scribner, 1978.

Ages 11–14. An 11-year-old discovers her love for her grandfather when she believes he is crazy. The family must decide what to do with grandpa, but the options seem cruel. Grandpa makes his own decision.

VanLeeuwen, J. *Oliver, Amanda, and Grandmother Pig.* Dial, 1987.

Ages 5–8. Oliver and Amanda are impatient with grandmother's limitations due to age until they learn to value her special qualities.

Warnock, N. K. *The Canada Geese Quilt.* Cobblehill Dutton, 1989.

Ages 8–11. Ten-year-old Ariel worries that life will change with her grandmother having had a stroke and a new baby soon to arrive. Ariel and her grandmother make a very special quilt together and both adjust to the new changes.

Whitman, S. *A Special Trade.* Harper & Row, 1978.

Ages preschool–5. A little girl helps an old man as he helped her when she was young.

Lesson 5

Death and Dying

Dear Mrs. Friedman,

Thank you for helping me to open up and not be afraid of seniors. I used to be scared of them.

Two years ago my Papa died. He died on my birthday. I couldn't help but think that because of me he died. So on my birthday I never really had fun. Since the program started I realized that it wasn't my fault. When I turned ten this year in April it was the first time since my Papa died that I had fun on my birthday. I still haven't forgotten my Papa, but now I think of his good memories. You did the best thing anyone could do for me. You made me realize it wasn't my fault.

— Jeslyn, 4th grade

LESSON OVERVIEW

I choose to treat this lesson differently than the others because as an educator, not a grief counselor, I do not feel qualified to present a lesson that implies this is the one good way to resolve issues surrounding death. Indeed I urge you to consult with parents and a school psychologist or grief counselor when a situation arises.

The death of an older adult during an intergenerational program has happened to me often enough that it leaves an indelible mark in my memory. I would like to share some of my experiences with you in an effort to put some perspective on the issue as it deals with intergenerational programming. And I would like to share those experiences in the context of concepts that are presented by Rabbi Earl Grollman in his book *Explaining Death to Children*.

Rabbi Grollman is one of many resources in the area of grief counseling with children. Certainly another expert in the field is Elisabeth Kubler-Ross. I urge educators to read the books listed in the Suggested Reading section of this lesson in order to better understand the area of death and dying in relation to children.

First, Rabbi Grollman claims that children definitely can understand the meaning of death and that it is important to present it without creating stories or imaginative myths that may lead to misunderstandings. Knowing this, I have always shared with students exactly what I know about the death, such as the cause and circumstances surrounding the death, of someone in our intergenerational program. I first, separately, tell the student whose special friend died (if that applies to the program) and then the individual student is with me when I tell the class what has happened. (I also call the guardian(s) before I tell the student, so that he/she is aware of the occurrence and can address it properly either when the child goes home or if they choose to come to school to meet their child.) In addition to telling what I do know about the death, I also explain what I don't know or don't understand. I share with students that death is equally difficult for adults and children; there is a lot that is not understood and emotions are valid at any age. I tell the children that death is final and therefore we will no longer see that person again.

Second, Rabbi Grollman states that children do experience grief and they should be allowed to express it. So, after the factual explanations, I share with students how I feel and I ask them to share, if they choose to, how they feel. There have been times when I have cried, and the children have cried. (Be sure to say that it is fine for boys to cry, too!) Although it is difficult, it is also cathartic. I am often surprised at how genuinely close I feel to the older adults in the program, and my reactions to a death often reflect that closeness. If the program involves a one-on-one relationship, children often are reluctant to admit they are relieved that it was not their friend in the program that died. I explain that it is normal to feel that way, and it is okay. But knowing that, we also have to be aware of the feelings of the student whose special friend did die. If the student most closely affected wants to share his/her feelings, fine. If not, we discuss in class what we can all do to help the student deal with this death.

Third, Rabbi Grollman believes that to help the child who has lost a loved one we must show empathy, understanding, and love, while making them accept the reality. When discussing in class what we can do to make the individual student feel better, or to make all of us feel better if it is a class program, I solicit ideas from the students. In the one-on-one type program, this is important for the grieving child to hear because he/she begins to feel the acceptance, genuine concern, and understanding by his/her peers. It is not uncommon for students to say, "You can share my pen pal (or friend)," or whatever the program guidelines decree. I will often raise the idea that the student's relationship with the older adult made that older adult very happy and that this relationship was a wonderful thing for the older adult to have in his/her life as he/she was dying or before death. (I have said this only after having been told it by so many family members, over so many years, and in so many circumstances. The relationships often carry a greater meaning than I would ever suspect, and it becomes obvious when, in lieu of flowers, some families have asked for donations to be made to the school or earmarked for intergenerational programs.) I usually ask the student to share an incident or story about the adult so that the students can "get to know him/her." Sometimes it is funny, sometimes simply factual. But the sharing helps the child get outside him/herself and accept the loss. And finally, I ask the students to suggest how we should proceed with the intergenerational program and how the particular student should proceed. Most of the time the decision is to wait awhile until the child feels ready to accept another special friend, and then find a new one. "Awhile" needs to be somewhat defined, because too long a wait is not productive, yet a grieving time is needed.

Fourth, Rabbi Grollman says that children often feel guilty for the death of a loved one, as if they caused the death. Although that may be minimal in a classroom intergenerational experience, the aging education that accompanies the program can assist in the recognition of the lack of culpability that can then be applied to other situations. The letter presented at the beginning of this lesson is a good example. I always make sure students understand that in this instance, or any other, nothing they did, or thought, or said could cause the older adult's death. And then I ask them to figure out why that is true based on how we know that person died. Relating the cause of death to biology often helps them understand the impossibility of their being the cause.

Perhaps, at this time, a few anecdotal stories that I have experienced may help support the ability of children to accept the death and may illustrate some of these concepts of empathy and understanding. I hope that they will provide reason for not shying away from intergenerational interactions because of the age or health circumstances of older adults.

An older adult died during a fourth-grade, pen-pal program. I told the woman's pen pal first, and then the class. I never said anything about the wake or funeral, I simply discussed with the students what happened, how we would miss the woman, and how as a group we could move on. That evening I went to the wake myself and was shocked to see about five students from the class with their parents. I approached the girl whose pen pal the woman was and asked her why she came. "I had to see her just once, and I had to say good-bye," she said. "Now I know what she looks like so when I reread her letters, I can picture her." I then asked the other students why they had come, because they had had no previous contact with the woman at all. "We came because our friend needed us," they said almost in unison.

A mother of four school-aged children shared with me the fact that her father had a stroke and was in the hospital. He could neither communicate nor move. Three of her children would not go to visit him because they were frightened and claimed they did not know what to say or do (certainly not a fear relegated only to children). The child who was in the intergenerational program went willingly and simply sat next to him, held his hand, and babbled on and on to him about anything. When asked how she was able to do that, she told her mother that in case he died, she wanted him to know that she loved him and was not afraid to be near him just because he was different now.

During an intergenerational program, a woman died unexpectedly. Her student friend shared some stories about her with the class and told them of the older woman's special love for gardening and flowers. When the class tried to help their classmate deal with the grief, one student suggested that sometimes having a visible remembrance of the person helps, as he had something of his grandfathers. But the student had no contact with the woman's family and was uncomfortable asking them for something. It was decided that the class would create something to make that visible remembrance, and they decided to plant a tree on the school grounds that would be in her memory. Through a fund-raising effort, and then in a ceremony that was quite emotional, they planted a tree and read a poem about the beauty of nature.

SUGGESTED ACTIVITIES FOR PROMOTING DISCUSSION ABOUT DEATH AS PART OF THE AGING EDUCATION CURRICULUM

To Encourage Empathy with Older People as They Experience Losses

This exercise is taken from the Ohio Aging Network Education Project: A Core Curriculum for Senior Service Providers, published in March 1993. The curriculum was funded by the Western Reserve Geriatric Education Center through a federal training and education grant from the Bureau of Health Professions, Health Resources and Service Administration. Its use is suggested only with an older, mature class, as it can be a very emotional experience. However, it is very powerful in reinforcing the concept of loss and in creating empathy with older people who may be experiencing losses all the time—spouses, friends, home, and so on.

1. Give each student three small pieces of paper and ask them to write one thing on each paper that is very important to them. It can be anything from a person to a possession to an ideal. Ask the students to hold up any one piece of paper and then go around the room, grabbing the piece of paper from each student's hand, crumpling all of them, and throwing them away. Tell the class they have lost what was written on that piece of paper and ask them what their feelings are.
2. Announce that one month passes, then another. . . . Now go around the room and pick one of the remaining pieces of paper from each student, crumple them, and throw them away. Tell students that they have now experienced a second loss. Ask students what additional feelings they have now.
3. Repeat with the other piece of paper if you choose, or stop here if the point has been made and it appears to be too emotional.
4. As a class, ask students to identify the items they wrote on their papers and list them. Ask students to hypothesize whether what they felt is similar to the real-life experiences of older people.

To Enable Students to Understand That Death Is a Normal Part of the Aging Process

This works especially well with young children and is a good introduction to the idea of birth, life, and death.

1. Have students plant flower seeds, watch them grow, and watch them die. Students should record their observations of the plant at the different stages of its life cycle.
2. Discuss with students about normal cycles of life and how everything that is living must also die. Encourage students to see the value of the flower in bring-

ing joy and beauty to those who see it. Discuss how everything has its own special value.

To See Death as Viewed by Different Cultures and Different Religions

Students can research and examine the meanings and rituals surrounding death in various cultures and religions. An understanding of the various customs allows a healthy respect for others but also allows us to see death as an integral part of life. There are many trade books that can be read in conjunction with this, especially surrounding the Native American cultures. (See the Bibliography at the end of this lesson.)

References

Grollman, E. A. (1967). *Explaining Death to Children*. Boston: Beacon Press.

Suggested Reading

Grollman, E. A. (1967). *Explaining Death to Children*. Boston: Beacon Press.
Kubler-Ross, E. (1985, c.1983). *On Children and Death*. New York: Collier Books.
Kubler-Ross, E. (1969). *On Death and Dying*. New York: Macmillan.
Siegel, B. (1995). Bereavement and Loss. In S. Parker & B. Zuckerman (Eds.), *Behavioral and Developmental Pediatrics: A Handbook for Primary Care* (pp. 343–347). Boston: Little Brown.

Suggested Bibliography for Use with This Lesson

Aaron, C. *Catch Calico*. Dutton, 1979.
   Ages 11–14. A 14-year-old deals with his grandfather dying while memories persist of his father's death and of a cat named Calico.
Aliki. *The Two of Them*. Greenwillow, 1979.
   Ages 5–8. This is a very sensitive story of the true and lasting love of a grandfather and his granddaughter who loves him more for himself than what he gives her. When he gets old, she cares for him; and when he dies, she grieves.
Bartoli, J. *Noona*. Harvey House, 1975.
   Ages 5–8. A young boy realizes that when his grandmother dies he still has wonderful things of hers to remember—her garden and cookie recipes.
Bunting, E. *The Happy Funeral*. Harper & Row, 1982.
   Ages 8–11. A young Chinese-American girl mourns her grandfather's death.
Burningham, J. *Grandpa*. Crown, 1984.
   Ages 4–6. A series of moments where grandpa and granddaughter share and ask questions. The ending implies death but no text identifies it as such. Deals with caring.
Carlstrom, N. W. *Blow Me a Kiss Miss Lilly*. Harper & Row, 1990.
   Ages 5–8. Sara and her neighbor are best friends. When the woman goes to the hospital and dies, Sara deals with her grief by remembering.

Clifford, E. *The Remembering Box*. Houghton, 1985.

Ages 8–11. Joshua enjoys a special relationship with his grandmother, who shortly before her death gives him a "remembering box" in which she places a girlhood picture of herself.

Curtis, G. *Grandma's Baseball*. Crown, 1990.

Ages 5–8. After her husband's death, grandma comes to live with her family, but her grandson doesn't like her because she is grumpy. Grandma's baseball brings them together and he understands more about grief.

DePaola, T. *Nanna Upstairs, Nanna Downstairs*. Putnam, 1973.

Ages 5–8. Boy has a relationship with his grandma and great-grandma and deals with the death of both.

Donnelly, E. *So Long, Grandpa*. Crown, 1981.

Ages 11–14. Michael and his grandpa share a special friendship. When grandpa gets cancer and is dying, Michael deals with a range of emotions.

Egger, B. *Marianne's Grandmother*. Dutton, 1986.

Ages 5–8. At home after her grandmother's funeral, a granddaughter remembers all the good times together and the special love they shared.

Fassler, J. *My Grandpa Died Today*. Behavioral Publications, 1971.

Ages 6–10. A little boy experiences and tries to accept the death of his grandfather.

Fosburgh, L. *Mrs. Abercorn and the Bounce Boys*. Four Winds, 1986.

Ages 8–11. Two boys without a father become friends with an older woman.

Fox, P. *Western Wind*. Jackson, 1993.

Ages 11–14. Because of a new brother at home, Elizabeth spends the summer with Gran and learns about life and death.

Gaeddert, L. *A Summer Like Turnips*. Holt, 1989.

Ages 11–14. While spending the summer at his grandfather's retirement village, Bruce helps gramps get over the death of his wife.

Goffstein, M. B., *My Noah's Ark*. Harper, 1978.

Ages 1–5. This is a very sensitive story of how a father made a Noah's Ark for his little girl, and added carved animals through the years and how she treasured it until she was 90 years old. Told by the old woman, it is love contained in an object.

Gould, D. *Grandpa's Slide Show*. Lothrop, 1987.

Ages 5–8. When the family visits grandma and grandpa they always show family slides. After grandpa dies, grandma continues with the show and the memories are even richer.

Harranth, W. *My Old Grandad*. Oxford, 1981.

Ages 1–5. After grandma dies, granddad comes to visit his family in the city. His grandson takes on a nurturing role and learns to love him. When granddad leaves, the boy cries.

Hazen, B. S. *Why Did Grandpa Die?* Golden Books, 1985.

Ages 8–14. An explanation of the death of a child's grandparent.

Hesse, K. *Phoenix Rising*. Holt, 1994.

Ages 12+. A 13-year-old girl learns about relationships and death when Ezra, who was exposed to a radiation leak, comes to live at her grandmother's home.

Hines, A. *Remember the Butterflies*. Dutton, 1991.

Ages 5–8. Holly and Glen spend a lot of time in grandpa's garden as he teaches them about butterflies and life. When grandpa dies, they learn to accept the loss, and it is the memory of grandpa's lesson that helps them discover the joy of spring again.

Hite, S. *It's Nothing to a Mountain.* Holt, 1994.

Ages 8–11. After the death of their parents, 13-year-old Lisette and her 9-year-old bother, Riley, go to live with their grandparents.

Holden, D. *Grand-Gran's Best Trick.* Bunner, 1989.

Ages 8–11. A young girl faces the sad experience of her beloved grandfather's death.

Johnson, A. *Toning the Sweep.* Orchard, 1993.

Ages 11+. Three generations come together when a dying grandmother prepares to move.

Joosee, B. *Better with Two.* Harper & Row, 1988.

Ages 1–5. Laura is good friends with her nextdoor neighbor, Mrs. Brady. When Mrs. Brady's dog dies, Laura brings presents, but Mrs. Brady only feels better when Laura gives of herself to her friend.

Jukes, M. *Blackberries in the Dark.* Knopf, 1985.

Ages 8–11. After his grandfather dies, Austin is not sure spending the summer with grandma will be fun. But when they express their mutual sorrow and try to enjoy the other's favorite activities, they learn they can have fun together.

Kroll, V. L. *Fireflies, Peach Pies, and Lullabies.* Simon & Schuster, 1995.

Ages 8–11. When Francie's great-granny Annabel dies of Alzheimer's disease, Francie finds a way to help people remember the real person rather than the shell she had become as the disease ran its course.

L'Engle, M. *The Summer of the Great Grandmother.* Farrar, 1974.

Ages 14+. Biography and memories of the author's summer as her mother dies and her daughter becomes involved.

LeTord, B. *My Grandma Leonie.* Bradbury, 1987.

Ages 1–5. Reassuring book about the loss of a loving grandmother. Simple and touching.

Lowry, L. *Anastasia Krupnik.* Houghton Mifflin, 1979.

Ages 8–11. Anastasia, an only child, is about to be a sister and is not happy. Her parents let her choose the name, and she vows to pick a bad one until the death of a senile, but beloved grandmother helps her decide.

Lyon, G. *Basket.* Orchard, 1990.

Ages 1–5. Grandmother had a special basket that held treasures but was lost for many years. After her death it was found and with it came all the memories of grandma.

MacLachlan, P. *Cassie Binegar.* Harper & Row, 1987.

Ages 8–11. A young girl feels guilty about the way she talked to her grandfather before he died. An insightful grandmother and eccentric relatives help her deal with her feelings.

Paulson, G. *Tracker.* Berkley, 1982.

Ages 11–14. A boy tracks a doe and at the same time deals with his grandfather's impending death.

Peavy, L. *Allison's Grandfather.* Scribner, 1981.

Ages 8–11. This is a very sensitive story of a young girl thinking of the good times she had with her friend and her friend's grandfather. The death of the grandfather evokes memories.

Polacco, P. *Uncle Vova's Tree.* Philomel, 1989.

Ages 5–8. Memories of Christmas at Uncle Vova's are wonderful because he was wonderful. When he dies, the miracle of his special Christmas tree, and the memories, grow.

Pomerantz, B. *Bubby, Me and Memories.* Union of American Hebrew Congregations, 1983.

Ages 8–14. The story depicts the loss felt by a young child after the death of her grandmother.

Sachs, M. *Thirteen Going on Seven.* Dutton, 1993.

Ages 11–14. When her twin sister begins to assert her individuality and her grandmother suddenly dies, Dezzy finds she is more mature than she thought.

Sorenson, J. *The Secret Letters of Mamma Cat.* Walker LB, 1988.

Ages 11–14. Grandma died and 12-year-old Meredith is not ready to let go.

Stevens, M. *When Grandpa Died.* Childrens Press, 1979.

Ages 5–8. A girl who loved her grandpa is angry when he dies because he left her. She learns to cry and talk it out.

Talbot, T. *Dear Greta Garbo.* Putnam & Sons, 1978.

Ages 11–14. Miranda and her grandmother face similar needs and struggles for independence as grandma adjusts after her husband dies and Miranda grows up.

Tiffault, B. *A Quilt for Elizabeth.* Centering, 1992.

Ages 8–11. After Elizabeth accepts her father's death, she and her grandmother begin a quilt using patches of his clothing.

Thomas, I. *Hi, Mrs. Mallory!* Harper, 1979.

Ages 5–8. Lil Bits and her best friend, a very poor old woman, have a lot in common. When Mrs. Mallory dies, Lil Bits learns how to cope.

Thurman, C. *A Time for Remembering.* Simon & Schuster, 1989.

Ages 5–8. A boy shares a special relationship with his grandpa. When grandpa is dying, he gives his grandson a job to do that will make grieving easier.

Tomey, I. *Grandfather's Day.* Boyds Mills, 1992.

Ages 8–11. Raydeen tries to mend grandfather's broken heart when he comes to live with them after the death of his wife.

Townsend, M. *Pop's Secret.* Addison Wesley, 1980.

Ages 11–14. A young boy describes life with his grandfather and his feelings about the man's death.

Wahl, M. *Grandfather's Laika.* CarlRhoda Books, 1990.

Ages 5–8. Matthew and grandpa love their dog, Laika, and enjoy nature. When Laika gets sick, grandpa and Matt learn about grief together.

Walker, A. *To Hell with Dying.* HarBra J, 1988.

Ages 8–11. Two children love their elderly neighbor and learn to deal with his death.

White Deer of Autumn. *The Great Change.* Beyond Words, 1993.

Ages 8–11. After grandfather's death, a Native American woman explains the circle of life to her granddaughter.

Wood, P. A. *Then I'll Be Home Free.* Signet, 1988.

Ages 11+. A girl deals with her grandmother's death and her grandfather's breakdown.

Wright, B. *The Cat Next Door.* Holiday House, 1991.

Ages 5–8. Visiting grandma and grandpa at their lake house is special. When grandma dies, her granddaughter doesn't want to return but a cat's surprise helps her remember her grandma in a special way.

Chapter Seven

Evaluation of Intergenerational Programs

CHAPTER OVERVIEW

As discussed in Chapter 1, the number of intergenerational programs in the United States is literally exploding. Yet the number of research or evaluative articles about those programs is not keeping pace (Kuehne, 1996). If we know, instinctively or otherwise, that these programs are indeed changing lives and communities, then we must communicate that information so that they will be continued. If we know that this field has an impact on human service delivery systems, then we must share that information with others in the field and those on the outside who need to be brought inside. This chapter discusses the evaluation process and provides concrete examples in the hope that you will be motivated to publish the results of your program.

REASONS FOR EVALUATING PROGRAMS

To Make a Case for a Program

Evaluations are used to make a case for a program. You have a great idea and want to "sell" it to your principal, superintendent, executive director, or manager. But it involves time, some money, and real commitment. To argue your case, you should have some proof that it will work and that it has measurable outcomes that will fulfill your goals.

To Assess the Program and Define Needed Change

Evaluations are used for quality assurance and for refining a program. How is it working? What changes do I need to make for it to be more successful? What do I need to change in the process to make the logistics work better or to better meet the goals and objectives?

To Ensure That Others Know about the Program

Evaluations are used to make others become advocates for the programs. Do the people in the community know about the program? Will it help the community? What populations are being served and will they become advocates for it?

To Ensure Program Expansion or Continuation

Evaluations are used for growth. Following the success of one program, what can be added to it, or subtracted from it, to make it even better? How have participants and community been changed by the program? Did it make a difference?

To Contribute to the Effectiveness of Other Programs in the Intergenerational Field

Valerie Kuehne (1996) explains that both research and evaluation are important for the growth of the field in general. She has four recommendations for the practitioner:

- Evaluate your program by becoming systematic about the development, by documenting the program implementation, and by documenting the impact from a number of different perspectives including the outcomes and the effects on participants and indirect participants.
- Evaluate your program based on your personal strengths such as skill in observation and communication.
- Share with other practitioners what you have learned about evaluation.
- Investigate what intergenerational programs and networks exist in your area, learn from them and share your information with them.
- Communicate findings in meetings, conferences, workshops, and publications.

INTERGENERATIONAL PROGRAM EVALUATION DIFFERS FROM OTHER PROGRAM EVALUATION

Bocian and Newman (1989) and Ames and Youatt (1994) propose that intergenerational program evaluation is unique because it presents the evaluator with many variables. These include wide age ranges (child-care programs through college students, and young-old through old-old), varying health status (well, active older adults through frail, bed-ridden older adults), and wide diversity for both young and old in socioeconomic status, educational levels, and living arrangements. As if in response to that concern, Aday, McDuffie, and Sims (1993) felt it necessary to study the impact of intergenerational programs on black adolescents because nothing in the literature had dealt specifically with that racial group. In addition to the individual variables, Bocian and Newman (1989) also pointed to the fact that even in administration and management of these programs there is not one administering agency, but there are collaborations that represent agencies with often completely different sets of objectives and goals.

Intergenerational program evaluation represents a unique opportunity and a unique challenge. To meet that challenge, researchers and evaluators have developed a variety of instruments that test the attitudes, life satisfaction, and self-esteem of participants in intergenerational programs. These include:

- Kogan Old People Scale, developed by Kogan (1961). This instrument consists of set of logically opposite statements. It is reliable and easy to administer.
- CATE—Children's Attitudes Toward the Elderly, developed by Jantz, Seefeldt, Galper, and Serock (1977). This instrument consists of three subtests: a word-association subtest that asks children to respond to questions that tap their knowledge and feelings about older adults, a semantic differential of ten bipolar adjectives, and a picture series identifying children's perceptions of people at varying ages.
- Testing Elderly Person's Attitudes Toward Children, developed by Seefeldt, Jantz, Serock, and Bredekamp (1982). This is a three-part test with sections that test the feelings older adults have toward children, older adult's knowledge of child development, and the frequency and level of interaction of the older adults with children.
- CPAE—Children's Perceptions of Aging and Elderly, developed by Rich, Myrick, and Campbell (1983). This instrument contains 20 items to which respondents express their level (five choices) of agreement or disagreement. It measures social, physical, and behavioral factors as part of the aging process.
- CAOPS—Children's Assessment of Old People Scale, developed by Cartensen, Mason, and Caldwell (1982). This instrument consists of a 20-item objective questionnaire that is similar to other instruments but was designed to "improve the predictive validity of the attitudes measured."
- APQ—Attitude Perception Questionnaire, developed by Nishi-Strattner and Myers (1983). This instrument was designed to test both young people's and older adults' attitudes toward each other. The same items and answer scales are used for both age groups, but the instructions for the older adults are to answer as they think the youth would, not what they themselves think.
- BPYC—Prosocial Behavior in Young Children Scale, developed by Dellman-Jenkins, Lambert, and Fruit (1991). This instrument "measured the frequency of prosocial behaviors directed toward the elderly by preschool-aged children." Children respond to six situations on a five-point scale after having watched six puppet stories. It tests the areas of helping, sharing, and cooperating with older adults.
- IEAS—Intergenerational Exchanges Attitude Scale, developed by Stremmel, Travis, and Kelly-Harrison (1996). They developed this instrument in response to a search of the literature in which they found no instruments that measured the attitudes of young and old toward the intergenerational interactions themselves. Consisting of 24 items with a five-point subscale measurement, this questionnaire was mailed to child and adult day-care center administrators.

PLANNING YOUR EVALUATION

Answering the following questions will help you develop the kind of evaluation that will best suit your needs.

- What do you want to know about the program?
- What do the funders want to know?
- What do the collaborators want to know?
- What parameters need to be identified in order to provide the information desired? What should you look for?
- What are the obstacles to obtaining the information needed? Will students understand the questionnaire and take it seriously? Will young children be able to fill out the form? Will participants cooperate? Do you have the money and time to do it properly? Do the staff members know how to collect the data or do they need to be trained?
- What is the methodology that will be used to gather the data?
- What is the best way to disseminate the information?

DEVELOPING YOUR OWN METHODOLOGY

Pre- and Posttest Questionnaires

Many researchers and evaluators devise their own attitudinal tests with questions that seem most appropriate to their own intergenerational program dimensions. Pre- and posttests are often given as a way to measure the changes, and the type of questions developed will depend on the type of information you need (Reinke, Holmes, & Denney, 1981).

For example, when I first began teaching about aging, many of the administrators of the schools in which I taught asked me to defend my position that children's attitudes about aging would be positively affected by this program. I developed a simple, one-page set of questions for children to answer and administered the pretest before I even introduced myself to the students. The posttest was given on the last teaching day of the class, approximately six to eight months later. I was surprised by how many students would say, "Hey, I answered these same questions a long time ago, but now my answers are different." Indeed in every case, the answers were significantly different and my position was well supported. Figure 7–1 is an example of the attitudinal test I gave to third- and fourth-grade students. I did not have a professional evaluator develop the questions, there was no statistical analysis of the data, and my sample size was too small to claim that this was a significant finding for all third or fourth graders. I simply presented the data in percentages of how children answered each question, identifying answers as either negative or positive based on words I anticipated receiving and my judgment as to their positive or negative impact. The administrators saw the results and agreed that important attitudinal changes were being made.

Observational Data

Qualitative, rather than quantitative, data are also valid indicators of the program's integrity. Because most educators are careful observers of their students and can detect even the smallest of attitudinal or behavioral changes, observation is an important tool

Figure 7–1 Questionnaire for Third and Fourth Graders

List three words that describe an old person.

_____

_____

_____

Complete these sentences:

1. I think old people are _____ .
2. Growing old is _____ .
3. When I grow old, I _____ .

Check true (T) or false (F) for each sentence as it applies to you.

1. I avoid older adults whenever I can.   ____ T ____ F
2. I never know what to say to older adults.   ____ T ____ F
3. Aging worries me.   ____ T ____ F
4. Most old people live in nursing homes.   ____ T ____ F
5. After retiring from work, life is usually boring. ____ T ____ F
6. It would be fun to be friends with an older adults. ____ T ____ F

in assessment. In my experiences, teachers noticed that students were willing to edit letters going to older adult pen pals but were reluctant to edit other classroom writing, that students were eager to write lengthy journal entries but only when the subject was their older adult partner, and that there was better classroom behavior on days that were designated for intergenerational interactions. In regard to the latter, a teacher once told me that a young boy who normally had disturbing behavior problems would hold a chair for his older adult partner and behaved impeccably during his interactions with her.

Another source of observational data that should not be overlooked is that by parents and others indirectly involved with the intergenerational program. Much of my anecdotal information comes from parents who have told me about attitudinal changes they noticed at home that I would have no way of knowing because of a lack of access to that part of the student's life. A parent once confided that she had been sad that her son seemed to have so little interest or concern for his grandmother. But during his involvement with an intergenerational program, his attitude changed dramatically, as evidenced by a day when schools were closed because of a blizzard and he called his grandmother three times to find out if she was safe.

I have sometimes developed questionnaires for parents. The questions explore the parent's own relationship with older adults and then ask them to evaluate, through statements that have a three-point scale, the impact of the program on their child. Questions include:

- How would you describe your overall feelings about older adults?
- Has *your* attitude about older adults changed as a result of your child's involvement in the program?
- How do you think this program affected your child's attitudes about older adults?

The effect of intergenerational programs reaches beyond the classroom (Stremmel, Travis, & Kelly-Harrison, 1996).

Interviews

Many educators regularly conduct interviews with their students to discuss whether self-directed goals are achieved. The interview procedure, therefore, is a good opportunity to discuss with students their attitudes and views of older adults, the aging process, and their own aging. Interviews are often conducted with very young children who cannot answer questionnaires (Kocarnik & Ponzetti, 1986), with older adults (Chapman & Neal, 1990; Kuehne, 1992), and with staff (Greene & Monahan, 1982).

In summation, intergenerational program evaluation is crucial to the growth of the field. Share your own findings and add to that growth.

References

Aday, R. H., McDuffie, W., & Sims, C. R. (1993). Impact of an Intergenerational Program on Black Adolescents' Attitudes Toward the Elderly. *Educational Gerontology, 19,* 663–673.

Ames, B. D., & Youatt, J. P. (1994). Intergenerational Education and Service Programming: A Model for Selection and Evaluation of Activities. *Educational Gerontology, 20,* 755–764.

Bocian, K., & Newman, S. (1989). Evaluation of Intergenerational Programs: Why and How? In S. Newman & S. W. Brummel (Eds.), *Intergenerational Programs, Imperatives, Strategies, Impacts, Trends.* New York: Haworth Press.

Cartensen, L., Mason, S. E., & Caldwell, E. C. (1982). Children's Attitudes Toward the Elderly: An Intergenerational Technique for Change. *Educational Gerontology, 8,* 291–301.

Chapman. N. J., & Neal, M. B. (1990). The Effects of Intergenerational Experiences on Adolescents and Older Adults. *The Gerontologist, 30* (6), 825–832.

Dellman-Jenkins, M., Lambert, D., & Fruit, D. (1991). Fostering Preschoolers' Prosocial Behaviors Toward the Elderly: The Effect of an Intergenerational Program. *Educational Gerontology, 17,* 21–32.

Greene, V. L., & Monahan, D. J. (1982). The Impact of Visitation on Patient Well-Being in Nursing Homes. *The Gerontologist, 22* (1), 418–423.

Jantz, R., Seefeldt, C., Galper, A., & Serock, K. (1977). Children's Attitudes Toward the Elderly. *Social Education, 41,* 518–523.

Kocarnik, R., & Ponzetti, J., Jr. (1986). The Influence of Intergenerational Contact on Child Care Participants' Attitudes Toward the Elderly. *Child Care Quarterly, 15* (4), 244–250.

Kogan, N. (1961). Attitudes Toward Old People: The Development of a Scale and an Examination of Correlates. *Journal of Abnormal and Social Psychology, 62,* 44–54.

Kuehne, V. S. (1992). Older Adults in Intergenerational Programs: What Are Their Experiences Really Like? *Activities, Adaptation & Aging, 16* (4), 49–66.

Kuehne, V. (1996). Evaluate Your Intergenerational Program: Four Recommendations for Human Service Practitioners. [Special issue]. *Southwest Journal on Aging,* 12 (1&2), 27–32.

Nishi-Strattner, M., & Myers, J. E. (1983). Attitudes Toward the Elderly: An Intergenerational Examination. *Educational Gerontology, 9,* 389-397.

Reinke, B. J., Holmes, D. S., & Denney, N. W. (1981). Influence of a "Friendly Visitor" Program on the Cognitive Functioning and Morale of Elderly Persons. *American Journal of Community Psychology, 9* (4), 491–504.

Rich, P. E., Myrick, R. D., & Campbell, C. (1983). Changing Children's Perceptions of the Elderly. *Educational Gerontology, 9,* 483–491.

Seefeldt, C., Jantz, R. K., Serock, K., & Bredekamp, S. (1982). Elderly Persons' Attitude Toward Children. *Educational Gerontology, 8,* 493–506.

Stremmel, A. J., Travis, S. S., & Kelly-Harrison, P. (1996). Development of the Intergenerational Exchanges Attitude Scale. *Educational Gerontology, 22,* 317–328.

Suggested Reading

Bringle, R. G., & Kremer, J. F. (1993). Evaluation of an Intergenerational Service-Learning Project for Undergraduates. *Educational Gerontology, 19,* 407–416.

Seefeldt, C., Jantz, R. K., Galper, A., & Serock, K. (1981). Healthy, Happy, and Old: Children Learn About the Elderly. *Educational Gerontology, 7,* 79–87.

Stremmel, A. J., Travis, S. S., Kelly-Harrison, P., & Hensley, A. D. (1994). The Perceived Benefits and Problems Associated with Intergenerational Exchanges in Day Care Settings. *The Gerontologist, 34* (4), 513–519.

Annotated Book List

(Books Not Cited Within Chapters)

Aaron, C. *Better Than Laughter*. Harcourt Brace Jovanovich, 1972.

Ages 11–14. Two rich brothers seem to have everything they want—except time, love, and understanding. The boys meet an 85-year-old keeper of the town dump who is struggling with his own issues of love, age, and consumerism.

Abercrombie, B. *Cat-Man's Daughter*. Harper & Row, 1981.

Ages 11–14. Thirteen-year-old Kate is kidnapped by her grandmother in an effort to make Kate's divorced parents consider Kate's welfare instead of their own.

Adams, P. *Who Cares About the Elderly People?* Child's Play, 1990.

Ages 8–11. Readers learn that older people and young people have a lot in common, and that there are many ways they can help each other.

Adler, C. S. *Fly Free*. Coward, McGee, 1984.

Ages 11–14. Older neighbor offers friendship to a lonely 13-year-old girl with an emotionally abusive mom and an absent father.

Adler, C. S. *Goodbye Pink Pig*. Avon, 1986.

Ages 9 +. An unconventional grandmother is a school custodian. A break with stereotypes.

Alexander, S. H. *Maggie's Whopper*. Macmillan, 1992.

Ages preschool–8. Maggie loves fishing with her great-uncle Ezra. Determined to catch a whopper of a fish this time, she does so just in time to save her uncle from a threatening black bear.

Alphin, E. *The Ghost Cadet*. Henry Holt, 1996.

Ages 9–14. Benjy is in for a surprise when he spends the spring break with a grandmother he has never met.

Anderson, L. *Stina*. Greenwillow, 1988.

Ages preschool–5. Stina and her grandfather spend the summer together and share the excitement of a huge storm.

Anderson, L. *Stina's Visit*. Greenwillow, 1991.

Ages preschool–5. The relationship between Stina and her grandfather during an idyllic summer together is explored. It includes tall tales by grandfather's friend on the island.

Ardizzonw, E. *Lucy Brown and Mr. Grines*. H.Z. Walck, 1971.

Ages 4–8. An orphan girl and old Mr. Grines are both lonely until they meet in the park and become friends.

Baldwin, A. *Sunflowers for Tina*. Four Winds Press, 1970.

Ages 8–11. A young girl in New York City looks for a way to brighten up her bleak back yard and her grandmother's empty life.

Bellairs, J. *The Mummy, The Will and The Crypt*. Dial, 1983.

Ages 9–12. Second in *The Curse of the Blue Figurine* trilogy. A boy and his grandparents are involved in a mystery.

Berenstein, S., & Berenstein, J. *A Week at Grandma's*. Random House, 1986.

Ages 5–8. Brother and sister experience some anxiety when they spend a week by themselves at their grandparent's house.

Berger, T. *Special Friends*. Messner, 1979.

Ages 5–8. Photographs enhance the text of a young person's wonderful relationship with an elderly neighbor.

Blos, J. *Old Henry*. Morrow Junior, 1987.

Ages 3–9. An eccentric old artist moves into an old, run down house and has problems with neighbors who expect him to fix it up.

Blos, J. *The Grandpa Days*. Simon & Schuster, 1989.

Ages 5–8. Philip wants to build something with grandpa during their week together, but first he has to learn the difference between wishes and good planning.

Booth, B. *Mandy*. Lothrop, 1991.

Ages 5–8. Mandy and her grandma share a special relationship. When grandma's special pin is lost, Mandy finds it for her.

Borack, B. *Grandpa*. Harper & Row, 1968.

Ages 1–5. A vision of her grandfather through a little girl's eyes. The two have a lot in common.

Borden, L. *The Watching Game*. Scholastic, 1991.

Ages 5–8. When they visit grandma, all four grandchildren watch for the fox who lives nearby and hope they have the chance to put out grandpa's hat, which is a sign to the fox that he has been seen.

Bosse, M. *The Seventy Nine Squares*. Crowell, 1979.

Ages 11–14. A boy on probation meets an old man who asks him to map every inch of his garden for him. When he finds out the man is an ex-convict, the boy defends him and learns about himself and others in the process. Good mentoring discussion.

Branscum, R. *Toby, Granny, and George*. Avon, 1977.

Ages 11–14. Toby has two missions: to preserve her home with her adopted granny and to save her farm from destitution. She does and in the process finds her mother, her first love, and solves a mystery.

Branscum, R. *The Girl*. Harper Junior Books, 1986.

Ages 11+. Left in the care of a cruel grandmother and a lazy grandfather in Arkansas, five children struggle to survive.

Bridgers, S. E. *All Together Now*. Knopf, 1979.

Ages 11+. A 12-year-old girl spends the summer with her grandparents. She encounters a number of unusual characters and fights to help a mentally challenged man avoid institutionalization.

Brooks, R. *Timothy and Gramps*. Bradbury, 1978.

Ages 5–8. A boy and his best friend, Gramps, share stories of adventure but at school the boy is shy. When Gramps tells one of his stories at school, Timothy begins to enjoy school more.

Buckley, H. *Grandfather and I*. Lothrop, 1961.

Ages 1–5. A boy takes walks with his grandfather and neither has to hurry so they look at lots of things. Special story of two people who have time for each other, but tends to be stereotypic.

Buckley, H. *Grandmother and I*. Lothrop, 1961.

Ages 1–5. The story of a young girl's comfort sitting on grandma's lap as she rocks back and forth. Special love between girl and grandmother, but tends to be stereotypic.

Bulla, C. R. *Shoeshine Girl*. HarperCollins, 1989.

Ages 5–11. Determined to earn some money, 10-year-old Sarah Ida gets a job at a shoeshine stand and learns a great many things besides shining shoes.

Bunting, E. *The Wednesday Surprise*. Clarion, 1989.

Ages 6–9. Anna and her grandmother spend every Wednesday reading together. The surprise comes on Anna's father's birthday when grandma gets up and reads for the first time, having learned from her "smart" granddaughter.

Bunting, E. *A Day's Work*. Clarion, 1994.

Ages 6–10. Francisco is so anxious to find work for his non-English-speaking grandfather that he lies about the man's qualifications for a gardening job. When the boss discovers the work has been botched, Francisco's grandfather teaches him a valuable lesson.

Buscaglia, L. *A Memory for Tino*. SLACK/Morrow, 1988.

Ages 8–11. An 8-year-old boy befriends an old woman and creates a beautiful memory.

Byars, B. *The House of Wings*. Dell, 1973.

Ages 8–11. A boy resents his parents leaving him with his grandfather. He runs away. Grandfather finds him and a blind crane. They help the crane and when the boy finds out his grandfather remembers every bird he nursed back to health, they become close.

Byars, B. *After the Goat Man*. Penguin Books, 1974.

Ages 5–8. An overweight, sensitive boy gains the insight and strength to overcome his problems through his search for and discovery of a friend's grandfather, known as a Goat Man.

Byars, B. *Blossom Promise*. Delacorte, 1987.

Ages 8–11. After a big flood, the Blossom family copes in their own way.

Caines, J. *Window Washing*. Harper, 1980.

Ages 1–5. A sister and brother spend a vacation with their funny and unconventional grandmother.

Caines, J. *Just Us Women*. Harper & Row, 1982.

Ages 6–9. A young girl and her Aunt Martha take a car trip that allows "just us women" to do whatever they like along the way.

Carlson, N. S. *The Family Under the Bridge*. Harper & Row, 1958.

Ages 8–11. An old man who doesn't want a family finds he is drawn to the children who live under the bridge and who need a family.

Carlson, N. S. *A Family for the Orphelines*. Harper & Row, 1980.

Ages 8–11. Fifty-one French orphans need a grandmother to complete their family, so they go looking for one.

Carlstrom, N. *Grandpappy*. Little, Brown, 1990.

Ages 1–5. A very special relationship is explored between a boy and his grandfather as they spend time together. Grandpappy offers advice (and his actions prove it is sound advice) on how to be a good person. Two special characters in a special book.

Caseley, J. *Apple Pie and Onions*. Greenwillow, 1987.

Ages 5–8. Rebecca loves her grandma but is embarrassed by something her grandma does. Grandma understands and wisely tells her a story that makes everything just right again.

Cazet, D. *Saturday*. Bradbury Press, 1985.

Ages 1–5. Barney and his grandpa make a fun day out of an ordinary one.

Cazet, D. *Great Uncle Fox*. Watts, Orchard, Richard Jackson, 1988.

Ages 5–8. A young rhinoceros meets his great uncle at the bus station and everything goes wrong.

Cazet, D. *Sunday*. Macmillan, Bradbury, 1988.

Ages 5–8. Barney's Sundays with his grandparents are never dull.

Clifton, L. *Lucky Stone*. Delacorte, 1979.

Ages 8–11. Tee loves hearing her great-grandmother tell how the lucky black stone had brought good luck to all its owners. Now Tee would have the stone, too.

Coats, L. J. *Mr. Jordan in the Park*. Macmillan, 1989.

Ages 8–11. This book reviews the entire life of Mr. Jordan, especially happy times in his favorite place, the park, where he now still enjoys quieter good times in his old age.

Coerr, E. *Chang's Paper Pony*. Harper & Row, 1988.

Ages 4–8. Chang and his grandfather live in San Francisco during the 1895 gold rush. Chang wants to buy a pony but is unable to buy one until he and his grandfather find a solution.

Cookson, C. *Mrs. Flannagan's Trumpet*. Lothrop, 1976.

Ages 11–14. While staying with his grandparents, 16-year-old Eddie helps his deaf grandmother in the struggle to free his sister and the household maid from white slavers. Takes place in 1890.

Coontz, O. *Hornswoggle Magic*. Little, Brown, 1981.

Ages 8–11. Using seemingly magical methods, a strange "bag lady" helps two children save one's father's newsstand, which is threatened by a huge vending machine.

Cosgrove, S. *Grampa-Lop*. Stern & Sloan, 1988.

Ages 1–5. Grampa-Lop may be a very old and gray bunny who is of no use to the older rabbits, but to the young bunnies of the thicket, he is magic.

Creech, S. *Walk Two Moons*. HarperCollins, 1994.

Ages 11–14. After her mother leaves home suddenly, 13-year-old Sal and her grandparents are together.

Dahl, R. *The Witches*. Farrar, Straus & Giroux, 1982.

Ages 8–11. A boy is turned into a mouse by the Grand High Witch of the World. He and his grandmother begin a war against the witches.

Davis, J. *Checking on the Moon*. Orchard, 1991.

Ages 11+. A country girl learns about working-class city folks by working in her grandmother's restaurant.

Denslow, S. P. *At Taylor's Place.* Bradbury Press, 1990.

Ages 1–5. Tory loves to go to Taylor's workshop and help him build weathervanes and bird feeders.

dePaola, T. *Tom.* Putnam, 1993.

Ages preschool–7. A boy and his grandfather have a special relationship.

Diller, H. *Granddaddy's Highway.* Boyd Mills Press, 1993.

Ages 4–8. Listening to the trucks roll past her home, young Maggie imagines heading west on Route 30 with her grandfather, driving one of those trucks all the way to the Pacific.

Dils, T. *Grandpa's Magic.* Willowisp, 1990.

Ages 1–5. A fantasy about a magic cane and the adventures of a boy and his grandpa.

Douglas, B. *Good As New.* Lothrop, Lee and Shepard, 1982.

Ages 1–5. When Grady's bear gets ruined by his young cousin only grandpa can make it as good as new.

English, K. *Big Wind Coming!* Albert Whitman & Co., 1996.

Ages 8–11. When Sarah and her family realize a hurricane is headed toward their farm, they prepare for it. After the hurricane passes, the family gathers in the doorway to survey the damage.

Fakih, K. O. *Grandpa Putter and Granny Hoe.* Farrar, Straus, & Giroux, 1992.

Ages 8–11. Twins Jzz and Roo find themselves in the middle of a nonstop war of one-upmanship, but their grandparents know how to stop it.

Fakih, K. O. *High on the Hog.* Farrar, Straus, & Giroux, 1994.

Ages 11–14. When Trapp's family plans to move from Iowa to New York City, she stays behind on her grandparent's farm for the summer. She discovers a long-kept secret that changes her idea of family and learns that moving on doesn't have to mean leaving behind what you love.

Fink, D. B. *Mr. Silver & Mrs. Gold.* Human Sciences Press, 1980.

Ages 5–8. Two people become friends and share many activities together.

Flora, J. *Grandpa's Ghost Stories.* Macmillan, 1980.

Ages 5–11. Three grizzly short stories told by an old man to his grandson.

Flory, J. *The Unexpected Grandchildren.* Houghton Mifflin, 1977.

Ages 5–8. Mr. and Mrs. Newton's life was orderly and quiet until unexpected grandchildren arrived.

Fox, M. *Shoes From Grandpa.* Orchard, 1989.

Ages 1–5. Grandpa gives Jessie a pair of shoes and everyone else adds to the outfit. Repetitive story as in *The House That Jack Built.*

Fox, M. *Sophie.* Harcourt Brace, 1989.

Ages preschool–6. Sophie holds onto her grandfather's hand as she grows up. He holds onto hers as he gets smaller and older.

Franklin, K. L. *The Old, Old Man and the Very Little Boy.* Atheneum, 1992.

Ages 5–11. The old, old man sits on a stump and shares his wisdom with the men and women of the village. Each morning the very little boy visits his old friend to hear his stories. Only when the little boy grows up does he understand the meaning of his old friend's words.

Gauch, P. L. *Grandpa and Me.* Coward, McCann, 1972.

Ages 1–5. A boy and his grandfather share good times during their summer at the lake.

Gerson, C. *My Grandfather the Spy.* Walker & Co, 1990.

Ages 11–14. On a long bus ride to Vermont, Danny sits next to an elderly man who is easy to talk to and is anything but boring. When the man leaves the bus without saying goodbye, Danny investigates to find out about him.

Gibbs, D. *Major League Melissa.* Bantam Paper, 1991.

Ages 7–11. Walter, with his grandpa as coach, finds enough players to form his own baseball team.

Goffsten, M. B. *Fish for Supper.* Dial Press, 1976.

Ages 3–6. This story describes grandmother's typical day of fishing.

Goldman, S. *Grandpa and Me Together.* Albert Whitman, 1980.

Ages 5–8. A girl spends an active day with her grandfather.

Gomi, T. *Coco Can't Wait.* Puffin, 1985.

Ages 5–8. A girl and her grandmother keep missing each other as they try to visit.

Gondosch, L. *Who's Afraid of Haggerty House?* Lodesate, 1987.

Ages 8–11. An 11-year-old girl befriends an old woman after the girl becomes alienated from her two best friends.

Graham, B. *Rose Meets Mr. Wintergarten.* Candlewick Press, 1992.

Ages 4–7. A young girl's attempt to retrieve her ball from a grouchy neighbor's yard changes the way they feel about each other.

Green, P. *Grandmother Orphan.* Nelson, 1977.

Ages 8–11. An 11-year-old shoplifter is sent to her tough grandmother's house for one week.

Green, P. *Uncle Roland, The Perfect Guest.* Four Winds, 1983.

Ages 8–11. A disruptive house guest offers to do the children's chores.

Greenfield, E. *Grandpa's Face.* Putnam & Grosset, 1988.

Ages 5–8. Despite grandfather's many different kinds of facial expressions, his granddaughter learns that his feelings for her remain stable and she can depend on his love.

Haas, J. *Beware the Mare.* Greenwillow, 1993.

Ages 8–11. Grandfather and Lily wonder why the horse they have just acquired is named Beware.

Hanft, P. *Never Fear, Flip the Dip Is Here.* Dial Books, 1991.

Ages 6–11. Flip, upset about not being able to play baseball very well, acquires self-confidence and sports skills from Buster, a former minor league ballplayer.

Hartling, P. *Oma.* Harper & Row, 1977.

Ages 8–11. A young orphaned German boy goes to live with his grandmother in Munich.

Haseley, D. *Shadows.* Farrar, 1991.

Ages 8–12. The mystery concerning the death of Jamie's father is somewhat relieved when his grandfather begins to teach him how to make shadow figures.

Havill, J. *Leroy and the Clock.* Houghton Mifflin, 1988.

Ages 5–8. A 5-year-old boy hesitates about his first visit alone with his grandpa. He expresses feelings via the hall clock.

Hayes, S. *Speaking of Snapdragons.* Lodestar, 1982.

Ages 11–14. A lonely, fatherless 11-year-old girl befriends an old gardener.

Hedderwick, M. *Katie Morag and the Two Grandmothers.* Little, Brown, 1985.

Ages 5–8. Katie has a fancy city grandmother and a plain island grandma who don't get along well. When city grandma's makeup helps island grandma win a prize for her sheep, everything is better.

Heide, F. P. *When the Sad One Comes to Stay.* Bantam, 1976.

Ages 11–14. A new girl in town befriends an old woman who fantasizes that the girl is her own daughter. Social-climber mother doesn't approve of the friendship, and the girl betrays her one friend and assumes her mother's values. Good discussion about values.

Heins, L. *My Very Special Friend.* Judson, 1974.

Ages 1–5. A 5-year-old tells about a special visit with great-grandma while mom is in the hospital.

Hellberg, H. E. *Grandpa's Maria.* William Morrow, 1974.

Ages 11–14. In the care of her grandpa following her mama's nervous breakdown, Maria learns to cope with uncertainties.

Hermes, P. *A Place for Jeremy.* Dell, 1989.

Ages 11–14. Jeremy switches schools in the middle of the year and goes to stay with her grandparents.

Hermes, P. *Take Care of My Girl.* Little, Brown, 1992.

Ages 11–14. When Brady's dad leaves her with her grandpa for six years, she learns to love Jake.

Hest, A. *The Purple Coat.* Macmillan, 1986.

Ages 5–8. Gabrielle's grandfather, a tailor, always makes her a new navy coat. But this year he agrees to make her a purple one and help convince her mother it is a good choice.

Hest, A. *The Crack of Dawn Walkers.* Puffin, 1988.

Ages 1–5. Every other Sunday Sadie gets to go for an early morning walk with her grandpa and she doesn't have to share him with anyone else. Next week will be her brother's turn, but for now, she and grandpa are together.

Hest, A. *The Go-Between.* Four Winds Press, 1992.

Ages 8–11. Grandma lives with her family, and granddaughter Lexi is the go-between when Murray and grandma are friends. Lexi finds there is more to their friendship than baseball. They love each other and Lexi helps that love become a marriage.

Hest, A. *Nana's Birthday Party.* Morrow, 1993.

Ages 6–11. Maggie wants to write a story for her grandmother's birthday, but lacks the inspiration.

Hest, A. *Weekend Girl.* Morrow Junior, 1993.

Ages 8–11. When her parents go away for the weekend, Sophie enjoys sharing her grandfather's hobbies.

Hickman, M. W. *Robert Lives with His Grandparents.* Albert Whitman & Co., 1995.

Ages 8–11. Robert is embarrassed to admit to his classmates that he has lived with his grandparents since his parents' divorce.

Holl, K. *Just Like a Real Family.* Macmillan, 1983.

Ages 9–14. June Finch, a 12-year-old, gets involved in a class project to adopt grandparents from a retirement home.

Holland, I. *Now Is Not Too Late*. Lothrop, 1980.

Ages 11–14. While spending the summer with her grandmother, 11-year-old Cathy learns about herself and her relationship with other people.

Hooker, R. *At Grandma and Grandpa's House*. Whitman & Co, 1989.

Ages 1–5. The joy of visiting grandma and grandpa is recounted by their grandchildren.

Hoopes, L. L. *Half a Button*. Harper & Row, 1989.

Ages 1–5. William and his parents visit grandpa and spend a happy day. William remembers the day every time he looks at the half button his grandfather gave him.

Houston, G. *My Great-Aunt Arizona*. HarperCollins, 1992.

Ages 1–6. An Appalachian girl, Arizona Houston Hughes, grows up to be a teacher who influences generations of schoolchildren.

Howker, J. *Badger on the Barge and Other Stories*. Viking Penguin, 1984.

Ages 9–14. Five short stories set in small towns in northern England. Each explores a brief but meaningful encounter between a youngster and a solitary old man or woman in a beautifully depicted rural setting.

Hutchins, P. *The Doorbell Rang*. Greenwillow, 1986.

Ages 5–8. Children are sharing cookies when grandma shows up with the best cookies of all.

Hynes, A. *Grandma Gets Grumpy*. Ticknor & Fields, 1988.

Ages 5–8. Five cousins spend the night with grandma and realize she is fun to be with until the children don't cooperate.

Jenkins, L. B. *Celebrating the Hero*. Lodestar, 1993.

Ages 11+. Camila learns there is more to her grandfather's life than legend had made her believe.

Jones, R. *Madeline and the Great (Old) Escape Artist*. Dutton, 1983.

Ages 11–14. Madeline doesn't like her new home and decides to run back to her old friends. She runs away with an old lady, and their escape is filled with unexpected things to learn.

Kantrowitz, M. *Maxie*. Parents, 1970.

Ages 5–8. On the day Maxie stays in bed because she thinks her dull routines are of no use to anyone, she discovers how many people really do rely on her.

Keams, G. *Grandmother Spider Brings the Sun, A Cherokee Story*. Northland Publishing, 1995.

Ages 6+. After Possum and Buzzard fail in their attempts to steal a piece of the sun, Grandmother Spider succeeds in bringing light to the animals on her side of the world.

Knotts, H. *Great-Grandfather, the Baby and Me*. Atheneum, 1978.

Ages 5–8. When his baby sister is born, a boy feels sad and lonely but his great-grandfather tells him a story to make greeting the new baby easier.

Konisburg, E. L. *From the Mixed Up Files of Mrs. Basil E. Frankweiler*. Atheneum, 1967.

Ages 9–11. Teenagers learn some important life lessons from an elderly woman.

Kraus, R. *Bunya the Witch*. Windmill, 1971.

Ages 1–5. People are mean to old Bunya and call her a witch. When they find out she really has powers, they try to be nice, but she tells them to leave her to herself and flies away.

Kroll, S. *If I Could Be My Grandmother*. Pantheon, 1977.

Ages 1–5. A young girl describes all that she would do if she were her grandmother.

Kroll, S. *Annie's Four Grannies*. Holiday House, 1986.

Ages 1–5. Annie has four grannies but they don't get along well together. At Annie's birthday party she changes that.

Kroll, S. *Patrick's Tree House*. Macmillan, 1994.

Ages 8–11. Patrick spends one week alone with his grandparents and is thrilled with his own tree house until someone tries to take it over.

Kroll, V. *Pink Paper Swans*. Eerdmans, 1994.

Ages 7–10. A friendship that crosses lines of age and culture.

LaFarge, P. *Granny's Fish Story*. Parents, 1975.

Ages 5–8. A granddaughter and a friend overcome the fear of thunderstorms when they visit grandmother in the country.

Lapp, E. *In the Morning Mist*. Whitman, 1978.

Ages 5–8. A young child and his grandfather set out on a fishing trip and find the countryside transformed by morning fog.

Lasky, K. *I Have Four Names for My Grandfather*. Little, 1976.

Ages 5–8. Open discussion and expressions of love between grandfather and grandson. Differences in age, wisdom, and physical size are seen in words and pictures.

Leonard, M. *Gregory & Mr. Grump*. Silver Burdett Press, 1990.

Ages 4–7. As Gregory faces a series of tribulations in trying to grow vegetables in his garden, he receives help from his supposedly grumpy neighbor, Mr. Grant. For each problem, the text offers several causes and asks the reader to choose the correct one.

LeShan, E. *Grandparents: A Special Kind of Love*. Macmillan, 1984.

Ages 8–11. Exploration of relationships between grandparents and grandchildren with advice about conflicts between them.

Levin, B. *The Trouble with Gramary*. Greenwillow, 1988.

Ages 11–14. Merkka's longing for a conventional existence is threatened by the art of her grandmother whose scrap metal collection offends the people in their village.

Levine, E. *Not the Piano, Mrs. Medley*. Orchard, 1991.

Ages 1–5. Going to the beach with grandma is fun but getting there is something else as grandma prepares to take almost everything she might ever need. And, after all that, they forget their bathing suits.

Lewis, R. *Aunt Armadillo*. Annick Press, 1985.

Ages 1–5. Aunt Armadillo loves books and creates a very exotic library.

Lexau, J. *I Hate Red Rover*. Dutton, 1979.

Ages 5–8. Jill does poorly with games at school until sharing her problem with grandpa helps her find a solution.

Lindburgh, A. *Three Lives to Live*. Little, 1992.

Ages 11–14. Garet is visited by Daisy, who is really his grandmother of 50 years before.

Lloyd, D. *Grandma and the Pirate*. Crown, 1958.

Ages 5–8. A boy and his lively grandmother go to the beach and he pretends to be a pirate.

Locker, T. *Where the River Begins.* Dial, 1984.

Ages 8–11. Two boys wonder where the river that flows gently past their houses begins. Grandfather takes them on a camping journey to find the beginning of the river.

MacLachlan, P. *Journey.* Delacorte, 1991.

Ages 11–14. When a mother leaves her two children with their grandparents, they feel as if their life will never be the same.

Magorian, M. *Good-Night, Mr. Tom.* Harper & Row, 1981.

Ages 11–14. A battered child learns to embrace life when he is adopted by an old man. Takes place during World War II.

Mahy, M. *Ultra-Violet Catastrophe!* Parents, 1975.

Ages 8–11. A girl and her great uncle share a walk in the country. Easy companionship of the young and old.

Mayer, M. *Just Grandma and Me.* Golden, 1983.

Ages 1–5. A boy and his grandma have a good time at the beach because he takes care of his grandmother and she helps him.

McCully, E. A. *The Grandma Mix-Up.* Harper & Row, 1988.

Ages 5–8. Young Pip doesn't know what to do when two very different grandmothers come to babysit for him.

McCully, E. A. *Grandma's at the Lake.* Harper & Row, 1990.

Ages 5–8. Pip and Ski have a hard time enjoying themselves at the lake with Pip's two grandmothers because they can't agree on anything.

McPhail, D. *Grandfather's Cake.* Scribner, 1979.

Ages 5–8. Peter and Andrew are taking a piece of warm chocolate cake to their grandfather who is tending the sheep, but the wonderful smell causes them to have adventures and creates problems as they protect the cake.

Moore, E. *Grandma's House.* Lothrop, 1985.

Ages 5–8. Summers at grandma's house are special because of the fun things they do but mostly because they are together.

Moore, E. *Grandma's Promise.* Lothrop, 1988.

Ages 1–5. A little girl and her grandma share time together and the girl learns she always has a place at grandma's house.

Mora, P. *A Birthday Basket for Tia.* Macmillan, 1992.

Ages preschool–6. Cecila wants to find the perfect present for her great-aunt's ninetieth birthday.

Morrow, L. K. *Dancing on the Table.* Holiday, 1990.

Ages 8–12. Jenny decides that she doesn't approve of the man her grandmother intends to marry.

Newton, S. *Rubella, and the Old Focus Home.* Westminster, 1978.

Ages 11–14. Rubella helps her lazy father run a hotel and decides to run away. She meets three old ladies whose ages total 228, who change her father and the whole town.

Nixon, J. L. *Maggie Too.* Dell Yearling, 1988.

Ages 8–11. A father who is about to remarry sends his daughter to spend the summer with her grandmother.

Numeroff, L. J. *Does Grandma Have an Elmo Elephant Jungle Kit?* Greenwillow, 1980.

Ages 1–5. Donald is worried that there will be nothing to do at his grandparent's house so he wants to take all his toys along.

Okimoto, J. D. *Take a Chance Gramps!* Little, Brown, 1990.

Ages 11–14. Twelve-year-old Jane Higgins is reluctant to begin a new school without her best friend, but advice from gramps helps. When the tables turn, Jane helps gramps take a chance at a dance for older adults.

Oldfield, P. *Simon's Extra Gram.* Children's Press, 1976.

Ages 5–8. Needing someone to read to him, Simon decides he needs an extra Gram.

Oneal, Z. *A Long Way to Go.* Viking, 1990.

Ages 7–12. Lika's life changes when her grandfather is jailed for fighting for women's rights.

Oppenheim, S. *Fireflies for Nathan.* Tambourine, 1994.

Ages 5–8. With the help of his grandparents, 6-year-old Nathan catches fireflies and keeps them in a jar.

Otto, C. *That Sky, That Rain.* Crowell, 1990.

Ages 1–5. As a storm approaches, a young girl and her grandfather take the farm animals in the barn and watch the rain.

Palay, S. *I Love My Grandma.* Raintree, 1977.

Ages 5–8. A young girl describes her relationship with her grandma.

Parsons, E. *The Upside Down Cat.* McElderry, 1981.

Ages 8–11. An old Maine fisherman and a boy love a cat they can't have.

Patterson, N. R. *The Christmas Cup.* Scholastic Paper, 1989.

Ages 8–12. Grandmother helps Megan find a use for the cup she impulsively bought at an auction.

Percy, G. *Max and the Orange Door.* Child's World, 1994.

Ages 5–8. An accident with orange paint helps Max, grandma, and grandpa have a vacation.

Peters, L. W. *Tania's Trolls.* Arcade, 1989.

Ages 8–12. Tania hopes that her piano-playing grandmother will give her special lessons before the spring recital.

Polacco, P. *Babushka's Doll.* Simon & Schuster, 1990.

Ages 5–8. Babushka's doll is special. She comes to life when Natasha wants to play with her, but she also teaches Natasha a lesson about being cooperative.

Polacco, P. *Thunder Cake.* Philomel Books, 1990.

Ages 5–8. Grandma helps her granddaughter get over her fear of thunder by collecting the ingredients and baking a thunder cake.

Pomerantz, C. *Timothy Tail Feather.* Greenwillow, 1986.

Ages 5–8. Grandfather tells Timothy a story with input from the boy. The real and the imagined intermingle. After the story Timothy tucks his grandfather and himself into bed.

Pryor, B. *Grandpa Bear.* William Morrow, 1985.

Ages preschool–5. Samantha Bear is too little to play with her big brother and too big for the baby, but she is just right to play with grandpa. Four chapters tell four stories of their adventures.

Rice, E. *Aren't You Coming Too?* Greenwillow, 1988.

Ages 5–8. A trip to the zoo with grandpa saves Amy from being lonely when everyone else is busy.

Rogers, P. *The Rare One.* Nelson, 1974.

Ages 11–14. An unhappy adolescent boy befriends an old man who lives in the woods. He writes a prize-winning essay about the old man but learns that winning at the expense of his friend's privacy is not good.

Saint James, S. *Sunday.* Albert Whitman, 1996.

Ages 1–6. No day is like Sunday! There's sleeping late and a delicious breakfast and reading the fat newspaper. Then, dressed in their Sunday best, the family sets out for church rejoicing in beautiful music and inspiring words. A subway trip to grandma and grandpa's makes the day a family day.

Scheffler, U. *A Walk in the Rain.* Putnam, 1984.

Ages 1–5. Jamie and his grandmother take a walk in the rain.

Schwartz, A. *Oma and Bobo.* Bradbury Press, 1987.

Ages 5–8. With the help of grandma, Bobo the dog learns to sit, stay, and fetch.

Schweninger, A. *On My Way to Grandpa's.* Dial, 1981.

Ages 3–7. Emily walks to visit grandpa, and all the comforting things she sees along the way remind her of the comfort and love she gets from him.

Seabrooke, B. *Looking for Diamonds.* Cobblehill, 1995.

Ages 5–8. A young girl shares a special visit with her grandparents in the country.

Shub, E. *Cutlass in the Snow.* Greenwillow, 1986.

Ages 6–12. Sam and grandpa are forced to spend the night stranded on Fire Island, where talk of pirates keeps them alert all night. In the morning they find a cutlass in the snow. This is a nineteenth-century tale based on a true incident.

Simpson, C. *Everything You Need to Know When Living with a Grandparent or Other Relatives.* Rosen Publishing Group, 1994.

Ages 12–17. An updated guide to coping with the sudden change of a live-in relative. Includes color photos.

Sinykin, S. C. *The Next Thing to Strangers.* Lothrop, 1991.

Ages 11–14. While visiting their grandparents at a trailer park in Arizona a diabetic girl and an overweight girl find friendship.

Sharmat, M. *Morris Brookside, a Dog.* Holiday House, 1973.

Ages 8–11. An older couple take in a stray dog and make him part of their family. When he finds a friend, they take him in too.

Skolsky, M. W. *Carnival and Kopeck and More About Hannah.* Harper & Row, 1979.

Ages 11–14. Hannah is excited that grandma moved so nearby and is excited to take her to the carnival in town. When Hannah upsets her grandma, Hannah realizes there are problems with living nearby too, but that problems can be worked out.

Skorper, L. M. *Mandy's Grandmother.* Dial, 1978.

Ages 5–8. Mandy and her grandmother learn that they do share things in common and can learn from each other. Excellent illustrations.

Spinelli, J. *The Bathwater Gang.* Little, Brown, 1990.

Ages 7–9. An all-girl gang gets into a harmless but heartfelt war directed by a grandmother.

Spurr, E. *Mrs. Minetta's Car Pool.* Atheneum, 1985.

Ages 5–8. Fantasy story of a car pool with an older adult who takes them on adventures.

Stevens, C. *Anna, Grandpa and the Big Storm.* Clarion, 1982.

Ages 4–7. Anna's grandfather is bored with city life until he and Anna are stranded on the 3rd Avenue El during the Blizzard of 1978.

Stevenson, J. *The Worst Person in the World.* Greenwillow, 1978.

Ages 1–5. The worst person in the world, an old man, was grouchy and had no friends until he met the ugliest thing in the world—a creature who convinces him to have a party.

Stevenson, J. *No Friends.* Greenwillow, 1986.

Ages 1–5. MaryAnn and Louie have no friends in their new neighborhood. Grandpa tells them of his adventures when he and his brother moved. Soon friends appear.

Stevenson, J. *There's Nothing to Do.* Greenwillow, 1986.

Ages 1–5. When his grandchildren are bored, grandpa tells them a story about the adventures with his brother.

Stevenson, J. *July.* Greenwillow, 1990.

Ages 5–8. Grandpa tells a story of visiting his grandparents every July and all the adventures he had.

Stoltz, M. *Storm in the Night.* Harper & Row, 1988.

Ages 5–8. During a nighttime thunderstorm, grandfather tells a story about a boyhood fear that helps the young boy understand himself and grandfather better.

Stren, P. *There's a Rainbow in My Closet.* HarRow 1979.

Ages 5–8. Grandmother takes care of her granddaughter while mother is on a trip. The girl is resentful until grandma notices her talents and becomes fun.

Tate, J. *Grandpa and My Sister Bee.* Children's Press, 1979.

Ages 1–5. Bee, age 3, helps grandpa plant wildflowers—but is she really helping?

Thesman, J. *When the Road Ends.* Houghton Mifflin, 1992.

Ages 10–12. Three foster children and an elderly invalid are abandoned by a cruel caretaker.

Titherington, J. *Sophy and Auntie Pearl.* Greenwillow, 1995.

Ages 1–5. Fantasy story. When Sophy discovers she can fly, no one believes her except her great-aunt Pearl.

Towne, M. *Wanda the Worry-Wart.* Pocket Paper, 1993.

Ages 9–14. Perpetual worrier Wanda tries to find a suitable mate for her divorced step-grandmother.

Tusa, T. *Maebell's Suitcase.* Macmillan, 1987.

Ages 4–7. An elderly woman sacrifices a treasured prize to help her friend, a young bird, make his first flight south.

Vigna, J. *My Two Uncles.* Albert Whitman, 1995.

Ages 11+. Elly's grandfather has trouble accepting the fact that his son is gay.

Voight, C. *The Homecoming.* Atheneum, 1981.

Ages 10+. When their mother abandons them, Dicey and her siblings seek out the grandmother they have never met.

Voigt, C. *Dicey's Song.* Macmillan, 1982.

Ages 10+. This story of Dicey's life with her "gram" in Maryland is a Newberry Award winner.

Waddell, M. *Little Obie and the Flood.* Chandlewick, 1992.

Ages 7–14. The story of Obie and his grandparents, who have little worldly goods but always have room for one more.

Waggoner, K. *The Lemonade Babysitter.* Little, Brown, 1992.

Ages 5–8. In spite of Molly's reluctance to have an old man for a babysitter, she finds they have more in common than they ever imagined.

Wahl, J. *The Fisherman.* Norton, 1969.

Ages 5–8. A girl goes fishing with her grandfather and although they don't catch fish, they find a bigger treasure.

Wahl, J. *Grandmother Told Me.* Little, Brown, 1972.

Ages 1–5. A boy's grandmother points out all sorts of things that he just misses seeing.

Wallace, I. *Chin Chiang and the Dragon Dance.* Atheneum, 1984.

Ages 5–8. Chin Chiang always wanted to dance the dragon dance with his grandfather, but when the time came he grew scared of failing. He runs away and meets an elderly woman who helps him gain confidence.

Walter, M. P. *Justin, and the Best Biscuits in the World.* Lothrop, 1986.

Ages 8–11. Ten-year-old Justin is surrounded by females in his family, and he doesn't want to help clean and keep house until he visits grandpa on a ranch.

Ward, S. *Punky Spends the Day.* Dutton, 1989.

Ages 1–5. Punky spends the day with her grandpa and makes a hideout, rakes leaves, and hears a bedtime story.

Weisman, J. *The Storyteller.* Rizzoli, 1993.

Ages 8–11. This story features an intergenerational friendship.

Westheimer, R. K. *Dr. Ruth Talks About Grandparents: Advice for Kids on Making the Most of a Special Relationship.* Farrar, Straus, & Giroux, 1997.

Ages 6+. This book advises readers to treasure their grandparents and suggests ways in which they might enhance their relationships.

Wild, M. *Our Granny.* Ticknor & Fields, 1994.

Ages preschool–8. A celebration of all kinds of grannies.

Willard, N. *High Rise Glorious Skittle Skat.* Harcourt, 1990.

Ages 8–11. As she is making a cake, a girl is visited by three angels who want a taste.

Williams, B. *Kevin's Grandma.* Dutton, 1975.

Ages 1–5. Amusing book about an unusual grandmother told by her imaginative grandson—and in comparison to his friend's more normal grandmother.

Williams, V. *"More, More, More" Said the Baby.* Greenwillow, 1990.

Ages preschool–K. A father, mother, and grandmother follow playful rituals with a baby.

Wilkinson, B. *Ludell.* Harper & Row, 1975.

Ages 11+. Ludell is an African American pre-teen being raised by her loving grandmother in the segregated South.

Wilson, G. *Granny's Fish Story.* Parents, 1975.

Ages 5–8. Grandmother wears blue jeans and sneakers, and is different than other grandmothers. She helps her granddaughter and her friend not be afraid of thunderstorms.

Wolitzer, H. *Wish You Were Here.* Farrar, Straus, & Giroux, 1984.

Ages 11–14. Bernie doesn't want to live with his stepfather and decides to move in with his grandfather instead.

Woodruff, E. *The Summer I Shrank My Grandmother.* Holiday House, 1990.

Ages 11–14. When Nelly visits her grandma for the summer, she is excited to find a chemistry set with magic formulas to make wishes come true. Nelly wishes her grandmother were small and then hopes she can reverse it when her grandmother turns into an infant.

Wright, B. R. *Getting Rid of Marjorie.* Holiday House, 1981.

Ages 11–14. Emily loves being with her widowed grandfather and is especially close to him since grandma died. But when grandpa returns from vacation with a new wife, Emily decides to get rid of her.

Yolen, J. *No Bath Tonight.* Crowell, 1978.

Ages 1–5. A little boy tries to avoid his bath until grandmother outwits him.

Zolotow, C. *My Grandson Lew.* Harper & Row, 1974.

Ages preschool–8. Lew wakes up in the night wondering where his grandfather has gone.

Zolotow, C. *I Know a Lady.* Greenwillow, 1984.

Ages 5–8. An elderly woman shares her garden and gives Halloween treats.

Index